For Ginnie

Contents

Preface

When colleagues, friends, and relatives learned that I was writing another book, the natural question was "What kind of book?" Depending on the state of my whimsy, my response ranged from "a self-indulgent intellectual autobiography" to "a selective literature review." In truth, the finished product is several things at once, but an exemplar of none of them. As a central theme I have tried to capture what is most intriguing about people's attempts to understand each other — their motives, their emotions, their traits, their attitudes—and in the process I have included some personal reminiscences and reflections. I wasn't quite "present at the creation," but my own career has wound in and out of the history of person perception research for nearly forty years. I have sustained a preoccupation with how we decide what another person is "really like," and how we try to control the identities that we hope others will confirm.

This preoccupation has led me to have great respect for the social context in which our everyday person perceptions are formed. The book champions an embedded view of person perception, stressing the ongoing interplay between our expectancies, our actions, our perceptions, and our attributions. The truly distinctive feature of social cognition is that we participate in the creation of our own social reality. The social world is not something that merely passes before us on the video screen of daily events; it is a world at least partly responsive to our actions in it: our choices and decisions to enter or to avoid settings and our attempts to influence and control the actions of those we care about. If the reader of this book fails to grasp this unique consideration of the perceiver's contributions to the reality he or she perceives, then I have certainly failed in my expository mission.

My own research is abundantly referenced in the pages to follow, but I have tried to achieve some balance by giving credit to those other research scholars whose work I find particularly solid and provocative. Undoubtedly, I have been more selective in treating the work of others and more indiscriminate in the inclusion of my own research. The practitioner of such self-indulgence inevitably runs the risk of inviting the conclusion that the research of others is more interesting and more important than that of the practitioner's. So be it. I have tried to reach a compromise between those scholarly compendia that cite everyone and everything and a tiresome litany of my own research contributions.

To facilitate this compromise, in the manner of narrative historians, I have used reference notes to spare the reader repeated confrontations with names and dates in the text itself. The interested scholar will, I hope, find solace in the endnotes, which contain self-protective caveats, discuss rather arcane but relevant controversies, or simply refer to specific sources listed in the bibliography.

In form, *Interpersonal Perception* is an outgrowth of a course I have taught advanced undergraduates for many years —first, at Duke University, and more recently at Princeton University. I am most familiar with what these audiences have wanted and needed to know over the years. Nevertheless, and quite naturally, I would be delighted if this book were widely read by psychologists and intelligent laypersons for what I dare to hope is a coherent presentation of an intrinsically interesting set of ideas. I have tried to hold jargon to a minimum and to accompany abstract propositions and conclusions with apt examples. I have aimed for a level of discourse that is sufficiently challenging for undergraduates and graduate students without daunting (or boring) those who have no background in social psychology.

In a larger sense this book represents a lifelong project of planning and writing up research and fine-tuning course presentations of the large literature in person perception. Such being the case, it would be impossible for me to acknowledge the many influences that have shaped my research goals and my perspective. I have known and surely been influenced by many illustrious innovators in the field, including Fritz Heider, Solomon Asch, Lee Cronbach, Jerome Bruner, John Thibaut, and Harold Kelley. Through the years I have been highly dependent on my graduate students, and I have been unusually fortunate in working with an outstanding collection of research and teaching assistants at Duke and at Princeton. Many of these have become major contributors to the person perception area and are represented in the chapters to follow. Of those current and former students who have been specifically helpful in preparing this book, I would like especially to express gratitude to Alane Brown, Joel Cooper, Daniel Gilbert, Linda Ginzel, George Quattrone, and Melvin Snyder. Others who read and helped to improve various chapters include David Myers, David Schneider, and William Swann.

The National Science Foundation has supported my research for thirty-five years. Certainly this book owes much to the Foundation's continued affirmation of interest in the topics discussed.

Mary Ann Opperman has typed, photocopied, raised questions, suggested examples, and in so many other ways reduced the burdens and increased the fun of writing this book. Every author should be so lucky!

I have never dedicated a book before, and it is most appropriate that I finally dedicate one to my wife, Virginia Sweetnam Jones. She has not read a word of this book and probably never will, but she has become such an arbiter and constructive critic of my thought processes that her influence is much greater than she could ever know. Her insights as a sensible, penetrating, and objective observer of the human scene need finally to be formally recognized.

Edward E. Jones
May 1990

Interpersonal Perception

The

Interpersonal Framework

This book explores how we come to understand what makes a particular person— including our own selves—behave in particular ways. How do we sense or figure out what a person is like "inside" from the way he or she acts at a particular time in a particular setting? Many everyday actions are routine or perfunctory. When we observe them, we don't learn much, if anything, about the actor. But the more interesting and meaningful social actions reflect decisions, and these decisions imply motives, and motives, at least some of the time, imply stable personality dispositions: values, beliefs, traits. When we perceive a person, we draw conclusions about that person, either rapidly and automatically, or thoughtfully and deliberately. In this book we shall be preoccupied with what determines these person perception conclusions and the consequences of drawing different conclusions for interpersonal relations.

To me this is a fascinating enterprise. I have always been excited by the challenge of trying to develop a penetrating and accurate account of how we use the evidence of behavior to construe the distinctive characteristics of the person behaving. There is something endlessly intriguing about trying to construe the private world of another person from observing outward appearances and actions. But even those who don't find this task intrinsically interesting can, I hope, be persuaded to concede that we can better understand how interpersonal relationships develop and change if we learn as much as possible about what people think they have discovered about others while interacting with them. Our actions toward others are shaped by our perceptions of them: We treat others as we perceive them, not as they may really be. A psychology of interpersonal relations that ignores the perceptual underpinnings of these relations would be almost inconceivable. It is very difficult to predict a person's behavior from his or her behavior in the past, unless you have some idea *why* that person chose the particular courses of action you have observed.[1] Did John miss your party because of an unavoidable crisis, because he simply forgot, or because he really did not want to be with you and your friends? Did your friend Mary do poorly on the final exam because she didn't study hard enough or because she just isn't very bright? Is the coach really angry at you, or is he just trying to get you to play with greater intensity?

The study of how people perceive each other's emotions, motives, and predispositions to act in certain ways is important precisely because these private conditions are usually not easy to discern in everyday life. People do not wear their hearts on their sleeves most of the time; they can and often do control displays of their emotions. They are very selective in revealing their aspirations and their ongoing thoughts. The meaning of their actions is often ambiguous because actions are multiply determined. Many of the determinants of their behavior are unknown (unconscious?) even to them. If, in fact, actions more directly reflected thoughts and dispositions, psychology would be a vastly different enterprise—and social life would be radically transformed. Imagine a strange corner of the Earth where people always say what they mean and mean what they say, where hearts are always worn on the sleeve. The actual ambiguity of behavior in all societies that we do know not only provides the challenge and the justification for this inquiry but is a central and controlling feature of interpersonal relations themselves.

In this book I will focus on the role of person perception in the course of ongoing social interaction. Person perceivers are not cameras; they are active agents who not only process information but also produce it. Our impressions of others normally grow out of our interactions with them. We respond to them and they to us; we (and they) are actors, perceivers, and target persons. Our actions flow from our understanding about the setting we are in and the characteristics of other persons in the setting. To illustrate a few of the major themes that we will analyze, let me begin with a homely example. On parents' night at my son's school, what do I learn about his teacher, Mrs. McCarver, when she introduces herself to me? Is her physical appearance important? Does she fit my image of other teachers that I have known? Are her remarks completely predictable from knowing the occasion and the setting? Do my emotions tell me anything about whether I would like to get to know her better? Does her response to me tell me anything new about myself?

This everyday example illustrates an important point: Understanding persons means that we have to understand situations. The decisions and actions that we strive to explain are embedded in a surrounding context of antecedent and impinging events. But the title of this book implies something else: Some of these impinging events are produced by us, the perceivers. The actions we observe are an interpersonal product, and in the interests of accurate understanding we should consider the extent to which they are shaped by our own prior actions. Thus, the "situation" that provides a context for the other's to-be-explained behavior typically involves the constraints, challenges, and opportunities inherent in our own appearance and behavior. If it is really important for me to determine the personal characteristics of my son's teacher, I should try to calibrate not only the general constraints of parents' night at a school, but the specific constraints on her of interacting with me as a parent and as a unique person, along with all the particulars these features add to the teacher's stimulus environment.

But maybe it is not important for me to concern myself with what Mrs. McCarver is *really* like — her beliefs, aspirations, interests, traits, and so on. I can essentially get in and get out of a brief encounter with my son's teachers without having to know or make inferences about any of these things. Although this book will focus on how we perceive the personal characteristics of others, it is important to keep in mind that what we need to know in any given social episode is a function of our *interaction goals*. These are determined in large part by the limits and opportunities of the current situation, as well as by our vision of prospective encounters with a target person.[2] This is a point made convincingly by William Swann,[3] who argues for the importance of such circumscribed encounter-relevant accuracy in person perception. Ours is a "bounded rationality" when we form impressions[4]: We need not be equally concerned with accurate inferences about all the personal dispositions of a target person; some behavioral dimensions are much more consequential than others in determining the fate of particular interactions, and these will naturally receive more attention in the chapters to come.

To set a framework for the chapters to follow, let me introduce some useful terms and try to locate them in a typical interaction sequence.[5] To set the stage with what I hope will be familiar actors and familiar props, consider the acquaintance process of Amy and Beth.[6] Amy is about to meet her college roommate, Beth, for the first time. Let's assume that Amy has received some limited prior information about Beth. She knows what town Beth is from, what secondary school she graduated from, that she is a nonsmoker, but little else. She also realizes that this is probably going to be a very important relationship — at least for the next year or so, if not for life. How can their first meeting be conceptualized in a way that will be useful for our future discussions of other interpersonal exchanges?

What the Perceiver Brings to the Interaction

Before Amy sets eyes on her roommate, we assume she has *expectancies*. That is, without her thinking carefully about it, she is probably carrying around a lot of implicit predictions about Beth based on certain feelings she has about Beth's age, the ethnic implications of her last name, the part of the country Beth comes from, and the fact that Beth is enrolling in this particular college. These expectancies are largely *category based*, since they reflect certain presumptions about general groupings in our society and are not richly informed by individuating facts about Beth as a person. As Amy gets to know Beth, we assume, these category-based expectancies will be discarded in favor of more tailor-made, *target-based* expectancies, those built around everything we know about a particular person.

Amy also has *normative expectancies* about the forthcoming meeting with Beth. She undoubtedly has a picture in her mind of what the situation will be like when she meets Beth. Though she may never have been in a similar situation, she nevertheless has some sense of what the norms are in a setting where two roommates meet — what level of formality is appropriate, how to strike a balance between modesty and self-promotion, how to be accommodating without being obsequious, and so on. Such normative expectancies are crucial in the person perception process because they provide the framework of expectation for evaluating an individual's behavior.

In addition to expectancies about Beth and the situation, Amy obviously brings her self to this initial meeting. She has a *self-concept* that has been constructed in large part from the many, many interactions she has had with others over the years. She knows that Beth will form a particular image of her, and she is more or less confident about what this image will be. Especially since this other person is bound to be significant in her life, she wants to project a particular identity: She wants Beth to see the kind of person she sees herself as being — or even better, she wants Beth to confirm the most positive aspects of her self-concept and to make her feel good about herself.

These aspirations may be woven into Amy's interaction goals. In any social interaction, the participants have things they want to accomplish. These things may range from the pure enjoyment of sharing pleasant anecdotes over coffee to the ulterior gratifications of persuading or exploiting another. These interaction goals, whatever they are, will determine in important ways not only the actor's own behavior, but what information the actor pays attention to and what he or she makes of the selected information. We would expect Amy's goals to be rather diffuse. There are some specific objectives, such as getting the better cot and the better bureau. But these objectives may be subordinate to the larger goal of coming across as a nice person—one who is willing to be reasonable and accommodating. Interaction goals will almost inevitably involve *strategic self-presentation.* This refers to those features of behavior that are shaped or influenced by the desire to create a certain impression in the more general interests of one's interpersonal power. Amy has a stake in getting Beth to like her and to respect her. Certain ways of interacting, of presenting herself, will achieve these objectives better than others. The concept of strategic self-presentation will be more thoroughly discussed in the chapters to come. For now we may merely note that interaction goals are typically inter-twined with self-presentational features. Figure 1-1 summarizes what the perceiver (Amy) brings to a social interaction (with Beth).

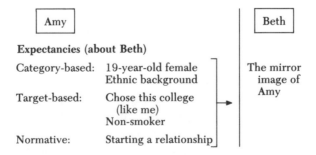

FIGURE 1-1 What the perceiver (Amy) brings to the interaction.

The Target Person and the Setting: The Information "Out There"

Amy and Beth meet — not in limbo or in a vacuum, but in a particular social *situation* that constrains (sets limits on) and channels their behavior in a number of important ways. I have already suggested that Amy has some general normative expectancies about this class of greeting situations, and these will be modified in various small or large ways as the greeting episode unfolds. In any event, there will undoubtedly be many aspects of the situation — the size of the room, the weather, which roommate arrived first, whether parents are present — that provide a backdrop for the evaluation of Beth's behavior. Amy's own behavior in the situation quickly becomes part of the situation to which Beth must react, and important research questions concern how and when perceivers like Amy become aware of and take account of their own role as part of the stimulus situation for others.

Then, of course, there is Beth herself, her appearance and her behavior. Since our Western heritage and democratic traditions emphasize the importance of "what's inside" and play down the moral significance of external appearances, it would be comforting to find that physical appearance plays only an incidental role in the formation of impressions. Unfortunately, the importance of *appearance cues* is almost impossible to overestimate in a first-impression situation. Such appearance cues include the attributes of commonly recognized physical attraction, clothes and grooming, facial expression, and posture. Experiment after experiment testify to the strong contribution of physical appearance features to the creation of positive and negative impressions.[7] The importance of such features is unfortunate not only from a moral point of view. To a research-oriented social psychologist, such cues are difficult to incorporate into meaningful theories in spite of their significant impact on impressions. It has become conventional to acknowledge their importance, but no one has a very precise idea how appearance cues enter into the person perception process.[8]

However much you have thought about variables contributing to first impressions, you are not likely to argue with the contention that the *behavior* of the target person (in this case Beth) is going to be a crucial determinant of the impression formed. It is obvious that Beth can "say the right thing" or alternatively behave in ways that only confirm Amy's "worst-case scenario." Beth can be charming, aloof, self-mocking, arrogant, insecure, nervous—as revealed in five minutes of conversational exchange. Behavior is the "figure" against the "ground" of situational and appearance cues.

Back to the Perceiver

Amy and Beth start to compare notes, discussing how long it took them to drive to campus, commenting on each other's wardrobes and intended majors, probing for mutual friends, going over any plans for dinner, checking on the time of the morning orientation session, and so on. In all probability, Amy and Beth are not only trying to carry on a responsive and coherent conversation, they are also trying (perhaps without intense self-conscious effort) to figure each other out, to anticipate each other's probable reactions in projected future encounters. At the conceptual level (i.e., with our jargon showing) Amy is perceiving Beth's behavior and interpreting it in the context of Beth's appearance and the normative constraints inherent in the situation. These interpretations can be seen as attempts to assign or attribute the causes of Beth's behavior, either to some characteristics of Beth or to the situation itself. Amy is making *attributions* about Beth's dispositions—her traits, values, motives; how Beth sees her self (whether she is self-confident or anxious); and very importantly, Beth's attitude toward Amy. She may also be withholding judgment, or attributing Beth's reactions primarily to the demands of this strange and novel situation. These attributions are the product of complicated cognitive processes that integrate behavioral and situational information with the prior expectancies of the attributor. Much will be said about making attributions in the chapters to come since I treat attribution processes as the central focus of interpersonal perception.

The View from the Other Side

Obviously, I could just as well have focused on Beth as the perceiver in this interaction and Amy as the target person. Each can be equally involved in forming impressions of the other, using the same kinds of information. Also, we have looked at but one quick pass through the interaction sequence. Amy's attributions will invariably lead to continuous revisions in her expectancies about Beth, as category-based expectations give rise to target-based ones. One might also suspect that in most interactions, over time, appearance cues will lose some of their salience and power. And appearance cues are not very stable in any event. When we grow to like someone who did not strike us as physically attractive when we first met, we usually see him or her as better looking over time and begin to wonder why we ever thought otherwise. (At least that is my experience.[9])

As Amy and Beth share more and a greater variety of social experiences, we would expect their attributions of each others' dispositions to stabilize and to be held with firmer and firmer conviction. Each person's attributions should also become interconnected in an increasingly complex knowledge structure as Amy's and Beth's experiences with each other accumulate. General attribute labels that Amy might have initially applied to Beth as a rough approximation become differentiated, qualified, and divided into subcategories to capture more accurately the idiosyncratic character of the multiple observations of Beth.

Finally, neither Amy's nor Beth's *self* is an unchanging anchor in the interaction sequence. Amy, of course, will never be exactly the same person after meeting Beth as she was beforehand or as she would have been if she had drawn a different roommate. Beth's responses to Amy not only affect

Amy's attributions of Beth's dispositional characteristics, but may in small and large ways affect Amy's view of herself. Less obviously, Amy and Beth will each be observing her own behavior, and under certain circumstances at least, these self-observations can set in motion changes in the self-concept. Figure 1-2 attempts to portray one swing through the interaction sequence, a sequence that forecasts the structure of the chapters that follow.

The remarks accompanying one fictitious example can hardly capture the richness of social interaction. My intent has been to provide, with the concrete assistance of Amy and Beth, an analytic framework for locating the research and ideas that I will be discussing in the chapters to come and to identify a few of the more important concepts that will be used. Something as complex as the interaction sequence, even as portrayed by the simple sketch above, cannot be studied

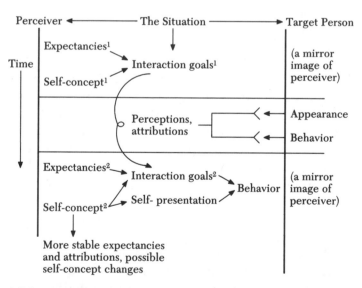

FIGURE 1-2   An attempt to summarize the beginnings of an interaction between two persons (a perceiver and a target person), emphasizing the role of expectancies and goals.

whole. We can perhaps observe what goes on from the outside, we can interview after the fact, we can introspect as one of the participants, but there is no encompassing single method that will reveal the mysteries of interpersonal perception in all its diversity of content and levels of meaning as one person holds a conversation with another.

Among the various methods available, the experimental approach is the strategy that appeals to me the most. Of course, I readily acknowledge that almost everything interacts with almost everything else in this world, and many of the most important things that happen to us in our social interactions occur in a time frame that cannot be compressed into the moments available for a psychology experiment. Putting that caveat aside, we can make constructive headway toward causal understanding of these rich, complex interaction sequences by entering them at various convenient points and studying part-processes or episodic cross-sections. The resulting task of sewing the cross-sections together presents a formidable but, I think, not insurmountable challenge. The trick is to find the most fruitful points of entry, to find tractable segments and investigate them without wrenching them so cruelly out of context as to distort their contributing characteristics in the sequences we set out to understand.

Most of the results described in the following chapters have been generated by experiments conducted at such tractable points of entry. Equally important, if not more so, most of the theorizing and conceptualizing was either suggested by or constrained by the thinking that goes with designing appropriate experiments. I shall write disproportionately about my own research in a way that, I hope, reveals what I learned by designing such experiments and by reflecting on what I think the subjects were trying to tell us.

The main point of this chapter is to hold up a framework for analysis, a scaffold to keep in mind if we want to understand the perceptual and cognitive features of social interaction. I shall repeatedly remind the reader that each examined segment is embedded in the dynamic flow of social behavior, as people meet, exchange glances, converse, argue, and evaluate each other. And if I occasionally forget, I hope the reader will have learned to provide the appropriate reminder.

Plan of the Book

Chapters 2 and 3 are intended to provide a useful historical and theoretical context for the remaining chapters. Chapter 2 considers representative early approaches to person perception and their evolution toward an explicit concern with how social information is processed by perceivers. Chapter 3 reviews the major models that have been offered to explain how people attribute the causes of behavior, a process that plays a central role in making inferences upon observing another's actions. The current status of these models is considered along with some newer variations focusing on different stages of the attribution process.

The remaining chapters are designed to capture what happens at different stages of the interaction sequence. The emphasis, once again, is on the interweaving of cognitive inferences and behavior during episodes of ongoing social interaction. Chapter 4 focuses on "expectancy effects," the structured prior information that each of us brings to our interactions with others — information both about the situation, about people in general, and about the particular target person we may confront. Chapter 5 pauses to consider the general issue of "situational constraint," the impact of which is often ignored both by perceivers and by psychological theorists. Chapter 6 deals extensively with one of the most common consequences of this general tendency to underestimate the role of situational constraint. Chapter 7 focuses on the goals of each interaction partner and the behavioral strategies that are associated with them. The sensitive perceiver must take into account the most likely motives of the target person in assessing the meaning of motive-relevant actions. Chapter 8 asks whether and under what conditions social interactions lead to changes in the participants' self-concepts. This can be viewed as the end of one journey through the interaction sequence: A sequence that starts with one perceiver's expectancies may end with important changes in a target person's self-concept. The stages of this mysterious kind of social transformation are discussed in the final chapter, giving a general survey of expectancies that sometimes lead to their own fulfillment (thus, "self-fulfilling prophecies") as two people interact over time.

Early

Approaches to Person

Perception

How should we proceed to study the decision processes that constitute interpersonal perception? When I ask beginning students this question, a number of themes commonly emerge in their responses.

First, there seems to be a widely shared belief that some people are better than others at figuring people out. We think of these abilities as being important for therapists, salesmen, politicians, and certain kinds of executive leaders. Perhaps, therefore, we could study person perception by learning about the personalities and socializing experiences of these "experts."

Second, many students believe that a good starting point for research is the fact that some people seem easier to read than others. What is it that makes one person's values and traits appear to be such an open book whereas another person is opaque and inscrutable?

Still other beginning students will assume that a natural starting point for research is the skill we all seem to have at reading emotional states. Everyone thinks he or she can tell when someone is happy or sad, anxious or relaxed; moreover, this accomplishment doesn't seem to depend on a great deal of skill or training. The ability to discriminate between emotions would seem to be a fairly straightforward topic of study. Can perceivers looking at snapshots reliably distinguish one person who is experiencing fear from another who is experiencing anger? How about mirth and surprise?

Finally, there are those who see obvious links between person perception and the kinds of personality assessments in which clinical psychologists engage. To the extent that there is a reliable and valid science of construing personality from projective and objective tests, from content analyses of interview data and observations of behavior under stress, these principles could be extrapolated to help our understanding of more casual judgments in everyday relationships. Thus, the royal road to a science of person perception may pass through an understanding of professional diagnostic wisdom. At least some beginning students believe that psychologists have the appropriate training to read unconscious motives in slips of the tongue, in dreams and fantasies, and in associative links revealed by the juxtaposition of certain conversational topics. To the extent that this training can be shared, everyone can become a more expert person perceiver.

I have always found it difficult to understand why people would approach a psychological topic in a particular way without at least some understanding of earlier attempts. The need for historical background is particularly clear in the study of person perception. Perhaps it is not entirely a coincidence that the topics featured in early person perception research bear a certain resemblance to the various suggestions of beginning students mentioned above. Before World War II, research efforts to learn something about how people perceive and judge each other involved (1) attempts to measure the accuracy of acquaintances trying to judge each other's self-ratings, (2) other attempts to characterize both accurate person perceivers and easily perceived target persons, and (3) attempts to draw the links among emotions, their expression, and the perception of them by others. These early efforts tended to be haphazard and occasional until the 1950s.[1]

The Harvard Symposium

In fact, a particular occasion can be conveniently chosen to mark the emergence of person perception as a distinctive subfield within social psychology. The occasion was a symposium held at Harvard University in 1957 under the auspices of the Office of Naval Research (ONR). The Harvard setting of the conference was appropriate since Jerome Bruner and his colleagues at Harvard had been instrumental in promoting a new and liberated interest in the perception of the natural world. This approach represented a revolutionary departure from looking at perception under highly restricted laboratory conditions; Bruner and his colleagues believed that artificial conditions rule out the kinds of motivational and experiential influences that are clearly operative when we perceive what is going on in the natural, everyday environment. The liberalized view of perception that Bruner and his colleagues favored — generally identified as the study of "social perception" — necessarily required the use of motivationally relevant stimuli in experimental studies — coins, tokens that had acquired value through reinforcing experiences, pictures of food or thirst-quenching drinks, and words that were either threatening or highly valued.[2] From this it was an easy and natural next step to consider the perception of persons, which concerns perhaps the most motivationally relevant stimuli of all.[3]

The participants in the Harvard symposium addressed many of the questions often raised by beginning students, but though they addressed many old concerns, they relocated them for the first time under the "person perception" label. Also, as it happened, the conveners of the symposium were indeed prescient: The invited participants represented a roster of those who either were or would be extremely influential in shaping the nature of this new area of study. The participants included

1. Solomon Asch, the author of an extremely important paper on how we form impressions of others that, among other things, shifted the concern away from the accuracy of person perception to the processes involved. Asch's paper showed how people organize or integrate different traits in the process of forming a coherent impression of the person to whom the traits are said to refer.

2. Jerome S. Bruner, already described as the father of the "new look in social perception," was very much a cheerleader in getting others (including myself) involved in the study of person perception.

3. Lee J. Cronbach, a distinguished methodologist and a constructive critic of earlier research that had been concerned with measuring the accuracy of interpersonal judgment.

4. Fred Fiedler, a student of leadership whose theory was based on individual differences in the social perceptiveness of the leader.

5. Albert Hastorf, who had done research on the measurement of empathy and was later the coauthor of an important person perception text.

6. Fritz Heider, the father of what later would become attribution theory.

7. Albert Pepitone, a student of the role of motivation in the judgment of others.

8. Paul Secord, a student of the perception of facial expressions.

9. Renato Tagiuri, an organizer of the symposium and a student of one person's perception of being liked or disliked by another.

I was also present at this meeting and was impressed by the range of topics discussed and the general emphasis on phenomenology, on the importance of learning at first hand how perceivers see their world. I had coauthored with John

Thibaut a paper for the symposium concerning the role of interaction goals in person perception. This and other papers prepared for the symposium later appeared in book entitled *Person Perception and Interpersonal Behavior*.[4] It can reasonably be argued that after its appearance, no textbook in social psychology could again be written without at least a chapter on the topic of person perception. Among other things, the conference and the book that followed wrenched the topic away from the more general topic of social perception (which included the study of social influences on the perception of nonsocial objects) and provided a suitable label for any pertinent textbook chapter.

More than thirty years have passed since this remarkable collection of researchers and theorists launched the person perception field. Prior to 1957, as I have suggested, the antecedents of a person perception field existed in a scattering of studies concerned either with the conditions of accuracy in judgments of personality traits or with the expression and perception of emotions. Subsequently the field of person perception developed as a concern with the motives, expectancies, and mental processes of a perceiver who confronts behavior "out there" and is asked to draw inferences about the actor from the actions observed. As noted in the first chapter, the title of this book is intended to imply a third phase in the development of the field: a phase characterized by the consideration of the intricate interplay of perception and behavior in the process of ongoing social interaction. But to plant the seeds for the chapters to follow, it is important to consider, as our heritage, several segmental perspectives on the perceiver of persons that were already prominent in the late 1950s. Each of these perspectives, or models, was represented by one or more contributors to the Harvard symposium. I shall try to capture their assumptions and central focus as a way of providing a useful historical background for the chapters to follow. The main lines of investigation anticipated in this symposium were

1. The perceiver as a reader of emotions

2. The perceiver as a good judge of personality

3. The perceiver as an information integrator

4. The perceiver as an attributor of causation

5. The perceiver as a motivated actor

The Perceiver as Reader of Emotions

How good are people at discerning the emotions being experienced by another? For many years this question was treated as a mildly interesting side issue; the more important question was presumed to be whether there is a consistent ant reliable connection between a felt emotion and its expression. Charles Darwin[5] was one of the earliest emotion theorists; he was convinced that such connections were indeed stable, that the character of each facial expression is universal and innately programmed, reflecting the residual outcome of evolutionary processes. Thus, a facial expression of disgust is a partial replica of the behavior pattern of vomiting, the baring of teeth in anger is an incipient portion of a carnivorous attack, and so on.

As research into the nature of emotion began to incorporate questions of perceptual identification and discrimination, however, these notions of innate and uniform connections between emotion and expression became more and more difficult to sustain. For one thing, the results were highly inconsistent from study to study, varying, it seemed, with changes in procedure. It is hardly surprising that this was the case. If perceivers are exposed to still photographs of the face, their ability to discriminate among experienced emotions depends in obvious ways on how far apart the emotions lie on various underlying dimensions along which facial configurations can vary. For example, I can easily distinguish between joy and anger and even between sadness and fear, but more subtle discriminations might be beyond me. Some of the early research efforts attempted to come to terms with such differences in the discriminability of emotions—the perceived "distances" between them—by erecting fairly elaborate dimensional theories.[6]

As psychologists began to experiment with different presentational formats—using live actors or moving picture scenarios instead of facial photographs, for example — it became readily apparent that a major determinant of our perception of an emotion is the situational context to which the target person is presumably responding. If we note that the target person is in the same room with a coiled cobra, we are likely to perceive his facial expression as fearful over a wide range of actual expressive possibilities. A woman standing by a coffin may be smiling, but even so, we are likely to infer that she is sad. The fact that contextual information is so obviously important in identifying particular emotions served to deflect researchers from a concern with the information that *was* contained in the face and in various nonverbal gestures. This decline in research attention was probably accelerated by "cognitive labeling" theories of emotion like that proposed by Stanley Schachter.[7] Schachter argued essentially that our emotions reflect the combination of a cognition and the experience of arousal. The cognition is essentially a label, an explanation that is attached to undifferentiated physiological arousal. Thus, the emotion is, in this theory, actually defined by the context. One might infer from this theoretical premise that emotional experiences are extremely labile and that the connections between experience and expression are neither uniform nor innate. However, this conclusion does not follow from inexorable logical deduction, and a Schachterian could still maintain that facial and bodily displays can be wired to particular self-labeled emotional experiences.

In any event, the skepticism concerning the consistency of emotional expression cues has recently given way to a renewed interest in the behavioral cues that reveal emotion. This new research has focused on the face as both a determinant and a reflector of emotional experience.[8] This research shows that people *can* accurately perceive emotions from facial displays without the aid of context, but the face is also typically involved in doing many things besides expressing emotion.[9] In fact, studies of "deception" and its detection propose that we have better control over facial displays than over bodily gestures and vocal quality.[10] As a consequence, these studies generally conclude, people are better able to detect intentionally concealed emotions from nonverbal body movements or from vocal features than they are from the face. We are skilled at erecting deceptive facial masks, but the body gives us away—a phenomenon some refer to as "emotional leakage."

The study of deception and its perception is now represented by a substantial literature,[11] but one that cries out for theoretical integration. As yet the field of deception studies is somewhat isolated from the broader fields of social attribution and person perception research. The issues raised are of obvious practical importance (for example, to courtroom juries, customs inspectors, and lie-detection agencies), and students of person perception *should* be able to say something about how emotions are revealed even when the person experiencing the emotion is attempting to conceal it. This is, after all, one of the skills that we normally associate with the gifted therapist, the shrewd diagnostician, and those "untrained" people among us who seem especially deft at penetrating the disguises and masks of others.

The Perceiver as Personality Judge

As indicated earlier in this chapter, a natural avenue of inquiry into the domain of person perception would be to identify those who are good, accurate judges of others and to find out what makes them so. One does not have to travel very far along this avenue, however, before realizing that there are many potholes, barriers, and detour signs. The biggest problem of all is deciding what we mean by a "good, accurate judge"—accurate with respect to what?

Without reference to any research, our everyday experience tells us that we are all rather skilled at judging others. If we watch a person behave in different situations, listen to her talk, evaluate her gestures, we should quickly begin to form certain generalizations about this person that will help us predict her behavior in new settings, especially those that are similar to the settings in which we earlier observed her. There is hardly anything surprising about this. We can be quite confident, and probably quite accurate, about our predictions as long as we are asked the right questions and don't have to get too specific. For example, I have been married to the same person for more than forty years. If you show me the weekly TV schedule and ask me to predict which shows my wife will watch in the next seven days, I can be accurate well beyond any reckonings of chance because I have made some fairly firm generalizations about the kinds of programs she tends to like. I could probably predict her responses on most self-descriptive personality questionnaires with considerable accuracy. And as for her responses on an attitude scale, forty years of information about her specific views and the values that underly many of them ought to leave me in a pretty good position to predict these.

But there are many predictive tasks that would defeat me. I have no idea what my wife will serve for dinner tomorrow, what she dreamed about last Thursday night, or what opinions she actually expressed in a luncheon with some old friends who were passing through Princeton. In other words, even under such conditions of extended knowledge and recurrent experiences there are many behavioral predictions that are beyond me. Nevertheless, by most criteria you would have to say I am a good judge of my wife's personality, and no one would be surprised either at what I can or what I cannot predict.

But this isn't what the layperson — or the psychologist, for that matter — means by a "good judge of personality." We don't mean someone who can observe another person for forty years and predict certain kinds of behavior. We mean someone who is better than others at figuring out the values, motives, and distinctive predilections of another on the basis of limited information. What kinds of abilities might be involved in such an achievement?

In order to answer this kind of question we have to think about research methods and their requirement for careful definition, comparison, and control. In a series of trenchant papers in the 1950s Lee Cronbach helped us realize the complexity of the accuracy question.[12]

One kind of question that linked educational and social psychology in the 1930s and 1940s was whether good teachers and therapists are more socially sensitive than poor ones. Attempts to answer such questions led to a fairly standard procedure in which target persons rated themselves on a number of self-descriptive questionnaire items and judges attempted to estimate what these ratings were from their knowledge about and experience with the target persons. Judges also rated themselves on the same scale, and in some studies they may also have served as target persons for other judges. For the convenience of exposition, let us assume that each item could be rated on a ten-point scale and the higher the rating on an item, the more favorable the description (of self or other).

Given this procedure, judgmental accuracy could be measured by summing the differences across items of the target persons' actual self-ratings and the judge's predictions of these ratings. One of Cronbach's important contributions was to show that such an accuracy measure is composed of a number of components, each of which might have different psychological significance or reflect a different kind of judgmental skill. Accuracy breaks down into the following components:

1. *Elevation*. This is the judge's tendency to use the same part of the scale in rating target persons that the target persons themselves use. In the present case this would mean that high elevation accuracy reflects the fact that the judge has a good idea in general how favorably people are inclined to rate themselves. The elevation measure is averaged over target persons as well as over items.

2. *Differential elevation*. This is the judge's tendency to rate individual target persons as favorably as they rate themselves, i.e., to use the same parts of the scale for individual target persons, summing across items. This would presumably depend on a judge's realization that some particular target persons have a higher estimate of themselves than others.

3. *Stereotype accuracy*. This is the judge's tendency to predict the average self-rating on each particular item. Summing across different target persons, in other words, how good is the judge at figuring out that the average person might rate him- or herself 7 on "generous" but only 5 on "witty"?

4. *Differential accuracy*. Finally, this is the remaining or residual tendency to predict an individual target person's self-rating variations across individual items — to predict correctly

that Susan rated herself higher on generous than on witty, whereas Barbara rated herself equally on both. This comes closest to what we intuitively mean by judgmental accuracy, though the fact that the other three components can also vary might mean that this particular component would be obscured by an overall measure of difference between actual and predicted ratings.

A simplified example illustrating this componential analysis of accuracy may be seen in Figure 2-1. An implication of this

		Target Person 1	Target Person 2	Target Person 3
	Item:	1 2 3	1 2 3	1 2 3
	Actual other:	3 6 9 (18)	3 3 3 (9)	1 3 9 (13) (40)
Judge A	Self	2 5 8	2 5 8	2 5 8
	Perceived other	3 6 8 (17)	2 6 9 (17)	3 4 7 (14) (48)
Judge B	Self	6 4 2	6 4 2	6 4 2
	Perceived other	2 4 7 (13)	2 4 7 (13)	2 4 7 (13) (39)
Judge C	Self	5 5 5	5 5 5	5 5 5
	Perceived other	9 6 3 (18)	5 1 3 (9)	6 5 2 (13) (40)

Accuracy Components:

1. Elevation:	$C = B > A$	
2. Differential elevation:	$C > B = A$	
3. Stereotype accuracy:	$B > A > C$	
4. Differential accuracy:	$A = B > C$	
Assumed similarity:	$A > C > B$	

Item		
1	2	3
2.3	4	7
JA 2.7	5.3	8
B 2	4	7
C 6.7	4	2.7

Conclusions:

Judge C is the most accurate in assessing the relative favorability of each target person's self-ratings.

Judge B is the most accurate in assessing the "population norms" for each item.

Judges A and B are equally accurate—and more accurate than C—in tracking the particular ratings of particular target persons.

FIGURE 2-1 Who is the most accurate judge—A, B, or C?

analysis of accuracy into its components is that judges of personality can be equally accurate for different reasons. One judge might be accurate because he is good at judging how positively most people feel about themselves, which happens to be true of the person being judged (differential elevation), another judge might be an expert at knowing how people in general feel about their standing on different traits (stereotype accuracy), and still another judge might be very good at discerning the relative differences in particular judges' ratings on particular items (differential accuracy), even though she doesn't do such a good job in estimating the overall levels or absolute values of the ratings. To complicate matters further, any one of these measures of accuracy can actually reflect *assumed similarity*. A judge may respond to the task of rating a target person by assuming that all target persons are pretty much like himself. If, by coincidence, a particular target person is indeed similar, this similarity-assuming judge would get unfair "credit" for being a good judge when he is in fact just a lazy judge who may have no insight into the person being judged.

In surveying the literature on the psychometrics of measuring accuracy in judging others, Cronbach reached the conclusion that the variation in predicting responses should never exceed the actual variation in responses and should ordinarily be much smaller. In other words, the more cautious, conservative judge will usually be more accurate than the overconfident "gambler,"[13] whether the judge is a psychologist or anyone else who would like to be accurate in assessing another. Cronbach's general advice was to be very conservative when attempting to differentiate individuals on the basis of inadequate data. The rule of thumb should be that the more inadequate your information about a target person, the more you should treat the target person as average in all respects on any interpersonal judgment task. This may explain why trained psychologists aren't necessarily more accurate than intelligent laypersons on interpersonal judgment tasks. If we grant that trained psychologists may be more sensitive to nuances in the data they are working from, the chances are very good that they will overestimate the data's reliability and significance.

In fact, a rather substantial literature documents the tendency of psychologists and laypersons alike to fill in the gaps in their knowledge of others with storylines that fit their implicit theories of personality better than they fit the data.[14] Even experienced clinicians are often unaware of the extent to which the stories they construct from Rorschach responses or therapy interviews, although making coherent sense, involve "illusory correlations" between data and theory.[15] The rest of us should also realize that much of our faith in our judgmental accuracy probably stems more from our sense of satisfaction with the constructions we have achieved in accounting for the behavior of important others than from their accuracy per se. At least, we rarely get the kind of clear feedback that convinces us that we were wrong.

It was Cronbach's constructive intention to alert thoughtless researchers to some of the problems in treating perceptual accuracy scores as if they always reflected the same kind of ability. An important consequence of his papers on interpersonal judgment, however, was to make researchers very skittish about asking *any* questions that involved assessing judgmental accuracy. As the field of person perception developed in the 1960s, the concern with judgmental accuracy was increasingly seen as a diversion from the more important and theoretically significant studies of the *processes* of interpersonal perception. But a more recent study by Susan Andersen revives the accuracy question in a context that has intriguing process implications.[16]

Andersen recruited twenty female undergraduates and had them prepare three brief personal interviews, later to be used by naive observers as a basis for forming their impression. During each interview, the speakers were asked to describe themselves as accurately as possible with respect to such topics as career, relationships with others, major decision conflicts, and "experiences that have shaped me as a person." In the first interview there were no further instructions. In the second interview, however, they were either instructed to emphasize their thoughts and feelings in dealing with these topics or instructed to emphasize their overt actions and deemphasize their thoughts and feelings. In the third interview they received the alternative behavior or thought instructions—whatever they did not do during the second interview.

Prior to the tape recording of these interviews, each speaker had rated herself on fifty-one self-descriptive items. In a final phase of the study naive observers listened to one of the three interviews of a randomly selected speaker and rated her on the same items. A simple measure of accuracy could be obtained by correlating the ratings of the observers with the self-ratings of the speakers.

The main finding of the study was that those observers exposed to the "thoughts and feelings" interview were significantly more accurate by this measure ($r = .52$) than those exposed to the "behavior" interview ($r = .37$). But what about the various components of accuracy identified by Cronbach? Since subjects were forced to distribute their ratings into a normal distribution, no measure of "elevation" could be obtained. Also, since only one person was rated by each observer, no relevant measure of differential elevation (favorability ratings of different subjects) could be obtained. However, there were two indications that the measures concerned something more than "stereotype accuracy." Each observer had also been asked to rate the typical female student on the same items. When these ratings were partialed out of the accuracy correlations, the superior accuracy of the thoughts and feelings interview over the behavior interview was even greater. Furthermore, when the observers' ratings of the speaker they heard were correlated with the self-ratings of speakers they had not heard, these correlations (an index of "stereotype accuracy") were much lower. In short, Andersen was able to show, by a fairly pure measure of differential accuracy, that private thoughts and feelings are more diagnostic of the self (departing more from ratings of the average student) than are one's behaviors: "[O]bservers who heard interviews emphasizing thoughts and feelings, rather than behavior, departed more from their baseline ratings of average students when making their actual assessments."[17]

The results of this study may strike the reader as an elaborate demonstration of the obvious, but arguments could and (as we shall see) have been made concerning the informational priority of actual behavior in assessing what an actor is really like. Furthermore, the study marks an interesting convergence of an older interest in judgmental accuracy and a more contemporary interest in what kinds of information are given priority in the impression formation process. So this is more than probing for what kinds of people make the best judge; it is an attempt to use an accuracy measure to shed light on what self-descriptive content is generally the most useful in construing another person the way that person construes herself.

The Perceiver as Information Integrator

If everyone behaved with complete consistency over time, and if all the information we received about another person were mutually reinforcing, the process of forming impressions would be fairly simple and straightforward. But, alas, people contradict themselves from time to time, they can violate our expectancies, and we often find that an acquaintance is described in different terms by different friends. Thus, part of the process of trying to understand another inevitably involves the integration of information about diverse traits that are said to characterize the person we are trying to understand.

A most important approach to information integration was launched by Solomon Asch in 1946.[18] This approach was exemplified in an extremely simple study. Asch believed and wanted to show that when diverse traits or characteristics are applied to the same individual, perceivers will nevertheless form a unitary impression and the traits will be seen to have a lawful relationship to each other. How does this take place? Asch assumed that some characteristics will be seen as more central than others, and these central characteristics will serve as a focus for organizing the impression into a coherent Gestalt or pattern. In the first experiment in his classic series of studies he presented a list of character traits and told subjects to form an impression of the person described by these traits. Some subjects were given the list "intelligent — skillful — industrious — warm — determined — practical — cautious."

Others were given an identical list with the exception that *"cold"* was substituted for *"warm."* The subjects then wrote a free description of the target person and checked the applicability of such adjectives as "generous," "wise," "honest," "persistent," and "reliable." Not surprisingly, the impressions of the warm person were generally more favorable than those of the cold person, but there were important variations in the adjectives checked as applicable. Almost all subjects saw both the warm and the cold target person as *reliable, important, persistent,* and *serious.* The percentages of those endorsing such adjectives as *generous, good-natured, humane, humorous,* and *altruistic,* were vastly higher (over 90 percent) for the warm than for the cold (between 8 and 31 percent) target person. In short, in spite of the fact that only one out of eight characteristics was varied in the stimulus list, there were striking differences in the resulting impression. And these differences could not be accounted for entirely by an undiscriminating shift in a positive or negative direction (i.e., a "halo effect").

Asch had chosen *warm* and *cold* because he thought they would prove to be central, organizing traits. When, instead, he substituted such peripheral contrasting traits as *polite/blunt,* no such dramatic differences were observed. Nor is the *warm/cold* contrast always central. When *warm* versus *cold* appeared along with "obedient — weak — shallow — unambitious — vain," the variation had much less impact. It was possible, in other words, to make central traits peripheral and peripheral traits central by changing the context provided by the other traits in the stimulus list.

Asch was most intent on demonstrating that the meanings of these characteristics interacted with each other to form an emergent synthesized whole, an integrated unity. In common-sense terms, we might say that the "intelligence" of a warm person is not the same as the "intelligence" of a cold person. The term *intelligent,* like all personal characteristics, carries a penumbra of connotations, a fringe of ambiguity. When another trait is presented along with *intelligent,* one meaning or set of meanings is selected from the available alternatives. Thus, the warm — intelligent person is, perhaps, creative and spontaneous in intelligence; the cold — intelligent person, on the other hand, might be seen by most subjects as crafty or analytical.

There was little surprise value in Asch's findings, but this series of studies was very important historically because it was one of the first attempts to get at the *process* of impression formation, rather than focusing on the validity or predictive utility of the product. Asch was not interested in saying anything about the accuracy of his subjects. He only wanted to begin an inquiry into how different bits of information are integrated in attempting to form a unitary impression of another person. The studies were also important in exemplifying a conveniently simple procedure for exploring the rules of integration. It is hardly surprising that hundreds of studies followed in which strings of adjectives were presented to subjects who were asked to record their impressions of a target person to whom they referred.

The most impressive program of such follow-up studies was that conducted by Norman Anderson and his students.[19] Anderson's purposes were quite different from Asch's, but the thrust of his work often posed a challenge to Asch's position of "emergent unity." Anderson wanted to develop a formal mathematical model of the integration of information having different valences for the judge, i.e., information falling at different positions on a scale from favorable to unfavorable. He chose to work largely with adjective lists that were supposedly descriptive of particular persons (in the tradition of Asch), but this was primarily a methodological convenience. Unlike Asch, he was not trying to capture the psychological essence of the impression formation process. He was more interested in a highly general model of integrative algebra and chose an aspect of impression formation to exemplify this model. (He subsequently attempted to extend the model to other domains of cognitive integration.) An early step was to have large numbers of subjects rate large numbers of traits on a favorability dimension. After some of the more ambiguous traits were excluded, the remaining traits could each be assigned a scale value. Then in subsequent studies subjects could be exposed to various combinations of prescaled adjectives and asked to indicate the overall favorability of their impression of the person being described. In this way, for example, one could discover whether the ultimate favorability judgment was more influenced by the adjectives coming first (a primacy effect) or last (a recency effect). By varying the numbers of adjectives in the description, one could also try to determine whether subjects averaged the valences of the adjectives in forming their impression or added them. If they added them, then the greater the number of positive traits to be integrated, the more favorable should be the resulting impression. The average, on the other hand, could remain the same.

Anderson's subjects generally showed a most impressive capacity to reproduce the averages of individual trait valences in their summary judgments. By and large, it was not necessary for him to take into account any "configural" Gestalt effects in showing how favorability information was integrated. Anderson's model treated each trait valence as independent evidence of favorability, and the model was remarkably successful in accounting for the summarizing judgments of his subjects. However, before we take this model too seriously as providing insights into the actual process of forming impressions about another person, it is important to consider the way in which Anderson typically conducted his experiments. Subjects were exposed to many different strings of adjectives arranged in counterbalanced order and were asked to judge the person supposedly described by each list. It seems reasonable to assume that this rather quickly became a boring task, one that would normally lead to various simplifying strategies, including a lazy averaging of apparent degrees of trait favorability, rather than a deeper concern about the semantic interaction among the traits in a given list.

Regardless of the merits of this particular contention, Anderson eventually conceded that there was, at least occasionally, evidence of the kinds of emergent integration for which Asch had earlier argued.[20] And, indeed, it seems obvious to me that such emergent integration is bound to occur under the proper conditions. What would these conditions be? I would propose that the meaning of perceived personal characteristics will be more likely to interact with each other (and form an emergent, configural Gestalt) to the extent that the perceiver is trying to understand a particular target person, the information about the target person seems valid and "realistic," there is some degree of semantic inconsistency, and the judgment required is not simply one of placing the target person on an evaluative dimension.

Indeed, in some more recent research Asch (with Zukier) has pushed his configural case even more strongly by asking subjects to reconcile conflicting or "discordant" pairs of traits in describing a person.[21] In individual sessions, subjects were asked to think of a person who is, for example, *sociable* and *lonely*. Other examples of discordant traits (traits that do not follow from each other and seem almost like antonyms or opposites) were

brilliant – foolish

hostile – dependent

ambitious – lazy

generous – vindictive

treacherous – sentimental

shy – courageous

strict – kind

cheerful – gloomy

Asch and Zukier found that subjects had very little trouble with even these rather severe integration challenges, and such challenges certainly were not typically met by taking an average of the two adjective valences. Unitary impressions were reached in a number of ways. For example, the *sociable – lonely* person was seen as a truly lonely person who covers up loneliness by appearing to be sociable. The *cheerful – gloomy* person was easily dealt with as "moody." The *brilliant – foolish* person was typically seen as intellectually brilliant but foolish in commonsense matters—the dispositions were segregated by assigning each to a different sphere of the person. And so on. Asch and Zukier recapitulate the argument that Asch initially put forth some twenty-eight years earlier: "Standing alone, a disposition is generally viewed in its most rounded, least qualified sense. When several dispositions come jointly, they qualify each other. The initial broad scope of each dispo-

sition is altered by the necessity to adapt the respective implications to one another. These resolutions point to probable
origins, boundaries, and causal sequences of the respective
dispositions."[22]

The Perceiver as Causal Attributor

Asch was concerned with the facility of human perceivers to
form uniform, coherent impressions out of information about a
target person that might seem quite discordant. His good
friend Fritz Heider was also concerned with the unitariness of
our social impressions and also very much influenced by the
configural emphasis of Gestalt psychology, but his approach
had a rather different point of departure. In a classic paper in
1944 Heider focused on our direct perceptions of behavior
and emphasized that just as we understand the natural environment by perceiving any change as the effect of some cause,
so we immediately understand behavioral effects in terms of
the causes that produced them.[23] Causes of particular effects
may sometimes be inferred through elaborate cognitive processes, of course, but Heider argued that cause and effect can
also form a natural Gestalt unit, one that is immediately perceived or grasped as such. Thus, behavior is often linked without reflection to its cause and perceived as a single, coherent
pattern.

Heider had been impressed and influenced by the research of Michotte, the Belgian psychologist who demonstrated the rapidity and uniformity of causal perception when
simple objects were seen to strike each other in a laboratory
display.[24] If object A struck B and B moved away, subjects
consistently saw this as A "launching" B (*l'effet lancement*). If
A struck B and they both moved together, subjects reported an
"entraining" effect (*l'effet entrainement*). Heider with Simmel
put together a film showing nonsocial objects (two triangles, a
box, a circle) moving around each other in ways that were
typically seen in anthropomorphic terms.[25] Subjects viewing

this short film readily endowed the moving objects with intentions, even with personalities, and constructed a story accounting for the movements observed. It is debatable whether we want to call this perception, but Heider viewed all perception as the conversion of stimulus energy into its "distal" cause, whether that cause was the flash of lightning in the sky or the flashing light of a police car seen in the rear-view mirror.

Heider blended this Gestalt view of the cause–effect unit with a dedication to *functionalism*. That is, one perceives one's environment in cause–effect terms because it is very functional do to so; it promotes one's own survival. Take perceived size constancies, for example. I see the person at the end of the hall as roughly the same size as the person walking three yards from me, even though the sizes of the two on my retina are vastly different. I see a red blouse as about equally red whether the person wearing it is in the light or in the shade. Similarly, it is functional to attribute constancy or stability to the patterns of behavior we observe in others. Behavior is not all random variation: Behavior is caused. People behave for reasons, and it is important that the otherwise chaotic world of interpersonal relations be rendered as stable (and therefore as predictable) as possible by our attributions of motivation and personal dispositions and by our recognition of the causal role of the target person's situation.

Although prone to stress the inevitable role of causal attribution in all forms of perception, of both physical and social events, Heider also emphasized the distinction between personal causality and impersonal causality. A major feature of this distinction is that impersonal causality is a matter of infinite regress: Each cause is an effect of a prior cause. We could trace a forest fire to the confluence of factors having a history as long as the origin of the first oxygen molecules in the universe. Personal causality, on the other hand, is more like a worker and his or her product. We can, of course, look at the worker from the infinitely regressive point of view of the natural sciences, focusing on the physics of converting raw materials into a product, but as perceivers we do not do so. We truncate the causal sequence, attributing the product to the worker, whom we see as causing it, as its origin, responsible

for its being good or bad. It is vital that human life be organized this way, for otherwise one can imagine the impossibility
of any form of social order. In the domain of law, to take the
most obvious examples of the social order, we could never
punish rapists, murderers, and arsonists if we lived only in a
world of impersonal causality; after all, any social outrage can
be ultimately "explained" at the level of genes and past experiences. An impersonal causal explanation of the forest fire
might necessitate an infinite regress, but a personal attribution
could stop with evidence of a carelessly thrown match.

To illustrate the importance of causal attribution in everyday social life, consider:

1. What a difference it would make in our behavior if we
thought the dentist was trying to hurt us because of his or her
underlying hostility.

2. We have learned that because salespersons and politicians are dependent on our good graces, we should take their
advice ("vote for me," "buy this") with a grain of salt.

3. Getting along with others is difficult if we continually
misread their intentions or fail to appreciate how things look
from their perspective.

4. Teachers and counselors need to understand what
causes poor performance in a student; otherwise the "rem-
edy" might exacerbate rather than improve the situation.

5. At the international level it is extremely important that
we accurately read the intentions of foreign powers—what
lies behind certain moves and maneuvers. This is most obviously true in times of war when military strategies are specifically designed to conceal or mislead the enemy about one's
intentions.[26]

Heider's celebration of the role of "phenomenal causality" in the perception of persons was a crucial first step in the
development of the attributional approach, which became the
major underpinning and the dominant perspective of contem-

porary person perception research.[27] We shall discuss this approach in greater detail in the text chapter.

The Perceiver as Motivated Actor

Among those present at the Harvard ONR symposium, I was perhaps the one most directly influenced by Jerome Bruner. Not only had he been both my undergraduate and graduate adviser, but I had spent six years at Harvard breathing the heady atmosphere of the "new look" in perception — so named by analogy to the "new look" in woman's clothing following World War II. Bruner's view of perception, which was functionalistic in a more psychodynamic sense than Heider's, included a perceiver whose perceptual and cognitive activities were in the service of his or her needs and personal adjustment to environmental contingencies. Bruner shocked and disturbed many traditionalists in the perception field by failing to draw a clear line between sensation and perception, on the one hand, and inference and cognition, on the other. He argued and, along with his colleague Leo Postman and their students, tried to demonstrate that motives and expectancies enter at a very early stage in the perceptual process and affect some of the most basic parameters of physical estimation, such as size, brightness, and color.[28] But above all, Bruner's position was that our perceptual activities are selective: We are alert and sensitive to need-relevant objects in the environment and to those that are most likely to occur. We will "see" them quicker, under less illumination, or as larger than objects not relevant to our needs or more unexpected. The perceptual apparatus is not, then, like a camera that objectively reconstitutes objects and persons merely in terms of light values. When the perceiver has a "hypothesis" or an expectancy about what is out there, it takes less evidence to perceive the expected object.

During the early 1950s there were extended arguments in the literature about the plasticity of the perceptual apparatus

—its sensitivity to needs and the effects of past experiences. Do we really see or hear expected and desired things more readily, or is it merely that we are more likely to *report* seeing them? The issue of where perceiving ends and responding begins did not seem particularly problematic to me as I began my own research dealing with the "perception of persons." After all, when we speak of person perception we are, at least much of the time, using "perception" almost in a metaphoric way. Although it may seem that we perceive behavioral causes immediately and without reflection, who is to know (and perhaps who should care) whether this is truly immediate perception or involves the rapid application of inference or experience-based judgment?

In any event, it seemed obvious to me that a realistic account of person perception had to involve a big bite of the "new look" orientation. Person perception could most fruitfully be seen as embedded in social interaction, where perceivers have interaction goals and purposes. John Thibaut and I argued in a paper written for the Harvard symposium, that a perceiver's interaction goals will influence both the behavioral and situational information selected and the inferential uses to which it is subsequently put.[29] We proposed a crude taxonomy of *inferential sets:* "value maintenance" (where the goal is to be liked or admired or to have one's beliefs supported), "causal genetic" (where the goal is to determine the causes or historical origins of the behavior observed), and "situation matching" (where the goal is to decide whether the behavior matches or violates a normative rule).

We saw value maintenance as the most ubiquitous or omnipresent of the interaction goals and divided this category into a number of subdivisions. The most obvious consequences of being in a value maintenance set are those illustrating the egocentricity of our perceptions of others. It hardly takes years of studying psychology to come up with some version of a proposition that emphasizes how we perceive others in a self-serving way; that we will, for example, perceive the traits and motives of others in a more positive light when their behavior supports our interaction goals.

Richard deCharms and I tested a slightly more complex version of this proposition.[30] Male college student subjects worked in small groups on a series of performance tasks. One member of the group was a role-playing accomplice who always failed the last task. In some of the groups, according to a prior understanding conveyed by the instructions, this meant that none of the real subjects was entitled to an available monetary reward. In the rest of the groups, receipt of the reward was contingent only on the subject's own performance (which was always rigged so that he was successful). In addition, some of the subjects had been led to believe that the tasks were pure measures of intellectual ability, others that the tasks were chosen especially because they were very sensitive to motivation—how hard a person was willing to try. When subjects rated each other on a number of traits at the end of the experiment, the accomplice was strongly disfavored only when his failure had deprivational consequences for the subjects and only when the tasks were alleged to be sensitive to motivation. Though the behavior of the accomplice was always the same, he was "perceived" differently as a function of the implications of his actions for the value maintenance goals of the perceiver.

To argue that our perceptions of and inferences about others are affected by the implications of their behavior for our own goals and purposes was not controversial even as long ago as 1957. It is certainly not controversial today. And yet it has not been easy to develop a cumulative body of research showing just *how* our goals shape the cognitive processes associated with person perception.[31] The role of interaction goals and purposes will be discussed in many different contexts in the chapters to come, especially in contexts concerning attraction and self-presentation. At this point, perhaps it is most useful to note that this discussion of interaction goals has implications for qualifying the importance of accurate and fully formed interpersonal judgments. As noted in the preceding chapter, William Swann has forcefully argued that when we look at the perception of persons in the context of their interaction with each other, it is clear that most of our interactions do not require us to know what the other person is *really* like in any comprehensive or deep fashion.[32] The important thing is to be able to predict that person's behavior in our presence. Most of the time, this kind of "pragmatic accuracy" is just as satisfactory for our social adaptation as would be the presumably richer assessments of a clinical diagnostician.

Summary

In the present chapter I have played the role of a selective historian, trying to identify the major themes in the study of perceiving persons that began to emerge in the decade following World War II. The 1957 Harvard symposium was an organizing focus for an important new field. Most of the main lines of investigation that have come to identify the field were represented by symposium participants. I have tried to identify these lines and to explain the distinctive perspective of each on the role of the perceiver. Perhaps the earliest concern was with the *perceiver as a reader of emotional expression*. This concern was a by-product of a more fundamental interest in the uniformity of emotional expression, but it raised some early questions about methodological issues. The questions were more sharply posed by studies focusing on the accuracy of the *perceiver as a judge of personality*. The main consequence of this approach was to increase our skepticism concerning the measurement and the meaning of accurate judgments of someone's personality. Just as this skepticism was beginning to close off interest in the perception of persons, a new focus on the *perceiver as information integrator* surfaced. Here the emphasis on the processes of impression formation resuscitated the research enterprise and linked it to broader processes of cognitive inference. No perspective was to prove as important as the view of the *perceiver as causal attributor*. This perspective was to lead directly into the attributional approach that has dominated and shaped person perception inquiries for the past two decades. Finally, we have noted the importance of recognizing that the *perceiver is a motivated actor* whose interaction goals shape the selective intake and processing of information about others. This, again, is a theme that reappears in many places in the chapters to come.

The

Attributional Approach

Perceiving others is synony-
mous with making sense of their behavior, and this activity
typically involves finding the cause or causes of that behavior.
In their wisdom as naive psychologists, perceivers try to
"find" appropriate causes in characteristics of the actor—
inferred dispositions that seem to explain why the actor behaved as he or she did. Starting with some understanding of
what the actor was trying to accomplish, the perceiver moves
quickly to consider: What were the actor's motives? Do these
motives suggest more enduring traits, values, beliefs, attitudes? The search for such personal characteristics is a central
feature of attributing causes for behavior. Perceivers engage
in such an attributional process to confer stable meaning on

their social surroundings. Attempts to understand this process engage us in the attributional approach. Since it is the approach I find most congenial and one that provides much of the interpretive context of the chapters to follow, I will identify its major features and review enough of its historical evolution to enable the reader to appreciate its distinctiveness.

Phenomenal Causality

Philosophical treatments of decisions about causation are an old story, but it was in 1944 that Fritz Heider first impressed psychologists with the relevance of causal attribution in his paper concerning phenomenal (or experienced) causality.[1] The basic premise of this initial contribution to the attributional approach was that behavior is perceptually linked to, and takes its meaning from, its causes. But just how are these causes assigned? For example, what are the rules people use in deciding whether an act was intended or accidental? And if intended, what does an act imply about the actor's personality? The kinds of actions we are likely to be interested in are those that have consequences — ones that produce certain changes or effects in the environment. But actions typically have more than one consequence. Which of the multiple effects of an action is likely to be singled out as the effect whose intent is seen as the cause of behavior?

A major step in the evolution of Heider's thinking was to address some of these questions by trying to codify the naive psychology of the man-on-the-street. Everyone is a psychologist in the sense that everyone has certain beliefs or implicit theories about human nature — about what most people want, about right or wrong, about the achievements people are capable of. Presumably, a solid understanding of naive psychology could provide the underpinnings of a comprehensive understanding of how people perceive and judge others and therefore of some of the major determinants of their interpersonal behavior. But is there any consistency about these beliefs and theories?

There are some reasons for optimism in proceeding on the assumption that my naive psychology is not too different from yours. After all, we have all been socialized into roughly comparable cultures, and our actions are bounded by similar physical opportunities and constraints as we go about our daily business. There are many regularities in our life that come with ready-made explanations. We learn that the sun never rises in the west and never sets in the east, that horses run faster than people, and that death is irreversible. We also learn that people get angry when they are frustrated or thwarted, that hard-earned victories are gratifying, and that "love is blind."

So the rules governing naive psychology are there, all right. There are some widely held theories about human behavior. But how can psychologists, in the role of objective scientists, identify or gain access to these shared conceptions of human nature? Heider's *The Psychology of Interpersonal Relations* represents an important attempt to tackle this project, though Heider recognized clearly that it was only a beginning.[2] In reviewing this attempt, it is important to keep in mind that I am *not* concerned with the accuracy of an actor's causal interpretation or with his or her view of the motivational implications of certain actions. These are irrelevant to the attributional approach. My only concern is with accurately characterizing this naive psychology, a psychology that could be profoundly wrong or stupid or full of errors. In fact, the empirical legacy of the attributional approach is a peculiar mixture of results showing how clever and discerning we sometimes are, along with results showing how limited, biased, and even simple-minded we can be in making certain kinds of inferences.[3]

Heider was willing to look for clues about naive psychological principles everywhere — in his own experience, in the revelations of visual art, in poetry, fiction, and drama, and in the results of psychological experiments and observational studies. But the main feature of his approach was to analyze a limited number of common language concepts — concepts used in everyday speech to describe subjective states and interpersonal events. Heider believed that the structure of naive psychology might be revealed by analyses of a limited number of key words like *desire, promise, pride, envy, like, own, benefit, owe,* and *request.* This analysis would not be concerned with etymology or precise definitions; it would be an attempt to think through the common usage of each term, its relationship to other primitive terms, and its implications for interpersonal relations.

Examples are scattered throughout Heider's work, but my favorite example is his analysis of naive beliefs about action, an analysis that, I believe, forms the centerpiece of his interpersonal relations book. The following discussion does not precisely follow Heider in every detail, but it is very much in the spirit of his analysis. Let us first think of an action (x), some behavioral decision or achievement that produces an effect or an outcome: John takes and passes an algebra test; Mary buys a new dress; Roger is in an automobile accident; Greg knocks off the crossbar while attempting to clear six feet in the high jump. Our attributional analysis begins with such x's; then we can proceed to think about what was necessary and sufficient for x to occur. Here the major distinction is between two of those homespun words in our common language, *can* and *try.* (*Luck,* a term referring to uncontrolled features outside the attributional system, events that were unforeseen and perhaps unforeseeable, also enters the analysis.) The important thing about *can* and *try* is that some degree of each must be necessary for an action or achievement to occur. For this reason, Heider conceived the relationship between them as "multiplicative," meaning only that if either *can* or *try* is zero, there will be no x, no achievement outcome. John may have all the algebra skill in the world, but he will flunk the test if he fails to try at all and does not record any answers. Obversely, maximum effort cannot guarantee an A average for a student of limited ability.

But we don't (and Heider didn't) stop there. To *try* implies directed motivation and thus requires both *exertion* and *intention.* And both of these qualities are generally perceived to be under the control of the actor. On the other hand, the actor presumably has less control over the *can* ingredient, partly because it depends on the state of the environment— on the difficulty level of the task, for example—and partly because we can only control our ability in the long run, through practice or training, and even then there are limitations imposed by our own genetic makeup. This presumed difference in perceived control was important in the experiment by deCharms and myself reported in the preceding chapter.[4] Recall that people reacted more unfavorably to a failing partner when the tasks were initially described as sensitive to motivational factors. We predicted this result on the grounds that letting the team down when you could have tried harder invites more scorn than letting the team down through a lack of ability.

As I have noted, *can* is a joint function of personal *power* (often ability) and what Heider called *Effective Environmental Force* (usually translatable as task difficulty). This suggests a somewhat different breakdown in terms of personal and environmental force — or more generally, characteristics we can attribute to the person and those we can attribute to the environment. *Effective Personal Force* is the product of *power* (usually ability) and *try* (exertion and intention), whereas *Effective Environmental Force* (especially task difficulty) is one of the ingredients (along with *power*) of *can*.

Heider describes the relationship between environmental and personal force as additive (rather than multiplicative, as between *can* and *try*) in potentially producing *x* because a high enough level of one can overcome the absence of the other. As an example, he considers a boat in the middle of a lake: Whether it reaches shore can depend on the strength of the rower (either aided or thwarted by the wind) or entirely on the wind (if the rower became injured or was asleep). Thus, the outcome could be achieved even if either personal force or environmental force were zero.

This naive analysis of action is summarized in Figure 3-1.[5] The two "trade-offs" embedded in this analysis are the most fundamental features of the attributional approach. Trade-off 1, which I will loosely refer to as the ability/effort trade-off, becomes the crucial feature of a vast literature on the psychology of achievement and on responses by both actors and observers to success and failure. Trade-off 2, the person/situation trade-off, is perhaps an even more fundamental feature in the person perception domain. Here the central attributional issue revolves around the relative contributions of the unique and distinctive features of the actor and the demands or constraints of the situation. It is this trade-off that becomes the focus of correspondent inference theory, to which I now turn.

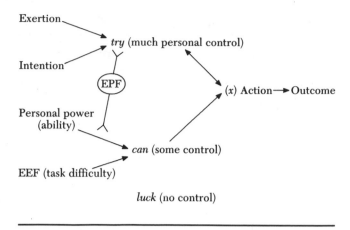

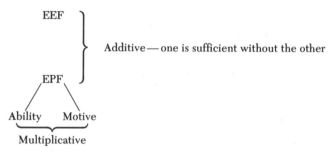

FIGURE 3-1   The naive psychology of action. (EPF = Effective Personal Force; EEF = Effective Environmental Force.)

Correspondent Inference Theory

In my view, the central problem of person perception has always been how people characterize others when observing their behavior. A first step is to realize that not all behaviors are equally informative. Why not? Various answers converge on the central issue of behavioral *choice*; freely chosen behaviors should be more informative than behaviors that are required or constrained by the situation. When hostages condemn their own country while held by terrorists, we are more likely to attribute their statements to coercion than to their own private attitudes. This seems obvious enough, but how could we take advantage of this to construct a theory of inferring dispositions from observed actions?

The first step in the development of correspondent inference theory was to recast choice in terms of behavioral alternatives and optional consequences.[6] That is, the meaning of an act—the significance for inferring intentions and ultimately dispositions—is contained in the effects of the act on the environment, not in the particular muscular movements or verbal patterns involved. If I get out of my chair and walk across my office to close the door to the hall, it is this consequence, this new environmental arrangement, that confers potential meaning on the behavior, not whether I closed the door with my left hand or my right hand or by kicking aside the doorstopper. We can begin to understand this simple act only by observing the effect on the environment (a formerly open door is now closed) and beginning to seek a plausible cause.[7] Causal analysis begins with the perception of an effect.

But even the briefest, simplest actions tend to have more than one effect. Closing the door may reduce the noise from the hall, change the distribution of light, give me a moment to decide what to say next, provide conditions for greater conversational intimacy, and so on. To make the point even more obvious, consider a more significant and important decision than closing my office door: A neighbor's son decides to join the marines. Now there is no question that the consequences of *that* decision are many, and we could reasonably spell out some of the major ones. In doing so, we would probably include many effects that would have followed alternative career decisions. If we knew, for example, that our neighbor's son was considering whether to join the marines or the air force, we could look at the effects of the chosen action and of the nonchosen action, and we would realize that many of the effects are common——leaving home, accepting military discipline, wearing a uniform, increasing the probability of danger, and so on. So the effects of most actions are not only numerous but common to actions perceived as alternative possibilities. Thus, behavior is informative to the extent that it is seen to involve choice among alternatives. These alternatives in turn are typically complex, involving multiple effects or consequences. Some of these consequences are common to the various alternatives considered; some are not. Logically, only the distinctive alternatives can be informative about the motives or intentions (the "causes") of the chosen action.[8]

It was this kind of reasoning that led to what Davis and I called a theory of correspondent inference. We chose "correspondent" to refer to those inferences a perceiver makes that treat another person's action at face value. A correspondent inference is a straightforward extrapolation from the behavior observed: The behavior is seen as corresponding to or reflecting an underlying disposition of the actor, and the consequences it achieves are not only intended but would be characteristically intended by the actor — they are representative of his or her behavior and characterize the actor as a person. Some examples of correspondent inferences:

Perceived Act	Inferred Intention or Disposition
He is eating a pickle.	He likes pickles (a preference).
"Reagan lied about Iran – contra."	Reagan is a liar (a belief).
"I love to feel free."	She loves freedom (a value).
He talks the most at a meeting.	He is dominant (a trait).
She solves a tough problem.	She is intelligent (an ability).
He says, "You're intelligent."	He thinks I'm intelligent.

Noncorrespondent inferences might include:

He says, "You're intelligent."	He flatters, intending seduction.
"The Union has gone too far."	He seeks ingratiation with company supervisors.
He spills wine on the white carpet.	It was only an accident.

Noncorrespondent inferences might also be drawn about an action (even one like punching someone in the nose) that would normally be quite diagnostic of the person but is an action that almost anyone would have undertaken under the same circumstances.

In various chapters and papers[9] my colleagues and I have offered different definitions of correspondence, some more technical and operational than others, but for present purposes the loose notion of "behavior at face value" should be sufficient. The perceiver who draws a correspondent inference essentially applies the same label to the act as to the disposition; for example, to call a person hostile after observing a hostile act would be to draw a correspondent inference. The preceding discussion of effects chosen and effects forgone has forecast the essence of correspondent inference theory. An inference would be correspondent to the extent that the effects chosen are distinctive from the effects forgone and can be described with a particular dispositional label (a trait, a motive).

But that's not quite enough because we still may be dealing with a distinctive set of effects or consequences that anyone would choose to bring about. In that case we probably would not think to label the person with reference to the consequences he or she seeks; that would be like attributing a love of swimming to a drowning woman or calling a soldier bloodthirsty for firing his rifle at the enemy. If a correspondent inference is to have reference to a distinctive set of personal characteristics, the theory had to include some reference to the popularity or inevitability of the chosen action — the extent to which not everyone would choose to act in the same way.

Behavior, in other words, can be informative about a person in two ways: because it could only have been enacted to achieve a distinctive effect and because the effect was not one that everyone would have sought to achieve. Behavior that is informative in both respects leads to a correspondent inference. This is represented in Figure 3-2.

The number of effects that are common to both the chosen and the nonchosen alternatives is an index of ambiguity. The more reasons there were for adopting a particular course of action, the less confident an observer can be that any of

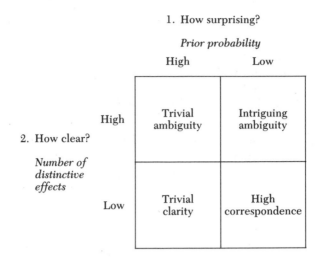

FIGURE 3-2   Determinants of correspondence.

these was especially important or determinative. Cross-cutting the number of distinctive effects are variations in the prior probability[10] or likelihood of the chosen action. If the act is only what could have been expected, then we treat the information as trivial. Some examples may be helpful here:

1. If Professor Williams closes the door because there is a deafening sound of an electric drill in the hall, an observer would be quite certain *why* she closed the door and would also be convinced that anyone else would have done the same thing under the circumstances. This would be a case of *trivial clarity*: The consequences of the action are singular or distinctive, and the action of closing the door when there is disruptive noise has a high prior probability. The results of the inference process are therefore clear but trivial from an informational point of view.

2. Let us imagine that Sam lives alone in a small Montana village with one movie theater at the intersection of the two main streets. Sam is observed going to see the Vietnam war movie *Full Metal Jacket* on a cold and rainy Saturday night. Can you infer that Sam likes Stanley Kubrick films? Or even that Sam likes war films? Here we have an obvious case of a

high number of effects associated with attendance at a movie and not with the alternative of staying home. Furthermore, since almost all of these effects would be viewed as desirable by most observers, the moviegoing act is not at all unexpected. Because of the many positive consequences of Sam's going to this movie, no observer could be clever enough to know which of these was crucial to Sam's decision to attend without knowing anything else about him. But the inference problem can be classed as a *trivial ambiguity* because most of the potential reasons for Sam's attending the movie are reasons why anyone would want to attend: The movie has been well reviewed, Kubrick is a famous director, the theater is warm and comfortable, the popcorn is good, and Sam will probably see many good friends — who also attended because there was nothing much else to do.

3. You, the observer, discover that Meg was given a full scholarship to Smith College, but instead, she chose to join the United States Coast Guard. The number of distinctive effects involved in this choice is colossal: Both the effects of being in the Coast Guard and the effects of not being a Smith student must be considered. The information is ambiguous, therefore, but it is an important, *intriguing ambiguity* because most people would not have made the same choice between these two alternatives. Asked to explain what kind of a person Meg is, the perceiver would have to consider many alternatives and would not be able easily to choose between them.

4. Max is on the college debating team. We overhear the coach ask him in preparation for the next debate whether he wants to defend or oppose the position that we should unilaterally dispose of our nuclear weapons. Max chooses to defend the disarmament position. Now it is conceivable that he made this choice because of the intellectual challenge that would be involved or because he has made some private agreement with a teammate, but a clear and plausible inference is that Max feels strongly enough about disarmament to prefer to take a position that even most pacifists would consider a little extreme. This would be a *correspondent inference* because there are few distinctive effects and the choice Max made does not have a particularly high prior probability.

This, then, is the essence of correspondent inference theory. Before considering any empirical tests of the theory or identifying some crucial problems of implementation, let me first present Kelley's covariation theory, one that bears many similarities to correspondent inference theory, along with some important differences, and one that has had an extremely important impact on the evolution of the attribution approach.

The Covariation Model

Correspondent inference theory grew out of a direct attempt to characterize the underlying logic of perceiving other persons. Harold Kelley's point of departure[11] was essentially the other side of the coin: How can we gain a stable view of reality when so much of it is mediated by the words and actions of others? Both treatments accept the general premise of a trade-off between the person and the situation: Perceivers view behavior as determined by the nature of environmental entities (the situation) or as reflecting distinctive predilections of the actor (the person), and the more they attribute something to the environment, the less likely they are to attribute it to the person. But the two models essentially cross the situation–person "bridge" in different directions. If Davis and I wanted to get past the influence of the situation to get to the person, Kelley wanted to discount the biases of observers to gain a clear picture of the situation.

Let us start with a convenient example that Kelley's model nicely handles. Joan tells us that she just read a wonderful book called *The Moviegoer* by Walker Percy. Shortly thereafter, we see a copy in a bookstore and try to decide whether we should buy it. A relevant question is whether Joan's response is simply an example of her idiosyncratic taste or her predilection to praise everything she's read, or whether it was specifically occasioned by the excellence of the book in question. In order to decide whether it is Joan (the person) or the book (the entity) we might review in our minds Joan's comments about other books. These comments might be high in *distinctiveness*

—this is the only book we have ever heard her praise—or low in distinctiveness—she is always gushing over everything she reads. We might also have checked with others who may have read the book. Joan's comments may reflect high *consensus* (many others agree with her) or a lack thereof. If Joan's praise of the book is high in both distinctiveness and consensus, we should be well on the way toward an entity attribution: We should be pretty confident that *The Moviegoer* is indeed a good book. This would especially be the case if the next time we saw Joan she again praised the book, or if she also praised the movie adaptation because of its fidelity to the book. We would have evidence of *consistency* over time and over modality.

Keeping this example in mind, let us try to follow a more abstract presentation of the essentials of Kelley's model.

1. We start with some *focus of judgment*. A perceiver or attributor wants to understand the nature of an entity. The entity can be anything in nature that elicits response: It can be a book, a theory, a Siamese cat, a sports car, an ethnic group, another person, or—and this opens very important new vistas—the self. Thus, I may use a person's response to help me understand another person to whom she is responding, and this other person might be myself. Or *I* might be the person responding, and I might want to know whether my response is idiosyncratic or entity determined.

2. The theory does not say much about the *nature of the response*, but it is clear from the examples given that it can be almost anything from an opinion or an emotional reaction (such as tears or laughter) to an approaching or avoiding action (buying a book or a marriage license, running from a tiger). The minimal feature is that the response can be interpreted as either triggered by a description of, or a preference for, the entity in question.

3. Next we must consider the *conditions of the response*, and here we reach the heart of the theory—the major independent variables, if you will. As introduced above, the major

conditions or variables are distinctiveness, consensus, and consistency.

4. The conditions of the response serving as the perceiver's focus of judgment determine the *attribution* that will be made. The dependent variables of the theory are the allocation of causation to the *person* (the actor whose responses are the focus of judgment), the entity to which the person is responding, or two ways in which persons and entities can combine. The attribution can be to both the person and the entity ($P + E$—as when we find out that Joan is an indiscriminate book lover, but everyone else liked *The Moviegoer*, too) or to some unique combination of person and entity ($P \times E$— Joan doesn't like any other book, but no one else likes *The Moviegoer*; there is something special, then, about the affinity between Joan and this particular novel). When the response serving as the focus of judgment is inconsistent, at attribution to circumstance is a final possibility. This is essentially a confession of ignorance, for the perceiver cannot otherwise account for the capriciousness of the actor.[12]

5. The theoretical premise that links the independent variable conditions to the dependent variable attributions is the covariation principle: If a reaction is always present when the entity is present and absent when it is absent, then the entity probably caused the reaction. So if Joan likes only this book, the book must be the cause of her reaction. From Kelley's model and this operating inference rule, the following predictions can be made:

Conditions

Dist.	*Consens.*	*Consist.*		*Attributions*
1. Hi	Hi	Hi	$\longrightarrow$	Entity
2. Lo	Lo	Hi	$\longrightarrow$	Person
3. Hi	Lo	Hi	$\longrightarrow$	Person × Entity
4. Lo	Hi	Hi	$\longrightarrow$	Person + Entity
5. Lo or Hi	Lo or Hi	Lo	$\longrightarrow$	Circumstance

Comparison of the Models

Kelley's covariation model represented a pivotal event in the evolution of the attributional approach.[13] Heider's book had attracted interest and praise, but the formulations of correspondent inference theory and especially Kelley's model led to a rediscovery of Heider's riches some ten years after the book was published. Kelley's model did several things that our presentation of correspondent inference had failed to do. His model explicitly dealt with sequences of behavior over time, whereas Davis and I had dealt in a somewhat similar way with options chosen and options forgone. The original form of correspondent inference theory was definitely a first-impression theory, dealing especially with the meaning of single acts or decisions by an unfamiliar target person.[14]

A second difference between the covariation model and correspondent inference theory was Kelley's explicit inclusion of self-attribution. In his view self-understanding (the attribution of self characteristics) is governed by the same variables as those involved in attributing dispositional characteristics to others. This was strategically important since it paved the way for Daryl Bem's self-perception theory.[15] In fact, a most important general virtue of Kelley's presentation was its connection with social comparison theory, dissonance theory, and Schachter's theory of emotional labeling.[16] With Kelley's able assistance, one could begin to see the broad relevance of attribution theory, not just for a particular understanding of person perception processes, but for a broader grasp of some of the most basic social psychological phenomena.

A major weakness of covariation theory was the primitive status of its dependent variables. An action can be attributed to the person, to the entity, or to circumstance. But in contrast to the case in correspondent inference theory, there is no concern with the content or level of the attribution, no clear way to specify what is being attributed. Perhaps it is fair to say that Kelley paid the price of dependent variable specificity by reaching for a more general and abstract formulation. Kelley's essay was more directly concerned with general issues of causal attribution—in the physical as well as in the social environment. He followed a model of the layperson-as-scientist. Davis and I were interested in behavior causation only if it were relevant to the attribution of distinctive personal characteristics (intentions, motives, and more stable trait dispositions).

No comparison of the two theories would be complete without emphasizing their many points of contact and similarity.[17] As noted previously, each deals in its own way with the basic Heiderian trade-off between situations and persons. Each contains a covariation principle, made more explicit by Kelley, assuming that the man-in-the-street is content to infer causation from correlation. More specifically, each assigns the same role to consensus or to the results of social comparison; if others respond the same way, the act is uninformative about this particular person.

But what of the principle in correspondent inference theory that we can only be confident of our inferences if the effects of observed action are relatively distinctive? Where does this notion appear in Kelley's covariation model? The answer is that it does not explicitly appear there, but Kelley did introduce it several years later under the felicitous label of *discounting principle*: "The role of a given cause producing a given effect is discounted if other plausible causes are also present."[18] The importance of this principle will be celebrated over and over again in the pages to follow. It is, in a way, but an extension of the basic idea of covariation, since it states that the more things that covary with x, the less certain we can be about which of these things really causes x. The other side of the discounting principle coin is the *augmentation principle*. The discounting principle assumes that all effects achieved by an action are facilitative, but suppose some are inhibitory; suppose some are costs instead of rewards. The augmentation principle would say that the greater the number of inhibitory effects following from an action, the more valued or diagnostic the facilitatory effects achieved. In the simplest terms, then, the more we are willing to pay for something, the more we must want it!

A classic experiment by John Thibaut and Henry Riecken illustrates the discounting principle.[19] Subjects were asked either to try to influence another subject to contribute to the "blood bank" (experiment 1) or to give them a much needed crossword puzzle dictionary (experiment 2). The influencing subjects were led to believe that they were either of higher status or of lower status than the recipients of their influence attempt. The recipients (role-playing confederates of the experimenter) eventually complied with the subject's request in all cases. When influencing subjects believed that they were of higher status than those complying with their request, they were uncertain about the reasons for compliance: The recipient of their influence might have complied because he liked the influencing subject and wanted to help or because he, being of lower status, lacked the social power to resist. The high-status subjects were in fact led to "discount" the compliance of the low-status recipients, treating it as an unreliable indicator of the recipient's liking for them or "spontaneous loyalty" to them. Low-status influencers, on the other hand, saw fewer distinctive reasons for the compliance of their high-status partners; they decided that the influence recipients must have liked them. We might call this a correspondent inference, or in Kelley's terms a person (rather than a situation) attribution. In any case, the differences between attributions by high-status versus low-status subjects illustrate both the discounting principle (in Kelley's terms) and the principle of distinctive effects (in correspondent inference theory terms).

To summarize, then, these two theoretical statements basically formalized some central features of Heider's naive psychology and attempted to characterize more explicitly the cognitive processes whereby perceivers allocate causation to the actor or to the environment. Correspondent inference theory more explicitly addresses the processes of person perception and can be readily applied to inferences about a previously unknown person acting in a particular way in a particular situation. Covariation theory is more comprehensive and more abstract, attempting to capture a general logic of attribution that applies to persons, things, and selves. The theories complement each other in many ways, and though they start from obverse orientations, they feature the same underlying logic of covariation and in most circumstances would lead to the same empirical predictions.

Empirical Support for the Models

A conventional view of the role of theories in psychology is that they contain, or can be used to generate, propositions that can be tested empirically. We can evaluate both correspondent inference theory and Kelley's covariation model in these terms, and they come off rather well. At least there are numerous studies whose results are consistent with one or both of these theories. In one early experiment that actually preceded the formulation of correspondent inference theory, Keith Davis, Kenneth Gergen, and I were able to show that behavioral deviation from a normative expectancy leads to an inference that is more correspondent than behavioral confirmation of the expectancy.[20] Subjects listened to a tape recording of a target person (allegedly) attempting to play the role of someone being interviewed for the job of a submariner or an astronaut. The "norms" for these positions were carefully spelled out beforehand, such that it was clearly noted that the ideal submariner was a gregarious extravert who enjoyed being with people in closely confined quarters, whereas the ideal astronaut was an introvert who could sustain him- or herself in social isolation for long periods of time. (This made more sense back in the days when single astronauts were sent into orbit for extended periods of time.)

In the subsequently monitored interview tape, the target person answered a series of standardized questions, either as an inner-directed introvert would or as an other-directed extravert would. The introvert's answers were "in-role" for the astronaut job and "out-of-role" for the submariner job. The extravert's answers were in-role for the submariner job and out-of-role for the astronaut job. Subjects listened to the complete interviews and were then asked to evaluate the extent to which the target person was truly inner- or other-directed. The results are summarized in Figure 3-3, which also presents the subjects' (basically accurate) recall of the target person's actual behavior. When the target person's interview responses were in-role, subjects could not tell whether the target person was inner- or other-directed. When the target person behaved in an other-directed manner and the role specifications called for an introvert, he was seen as truly other-directed. The

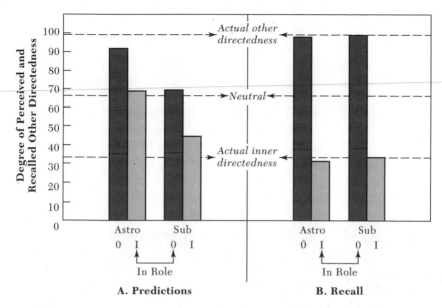

FIGURE 3-3 Degree of perceived and recalled other directedness. (From Jones, Davis, and Gergen, 1961.)

obverse was true of the inner-directed actor given a submariner role.

How do these results map into correspondent inference theory? I would suggest that the major variable is the number of distinctive effects. In the two in-role conditions we can identify (speculatively but reasonably) a number of different effects. For example, the target person who gives inner-directed responses in the astronaut role could be achieving at least the following effects:

1. Expressing a true preference for inner-directed settings

2. Showing a desire to cooperate with the experimenter

3. Showing sufficient cleverness to select the required answers

When the target person behaves in the same manner in response to instructions to come across as a submariner, the number of distinctive effects is reduced essentially to one: expressing a true preference for inner-directed settings. We could add that this is *at the expense* of appearing uncooperative and/or rather dimwitted. The results of the astronaut–submariner experiment can thus be interpreted in terms of a distinctive effects analysis, but they also exemplify Kelley's discounting principle, as well as the augmentation principle, the other side of the discounting coin. In-role behavior is discounted because there are more readily available causes of the behavior than in the out-of-role condition. Out-of-role behavior exemplifies the augmentation principle because there are reasons *not* to engage in the behavior (one would appear stupid and uncooperative, for example) that are apparently overcome by the motive to express one's true identity. Subjects therefore make an augmented correspondent inference.

But what of the prior probability principle? In a slightly later study specifically designed to test correspondent inference theory, Victor Harris and I asked subjects to read essays that were either favorable or unfavorable to Fidel Castro's regime in Cuba.[21] These essays were allegedly written as answers to examination questions in a political science course. Some subjects were led to believe that the essayists had no choice, had been forced to make the best case they could for Castro in one condition of the experiment and against him in another. Other subjects were told that the essayist had been able to choose a side; the examination question simply asked them either to defend or to oppose Castro in their answers.

The choice/no-choice variable seems to be a clear manipulation of the number of distinctive effects, with the no-choice condition comparable to the in-role condition of the astronaut-submariner experiment. We would expect subjects to be more uncertain about the true attitude of a target person who had been mandated a particular position than about one who could choose. But since the vast majority of undergraduates in the 1960s could have been expected to be against the Castro takeover in Cuba (and thus endorsement of Castro would have been low in prior probability), the degree of choice should not have made as much difference when their anti-Castro statements confirmed the subjects' expectations. Figure 3-4 shows that both the distinctive effects variable and the prior proba-

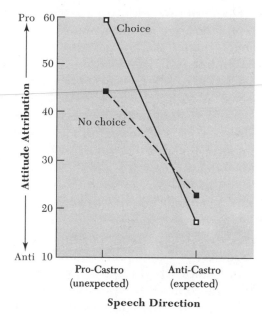

FIGURE 3-4 The attribution of attitudes to a target person writing a pro-Castro or anti-Castro essay. (Adapted from Jones and Harris, 1967.)

bility variable played a role in the results. The most correspondent inference (in other words, the inference that most strongly departs from prior expectation) occurred when the essay was pro-Castro under conditions of choice. When the essay was anti-Castro, the role of choice was incidental: The cultural desirability of the position was so high that subjects presumably assumed the target person was actually against Castro whether or not he was given the choice of position in the essay.

The trouble is, however, that these results are not very exciting. You the reader are probably saying something like, "Well, of course, we attribute attitudes more confidently when someone expresses an unconstrained opinion than when that person is constrained to adopt a particular stance toward an issue. Do we need a theory that can predict this obvious commonsense finding?" Perhaps not, but there are other features of the Castro experiment's results that suggest a rather different role for our theory than that of trumpeting the prediction of correspondent inferences under obvious conditions of behavioral freedom. In addition to the obvious findings outlined above, the figure contains a nonobvious anomaly. The essayists who had no choice were nevertheless attributed attitudes somewhat in line with the positions they expressed. This could not have been predicted by correspondent inference theory, and it seems to fly in the face of logic and common sense. Why should someone who is clearly constrained by an imposed requirement (in this case, an examination question) be held accountable for an unpopular position he or she has been forced to endorse? And (to get ahead of our story) this bias in the direction of correspondence under no-choice or limited-choice conditions turns out to be an extremely robust and replicable phenomenon, one that cannot be explained away as an artifact of particular experimental conditions.

The consequences of this "correspondence bias" are extremely important, and I shall discuss them in detail in Chapter 6. In the present context, the point I would like to make is that the identification of this anomalous tendency illustrates another function that can be served by a theory. As my students and I have tried to work with correspondent inference theory, we have come more and more to regard it as a model that presents a rational baseline against which to evaluate the biased attributions offered by the subjects rather than a valid predictor of these attributions. The theory is one that suggests how people should ideally behave, given ample time and sufficient cognitive resources. The model becomes useful, then, not only because it enables us to predict on many occasions how people do make attributions, but also because it helps us identify where they go wrong under certain circumstances. To give a second example of this function of a theory, correspondent inference theory (as well as commonsense logic) would give equal informational emphasis to effects chosen and effects forgone. That is, the effects I could have chosen but didn't choose should be just as informative as the effects that I chose. But people do not conform to this logical prediction, as Darren Newtson has shown,[22] and we are once again confronted with an intriguing puzzle—a puzzle that might well have gone undiscovered without the impetus of correspondent inference theory.

Kelley's covariation theory has some of the same potential as correspondent inference theory for identifying inferential mistakes, but the most relevant research has placed greater emphasis on verification of the theory's basic premises regarding distinctiveness, consensus, and consistency variables. A major study by Leslie McArthur showed how college student subjects generally used the principles embedded in Kelley's theory when they tried to account for the outcome of a variety of behavioral vignettes.[23] Her study was very complicated in its procedures, but in essence the vignettes were used to vary distinctiveness, consensus, and consistency and to elicit attributions to entities, persons, circumstances, and various entity–person combinations. Some examples follow:

Joan laughs at the comedian

Almost everyone laughs at the comedian

Joan does not laugh at almost any other comedian

In the past Joan almost always laughed at the same comedian

Here, with this example, most subjects made an *entity attribution*: Since distinctiveness, consensus, and consistency are all high, this is exactly what Kelley's theory would have predicted.

Sue is afraid of the dog

Hardly anyone else is afraid of the dog

Sue is afraid of almost all dogs

In the past Sue has been almost always afraid of dogs

Here, consensus and distinctiveness are both low, so the theory would have predicted a *person attribution*: Sue is a fearful person. This is what the majority of McArthur's subjects concluded. Other vignettes presented subjects with evidence that could not so conveniently support simple person or entity attributions. For example:

Bill thinks the teacher is unfair

No one else thinks the teacher is unfair

Bill thinks that none of the other teachers are unfair

In the past, also, Bill has thought that this teacher was unfair

Here, the only reasonable conclusion is that some *combination* of this *person* (Bill) and this *entity* (the particular teacher) is an important cause of the judgment of unfairness.

Though McArthur's study was generally supportive of Kelley's theory, she also found that subjects were more inclined overall to make person attributions than to make entity attributions. This preference is consistent with the observation of correspondence bias identified by Harris and me. McArthur also found that the consensus variable was not as powerful as Kelley's theory assumed; it was overshadowed by the effects of distinctiveness and consistency. Later research has shown that this muted role of consensus may have depended on particular conditions (such as the order of presentation and the particular vignette formats selected from the total array of possible vignettes[24]) in the McArthur experiments. In any event, the importance of consensus has certainly been documented as a variable affecting the inference process in person perception, whether or not people tend to endow it with the same strength as the theory would predict.

What is the "Real Cause" of an Event?

Several recent papers have attempted to extend or qualify Kelley's covariation model in a number of respects. There seems to be little controversy over the cases when consensus, distinctiveness, and consistency point clearly in the direction of person attribution (LLH) or entity attribution (HHH). But many words have been written concerning the ambiguous LHH and the HLH cells. Much of this controversy is arcane and not particularly relevant for our understanding of interpersonal perception. However, these more ambiguous cases, or cases in which the potential sources of variation are not fully specified, do raise some interesting questions about what perceivers select as a *cause* and what they treat as merely a *condition* of an event. The issue becomes relevant to anyone who has to answer the question "Does birth cause death?" Surely, you cannot die if you are not born, and no one who is alive can expect to elude death. Is this an example of Kelley's covariation principle? On what grounds can we say, "No, that's not what I mean by cause and effect."

One kind of solution is to argue that we treat as causal that which is "abnormal," that which departs from our experience-based expectations concerning the way things usually are.[25] This certainly seems consistent with the thrust of correspondent inference theory and its emphasis on expectancy violations and information gain. And it seems to cover adequately many commonsense examples: We don't say the house fire was caused by oxygen, even though it normally would not have occurred in the absence of oxygen, and we don't say the cause of someone's death was her birth, unless, indeed, there was something abnormal about the birth itself. Much of the reasoning behind this kind of "abnormal conditions" model focuses on the communication value of the particular condition selected as causal. When we are asked to explain why an event happened, we take into account what the audience already knows and focus instead on what amounts to new information. We say someone died because of cancer, not because he stopped breathing or because he was born. Everybody knows that the cessation of breath covaries with death and that all living things eventually die, but not everyone dies of cancer.

Ann McGill has moved the ongoing discussion of these issues away from the social communication rationale to a broader view of the *causal context*.[26] She follows Kelley (and most of the rest of us) in stressing the importance of covariation but emphasizes the role of surrounding context in making certain dimensions of covariation more salient than others. In one of her demonstration experiments, for example, she asks subjects to record the reasons why they (or their best friend) chose the college major they did. Some subjects were asked why they (or the friend) *in particular* might have chosen the major; other subjects were asked why they (or the friend)

chose the college major *in particular*. As expected, subjects in
the former condition tended to think of covariation along the
consensus dimension (the actor in comparison to other people)
and dwelled on relevant personal characteristics. Subjects in
the latter condition tended to think of covariation along the
distinctiveness dimensions (e.g., economics versus other
majors) and speculated about the pros and cons of different
disciplines.

In other experiments McGill shows how broad manipulation of the behavioral context will in and of itself point attributors toward making certain comparisons while ignoring others.
One of the contextual determinants is certainly the kind of
knowledge implied by the particular question getting at a
subject's attribution of causation. Somewhat paradoxically, if
the experimenter asks the subject why he or she did so well on
a task of solving anagrams previously described by the experimenter as extremely difficult, the subject attributes success to
"something about the task." On the other hand, subject attribute failure on difficult anagrams (where failure might be
expected and readily attributed to task difficulty) to "something about myself." A reversal of these attribution tendencies
occurs when the anagrams are initially described by the experimenter as moderately easy. McGill's explanations for
these rather strange attributional choices have to do with pre-
supposed knowledge versus new information. Since the anagrams have been presented by the experimenter as difficult
(or easy), there is little point in repeating this information
when asked to explain failure (on the difficult anagram task) or
success (on the easy anagram task). Therefore, subjects are led
to focus causally on themselves when outcomes are consistent
with expectations and on the task when outcomes are inconsistent with expectations.

It is difficult to be precise about the role of audience
knowledge and expectations when we report our attributions.
It certainly makes sense that we will focus on aspects of ourselves or the situations that seem to us special (abnormal?) and
that are not self-evident or clearly known by the audience.
There is little reason to assume, however, that this is the only
reason we select certain potential causes rather than others. I
am not inclined to question the underlying logic of the attribu-

tional approach—that causal perceptions and inferences are part of the necessary and inevitable result of our persistent attempt to make usable sense out of the events that are relevant for our choices and action decisions.

The Failings and Value of the Attributional Approach

I have given but a highly selective account of the voluminous research relevant to Heider's causal trade-offs, correspondent inference theory, and Kelley's covariation theory. I have tried to characterize the evidence by describing a few early experiments and attempting to generalize from them. My conclusion from these (and many other) studies is that these attributional approaches have some general predictive power over a wide range of person perception instances. Since they share many of the same basic trade-off assumptions, we would not expect to find experimental evidence that favors one version of "attribution theory" over another. Indeed, none is available. Each theory seems to capture important ingredients of the inference process, and the empirical results do show the ease and reliability with which people operate with Heider's person–situation (person–entity) trade-off. On the other hand, the theories fall far short of covering and explaining many features in many person perception experiments. This "failing" can be converted into a useful function if the theories are seen as providing baselines of what could be reasonably expected from a logical analysis of available information. Re sults that are anomalous in terms of theoretical predictions can thus help us move beyond the simplest kinds of commonsense verifications into more provocative domains involving numerous puzzles and questions. Many of the discussions in chapters to follow will address these puzzles and attempt to account for the lack of fit between selected empirical findings and the traditional attribution theory formulations.

Two-Stage Models of Attribution

Heider was attracted to the position that all perceptions are really causal attributions. The conversion of "proximal" stimulation—the physical energies that reach our receptors—into the visual perception of any "distal" object can be seen as an attribution of what caused the particular pattern of light on the retina. The idea of an immediate apprehension of causation was also very much a part of Heider's Gestalt orientation to the attempt to characterize perception. It certainly seems to fit common experience that causal attributions are often contained in the act of perception itself: We are not aware of any thinking or inferring when we steer a car through heavy traffic or maintain size constancy while watching a friend walk toward us. And yet Heider willingly conceded that some causal attributions may involve more complicated modes of thought. The school counselor who ponders the trade-off between effort and ability in a problem student presumably engages in considerable reflection in the attempt to make an appropriate attribution for the student's school failures.

As I have implied in discussing Heider's approach to phenomenal causality in the preceding chapter, the question of whether causal inferences can really be immediate or whether they are always inferred never seemed very important to me—largely because of the absence of any appropriate method to answer the question in any specific instance. In recent years, however, the issue of different stages in the attribution process has emerged in new and provocative formulations. I am no longer confident that the question of perception versus inference can be glibly ignored.

One of these formulations emphasizes an "ecological" approach to social perception, an approach derived from J. J. Gibson's emphasis on the analysis of stimulus structures.[27] Leslie McArthur and Reuben Baron, who favor this approach, argue that much of the information contained in the environment is prestructured to convey immediately the stable meaning of events.[28] This prestructured information comes to us in a form that most readily facilitates effective and adaptive action. As McArthur and Baron note: "It can be hypothesized that perceptual systems have evolved to be sensitive to the types of structural information available in a given ecological niche."[29] They go on to argue, "Certainly it is as adaptive to differentiate male from female and prey from predator in the social environment as it is to detect properties of the physical environment. Similarly, the helplessness of babies, the look of fear or anger, and ravages of disease require fast and sure recognition if our species is to survive."[30]

We become perceptually attuned to our environments not only through such evolutionary adaptations to our "ecological niche," but also through perceptual learning in line with our particular goals and concerns. Thus, the ecological approach assumes that the perceptual apparatus is consistently "retuned" as a result of interactions with the environment and that "on-line" adjustments are continually made in the perceptual apparatus.

Ecological theorists want to argue, then, that people become sensitized to, or especially prepared to take in, certain environmental events that are then perceived without inference or reflection. What kinds of evidence are adduced to support this approach? Much of the "evidence" is hypothetical at this point, and based on functionalist arguments: "[O]ne would expect social stimulus information to specify benevolence versus malevolence, ingroup versus outgroup, and gender and sexual receptivity. Similarly the adaptive value of detecting structural invariants such as physical strength and illness, mental astuteness and insanity, and social dominance and dependency argues for their specification in the stimulus environment that people project."[31] Thus, the ecologists have a strong tendency to argue backwards from what is adaptive to how information is most likely structured in the environment and made salient to the organism.

Some fairly impressive evidence does come from the realm of perceiving emotion in particular patterns of facial movement. Indeed, we are learning more and more about the invariant stimulus patterns — configurations of facial and bodily gestures — that characterize the more important (i.e., adaptively significant) human emotions.[32]

To me, the most intriguing evidence of what the ecologists refer to as prestructured information in the environment is that derived from a particular paradigm especially associated with the Swedish perception psychologist Gunnar Johansson. This paradigm involves photographing persons in the dark with pinpoints of lights attached to a limited number of body parts. In one study, though the film depicted nothing but ten bright dots, each moving in its own path, perceivers could readily and easily detect a walking or running man; perceivers could similarly detect that two persons were dancing when ten lights were attached to each dancer.[33] Even more impressive, Kozlowski and Cutting showed that a person's gender can be recognized from the moving lights as he or she walks in the dark.[34]

Though I find such perceptual achievements fascinating, I don't know quite what to make at this point of the ecological approach to the broader field of person perception. I would certainly agree that we need to know more about the stimulus environment, especially those characteristics that lend themselves to stable and meaningful perceptions of motives, emotions, abilities, and other adaptively relevant behaviors. The promise of studying temporal patterns of movement is worth pursuing systematically. We obviously learn a great deal about a person from his or her gestures and from other nonverbal accompaniments of more salient verbal behaviors. I also feel comfortable with the notion that we each become perceptually attuned to the more relevant recurring events in our environment, and one result of such attunements is immediate or very rapid perception of meaning, including the perception of social causation. Many of our social perceptions do appear to be quite automatic, occurring in the absence of elaborate inference processes. On the other hand, many of the most interesting aspects of person perception do involve such processes, and what we need is a theory that explicitly relates perceptions to inferences, assuming that we can distinguish between them.

A recent paper by Yaacov Trope attempts to do exactly this.[35] Trope is concerned, as we were in formulating correspondent inference theory, with the problem of attributing dispositions to others. The major innovation of Trope was to propose a two-stage model by drawing a distinction between *identification* processes and *dispositional inference* processes. The idea of identification processes is compatible with the ecological approach of McArthur and Baron. Trope suggests that incoming stimulus information is first identified in terms of attribution-relevant categories. As McArthur and Baron put it: "Success in a difficult task will be attributed to ability if little effort is present, but not if there is a great deal of effort. But, what information communicates effort?"[36] Trope would say that the answer to this lies in the identification process. Similarly, we perceive a remark as friendly or unfriendly; in doing so, we have applied an attributionally relevant category to ongoing behavior.

How does this identification process work? How do we decide that Susan's behavior is friendly rather than un-friendly? Here Trope makes the important point that the perceiver actually works with three sources of information and assigns meaning as a result of interactions among them. There is the *behavior* itself, there is the *situation* in which it occurs, and the perceiver approaches the behavior and the situation with certain kinds of prior knowledge (*priors*). In other words, the perceiver comes to the situation with certain expectancies, either based on the particular target person's behavior or on the behavior of other similar persons in similar situations. A crucial step in Trope's argument is that each category serves as a context for the other. So the behavior is more likely to be identified as friendly if the situation is one in which people are usually friendly — for example, a cocktail party. Since a person can cry when either very happy or very sad, crying itself is ambiguous with regard to the underlying emotion, so we are often dependent on the context to interpret the significance of tears: We decide that a person is crying out of sadness when his house trailer has been destroyed by a tornado and with joy when she has won the Miss America contest.

A similar contextual argument applies to priors. If the target person is friendly (known for many friendly overtures in the past), we are more likely to decide that an ambiguous act we just witnessed was a friendly one. In other words, we assimilate the meaning of the behavior we see to our expectations about what was most likely to happen (a well-established phenomenon that we shall discuss extensively in the following chapter).

These considerations may seem fairly obvious by now. What is not quite so obvious is that *behavior* can serve as a context to help in establishing the meaning of the *situation* and of *prior cues*. When the losing basketball player cries in the locker room, we infer that this was a very important game. When we see a man laughing uproariously at something that isn't terribly funny, we may revise our prior assumption that he is characteristically a somber individual.

So far so good, but how does it help us to realize that everything influences everything else? Here Trope notes the crucial role of *ambiguity*: The more unambiguous cues provide the context for understanding the meaning of the more ambiguous cues. If the situation is clearer than the behavior, the situation will shape the perception of the behavior more than vice versa. If the behavior is unambiguous and the situation is uncertain, the behavior will shape the meaning of the situation. Thus, we have an identification process in which the three identifications (I_s, I_b, I_p) "are themselves outputs from a process that transforms the initial situational, behavioral, and prior cues (α_s, α_b, and α_p, respectively) into more abstract representations."[37] These identifications, then, become the starting point for the second stage in the model: the dispositional inference process. From this point on, given the ways in which the situation, the behavior, and the priors are now identified, the standard logic of correspondent inference theory applies. In other words, the attribution of a disposition (D) is positively related to I_b and I_p but negatively related to I_s. Behavior identified as friendly gives rise to an attribution of "this is a friendly person" to the extent that we have seen that person behave in a friendly way in the past (priors create the expectancy of friendliness) and to the extent that we have not identified the situation as one that always leads everybody to behave in a friendly way. So here is our old friend, the basic trade-off between the situation and the person, embedded in a rather complicated two-stage theory of attribution.

Figure 3-5 attempts to capture the essence of the two-stage model. In order to understand how the two-stage model might work in a particular instance, let us invent an example. You, the perceiver, attend a Chamber of Commerce dinner in Spartanburg, South Carolina, to hear a speech by someone who might become a candidate for the United States Senate. He comes out very strongly in his speech for import tariffs to protect the American textile industry (this is the behavioral cue, α_b). When and if he becomes a senator, it is important to know whether he will push for this tariff—in other words,

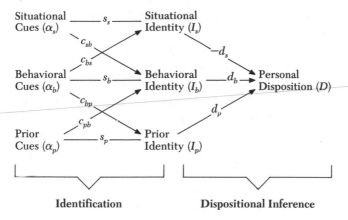

FIGURE 3-5 A two-stage model of dispositional attribution. (From Trope, 1986.)

there is an attributional problem of how strongly our target person believes (D) in protectionism. What kinds of further information might influence how we make this attribution? Before the speech began, you came into the situation with some priors (α_p). You knew the speaker was a Democrat, and given the particular political climate at the time, you could probably have inferred a generally protectionist attitude from that fact. This would have some contextual effect on the identification of the behavior as strongly protectionistic, though in fact the behavior was quite unambiguous.

But the behavior might serve as a context influencing the readjustment of priors. For example, suppose the speech reminded you that the speaker's father was imprisoned by the Japanese and you had heard that the speaker was very bitter about reconciliation with a former enemy country. This might lead you to readjust your priors in the direction of a stronger expectation that the speaker feels strongly about protectionism. On the other hand, before the speaker made his protectionist remarks, you had failed to think about the fact that the meeting was held in the auditorium of Cannon Mills and that there are many textile officials on the dais. Now the speech behavior suddenly makes salient the nature of the situation and the most likely sympathies of the audience. The situation is therefore identified, partly because of the role of the behavior as a context, as one that strongly facilitates a protectionist declaration.

Given these ingredients, the dispositional inference process would then take place in the second stage. The outcome would depend on how strongly the situational identification weighs in as a discounting factor. Probably the unambiguous strength of the speech, coupled with the newly adjusted priors, would lead you to expect that the speaker would come out in favor of the protection of the textile industry even in other surroundings. In other words, you would attribute a rather strong disposition to him. But if the constraints of the setting were seen as even less ambiguous than the speech, a perceiver might conclude that the speaker doesn't truly favor a protectionist approach and would not fight strongly for one if elected.

The value of the theory is that it enables us to understand certain research results that are otherwise difficult to explain. Melvin Snyder and Arthur Frankel conducted an experiment on the perception of emotions.[38] Subjects watched silent videotapes of a female college student who in fact was being interviewed about her "experiences last summer." Half the subjects were told that she was answering a series of rather innocuous questions about political issues, whereas the other half were told that she was answering a series of rather anxiety-provoking questions about sexual practices and experiences. Not surprisingly, at the identification stage, subjects clearly saw her as more anxious in the latter condition than in the former. They were then asked to make an attribution regarding dispositional anxiety; in other words, they were asked to assess whether this particular person on the tape was an anxious person in general. Now the discounting principle would normally predict that subjects in the "politics" condition would judge the target person to be characteristically more anxious than subjects in the "sex experience" condition. This should be true because any signs of anxiety in situational conditions that would not normally arouse anxiety would indicate an unusually anxious person, whereas anxiety in a condition that would arouse anxiety in anybody is hardly diagnostic of a disposition to be anxious. In fact, the results showed the opposite to be the case. The undergraduate was judged to be more dispositionally anxious in the sex condition than in the politics condition.

Trope's two-stage model helps us understand why these results might have occurred. A major factor is the contextual influence of the situation on the identification of the behavior. The important thing to note is that the situation was much less ambiguous than the behavior and therefore we should expect strong contextual influence from the situation toward the particular behavioral identity. This would occur at the identification stage. Then as we move to the dispositional inference stage, the situation that was a positive contributor to dispositional inference in the identification stage now becomes a negative influence. It makes sense to assume that the positive influence in the identification stage was stronger than the negative influence in the attribution stage. This, then, becomes a sensible accounting of the results in terms of Trope's theory.

Trope himself did several experiments on emotion identification that clearly demonstrate this role of differential ambiguity. He systematically manipulated the ambiguity of facial expressions and the ambiguity of situational contexts. As Snyder and Frankel found, when the faces were ambiguous and the situations were not, situationally appropriate emotions were perceived and the target persons were assumed to have dispositions in line with these emotions. On the other hand, when the face was unambiguous, the discounting/augmentation principle came into effect. Thus, an ambiguously calm person was seen as less fearful (dispositionally) when his or her calmness was in reaction to a horror film, a Doberman pinscher, or a swarm of bees.

Interestingly enough, Snyder and Frankel found that the discounting/augmentation principle operated when the behavior was presented before the situation was described. Thus, people who were *subsequently* told that they were watching a sexual experience interview must have reached back in their memory and decided, "That person seemed really calm in what must have been an arousing situation," and therefore determined that the person was dispositionally calm.

The full fruits of Trope's model have obviously yet to be determined, but I think it is an important addition to the theoretical arsenal of the attributional approach. A number of other dual process models seem to be in the atmosphere at the present writing, and I see this as an exciting new development in the enrichment of attribution theories. Clearly there are a number of remaining mysteries in the automatic processing of social behavior. A number of fascinating things occur beyond a level of our awareness in the very *production* of information to begin the more elaborate processes that we refer to under the label of attribution.

When Do We Make Attributions?

Can we "perceive" other people without automatically attributing causes for their behavior? Although Heider was attracted to the basic idea that behavior and person form a natural causal unit, this question raises an important issue that has recently received attention. Bernard Weiner has highlighted the methodological problems of determining whether attributions are spontaneous or merely forthcoming when researchers ask subjects what caused the behavior they just observed.[39] How can one know that an attribution a subject records on a postexperimental questionnaire actually would have existed in the absence of the question eliciting it? Weiner attempts to answer this question by looking at the small sample of existing studies in which spontaneous verbalizations of attributions were recorded either in experimental studies or archival reports (e.g., of corporate activities). His conclusion is that spontaneous attributions are very common, particularly when outcomes are negative or unexpected.

This conclusion has been seconded by others who have distinguished between immediate disposition or trait assignments, on the one hand, and more elaborate causal attribution inferences, on the other.[40] David Hamilton, for example, argues that subjects package consistent information about a person with little effort, summarizing the package in trait terms. However, when subjects were asked to make a person or entity attribution and the information was inconsistent, subjects took longer to reach a conclusion and they remembered the incongruent information items better on a later retest. Hamilton argues from this and related evidence that attribution only occurs in the overall "information-processing" sequence when incongruity interrupts routine processing and forces the perceiver to answer the question "Why?"

I have no trouble with the idea that more cognitive effort will be involved when a perceiver is forced to resolve inconsistencies in the information than when inferences can be easily and routinely made. Hamilton's experiments are interesting reminders that cognitive effort and attention will vary with the degree of integrative difficulty posed by an information-processing task. I am not convinced that "spontaneous" attributions do not occur when events are expected or information is consistent and not problematic. As noted earlier, there is a sense in which all perception involves an attribution to the "stable," "distal" object. Here is seems important to determine whether attributions occur spontaneously — whether they are an inevitable or integral part of processing information — and whether the processing of information requires an *attributional search*. To me these are two different questions. I can believe that some attributions are easier and more automatic than others, but whether we want to restrict the word *attribution* to deliberate, effortful attempts to answer the question "Why?" seems to me almost a matter of taste. We shall subsequently (in Chapter 6) confront a related approach to the effort involved in solving various attributional problems.

Concluding Remarks

In this rather long and difficult chapter I have tried to compress the essentials of the attributional approach, concluding with some recent emphases on the immediate reading or perception of behavior. I suspect that the reader may wish to return to this chapter from time to time since it sets the stage for much of what follows. The main thing to remember is that there is a great deal that we do not understand about how behaviors and situational contexts are immediately coded and labeled and that attributional theories also have their limitations even at the more inferential stages of the process. As noted, and as we shall continue to see in the chapters to come, attribution theories do have important descriptive and predictive value, but in a number of important respects they also serve as logical baselines against which to identify various biases and mistakes in the inference process. In the next chapter we shall begin our systematic study of the perception–interaction sequence by trying to organize what is known about expectancy effects in interpersonal perception. In other words, we turn to the role of what Trope has called "priors."

Expectancy

Effects

A cornerstone of anyone's naive psychology is that one person never observes or interacts with another person without having some expectations about that other person's probable actions in the imminent future. The expectations may be vague, they may involve a cluster of probabilities, but they are inevitably less than infinite and more than zero. Expectations can thus range from predictions that border on banal certainties (the truck on the cross street will stop at the red light) to the most hypothetical of hunches (she will think my sarcastic rejoinder is funny and will not respond in anger). I would like to collect all manner of expectations, predictions, hypotheses, and hunches about a target person's upcoming behavior under the commodious label "expectancy." Expectancies are obviously important when we are driving a car, being interviewed for a job, asking an acquaintance for a date, or telling an off-color joke to an unfamiliar audience.

Expectancies are also essential features of person perception even when we are passive observers of a social scene. When we see a person in a situation, we inevitably attempt to coordinate the actions we observe with the actions we expected to observe. These expectancies, in turn, are just as inevitably a product of our past histories as actors on, and observers of, the human scene. We have at least some idea of what situations call for and how most people behave in them. Beyond this, we have more differentiated ideas about how particular kinds of people behave in particular kinds of situations.

In the preceding chapter, expectancy notions were prominent in the attribution theories discussed.[1] Correspondent inference theory includes assumed desirability as a major variable, suggesting that behavior in line with social or cultural expectations is relatively uninformative about the actor. For Kelley expectancies have three different forms of representation: in consensus (expectancies about other people), distinctiveness (expectancies about situations), and consistency (expectancies about behavioral stability). Consensus is the most obvious source of perceiver expectancies, but the role of distinctiveness obviously implies that we have seen, or know about, the target person's response to entities similar to the one currently being encountered. Consistency information involves observations of a person's responses to the same entity over time, of course, observations necessarily implying the development of an expectancy that may or may not be confirmed. For Trope, there are priors—what the perceiver brings by way of prior knowledge to the task of observing a particular target person in action. Trope says little about the role of such priors, but he obviously considers them important enough to be included as a major variable in his theory of dispositional attribution.

Among other things, consideration of expectancies liberates us from a sterile preoccupation with first impressions and points us in the direction of saying something about the development of one person's understanding of another's dispositional tendencies. To understand such evolving impressions, we need to know where these expectancies come from and what role they play in the selection, organization, and attribution of new information conveyed by a person's behavior.

Category-based and Target-based Expectancies

Expectancies presumably reflect the experiences of the perceiver. I think it is useful to distinguish two different kinds of prior experiences. First, there are experiences with broad categories of persons—men, women, old people, infants, yuppies, Hispanics, southerners, bankers. Each of us has expectancies of varying clarity and detail about each of these categories. Daniel McGillis and I have previously called these category-based expectancies.[2] A second class of expectancies can be called target-based since they reflect prior experience with, or at least information about, the particular target person being assessed. I think this will turn out to be an important distinction, especially in understanding how perceivers handle expectancy violations.

Catetory-based expectancies can be further subdivided into dispositional and normative variations.[3] *Dispositional expectancies* reflect a belief that group members share similar dispositions: Nurses are nurturant; children are impatient; Italians are romantic. Dispositional expectancies are typically cognitive extrapolations from past experiences with other members of the category to which the target person belongs. We have different dispositional expectancies that are primed or triggered when we encounter waiters, dentists, or homosexuals. In any given case multiple schemas (e.g., homosexual waiters) may be activated. In such cases, the resultant expectancy (a probabilistic forecast of behavior) will be a complex function of the combined dispositional expectancies interacting with expectancies about the situation.

Normative expectancies are more strongly situation bound and introduce the additional consideration of social rules and social sanctions. We often expect people to behave in a certain way because, behaving otherwise, they expose themselves to ridicule, prosecution, or some other form of social penalty. Thus, we expect almost all subway riders to put tokens in the fare turnstile, we expect guests to express their appreciation to hosts, and we expect subordinates to avoid disagreeing in a supercilious manner with their superiors.

The key feature of category-based expectancies is their probabilistic quality. We may have a schematic expectancy that the Irish "drink for what ails them" but not be particularly surprised when we meet an Irish teetotaler. It is important to know the extent to which an expectancy is probabilistic, because when probabilistic expectancies are disconfirmed, they may be quickly treated by the perceiver as irrelevant for making further judgments about the individual. Probabilistic categories tell us what is most likely to happen; when it does not happen, we may simply move on to other categorial information. We may not modify our schema about the drinking Irish, but we will no longer think about the schema's implications as we interact with this particular Irish teetotaler.

I would not go so far as to insist that category-based expectancies are probabilistic is this sense. We may end up thinking our teetotaling Irish friend is a secret drinker. But relative to target-based expectancies, their probabilistic nature is more apparent. *Target-based expectancies* can vary in the degree of generalization they require from past observations of the same person. In more technical terms we can say that they vary on a dimension from replicative to structural. The replicated expectancy would be involved when we see our target person behave angrily in situation x, and it is important for us to predict his or her behavior in a highly similar situation again. We expect anger because we have learned that future behavior tends to replicate past behavior when all the relevant factors are the same. Structural expectancies are involved when we have a complex cognitive schema or an implicit theory of personality that entails a variety of subtle predictions concerning hostile people and the circumstances under which they express their anger. Our predictions may reap the benefits of such complex cognitive structures even though we have never previously seen the actor in this particular setting. Target-based expectancies are less probabilistic than category-based expectancies; when they are discon-firmed, there is greater reluctance to decide that the expect-ancy is irrelevant and inapplicable.

But before going more thoroughly into the effects of ex-pectancies, let me point to a problem in maintaining some of the distinctions I have proposed. The alert reader may have realized that many of the examples of category-based expect-ancies are, at least to some extent, target-based expectancies as well. The problem is that many categories are to some degree selected by the category members. People either have chosen to belong, or the category is an end point of earlier selections. National origin, birth order, gender, age, and a few other categorizations can be treated as "random assignments," but occupational categories, religious affiliations, club mem-berships, alumni affiliations, and many other groupings are not. When we learn that a target person is a Stanford graduate, the expectancies generated are based in part on the further assumption that (1) the target person probably wanted to go to Stanford, which tells us something about a particular set of preferences. (2) Once matriculating at Stanford, the target person apparently liked it well enough to stay the course, and (3) must have been influenced in certain predictable ways by his or her experiences there. Membership in the Stanford graduate category thus tells us something about the target person's past behavior, and this something might qualify the knowledge as a target-based expectancy. I will concede that there is a dimension of variation ranging from pure examples of categories having no complications concerning the prior behavior of the target person, through mixed cases of catego-ries with target-based features, to directly observed actions of the target person. As we move from pure category-based to pure target-based expectancies, moreover, the expectancies become less probabilistic and more constraining. Thus, such mixed expectancies may affect our estimates of the degree or strength of an inferred disposition rather than affecting proba-bility judgments about the existence of the disposition in the first place.

An analogy may clarify the distinction between category-based and target-based expectancies. If I am told quite accu-rately that a jar contains eighty yellow and twenty blue jelly beans, I will have a category-based expectancy about that particular jar. When I close my eyes and reach into the jar I will expect to (the odds are that I will) pull out a yellow rather that a blue jelly bean. I know, however, that I could be wrong. And if I pull out a blue jelly bean, I am not likely to perceive it as having a yellowish tinge. It seems to me that many category-based expectancies in the social world have this same quality. Let us say I have category-based expectancies that most Canadians are interested in ice hockey, most electrical engineers are men, and most Japanese people are industrious. If I then meet a Canadian, and electrical engineer, or a Japanese person who does not fit the relevant expectancy, the expectancy will not influence how I see the person on the dimension involved. I know that there are Canadians who could not care less about ice hockey, I know that there are female electrical engineers, and I know that there are lazy Japanese people. I will usually be right if I expect the opposite, but when the expectancy misleads me, I do not have to go through any elaborate cognitive activity or distort my perception.

In contrast, if you can imagine that I have been reliably told that a particular person is extremely conscientious and hard working and I then learn that this same person tends to keep very short working hours, I have a different sort of problem than I did in a category-based case. If my initial expectancy is a strong one, and I am committed to it, I will most likely go through some cognitive work to make the subsequent information fit my earlier expectancy. I simply may not notice that the person works short hours, or I may assume that the person takes work home; if all else fails, I may convince myself that the quality of the person's work is greater because of the intensity of effort while on the job.

Carolyn Weisz and I conducted two experiments generally corroborating the proposition that violations of target-based expectancies are more difficult to handle and produce more cognitive stain than violations of category-based expectancies.[4] Expectancies were constructed *de novo* about a particular boy or a group of boys. The information provided suggested that the boy (or group) was essentially passive and nonaggressive. With this expectancy-establishing information, subjects in the category-based condition made the same predictions about a new boy from their group as did subjects in the target-based condition about their target boy. All subjects were then exposed to an audio tape presenting a boy acting very aggressively—he was either from the target group or he was the target child. Both category-based and target-based expectancies were therefore violated by the same observed episode of aggressive behavior.

In spite of the equal predictive strength of the two expectancies, subjects responded differently when the expectancies were violated. Those in the target-based condition were more reluctant to abandon their expectancy. In their final impression they saw the child as more friendly, more cooperative, and less irritable than did those in the category-based condition. Target-based expectancy subjects were, however, much less confident about their resulting impressions than were category-based expectancy subjects. Apparently, category-based expectancy subjects had little difficulty discarding a strong expectancy about a particular child when they confronted one who behaved like an atypical group member. I shall return to some other features of this study in the discussion of stereotypes.

Resolving Informational Conflict: A Brief Review

Only a few things can happen cognitively when a person tries to reconcile two conflicting, discrepant, or contradictory pieces of information about the same entity: Either piece of information can be ignored, forgotten, explained away, or otherwise discounted. Alternatively, some kind of compromise can take place; for example, the information can be averaged along a dimension of general evaluation. The effort to determine the conditions favoring each of these general outcomes becomes a fascinating and important scientific game.

Common sense, an abundant collection of empirical studies, and theories like Trope's, help us to identify some of the most likely factors affecting the resolution of such informational conflict. Two such factors are *commitment* and *ambiguity*. There are various ways that perceivers can be committed to an expectancy. Any kind of evidence about a person usually leads the perceiver to form an opinion about the person to which he or she will feel at least minimally attached. The more authentic the evidence seems, the stronger will be the perceiver's commitment to the resulting impression. Such feelings of commitment are also strengthened by recording one's opinion or expressing one's views to another person. Any such committing activities increase the resistance to subsequent information that might otherwise disconfirm the expectancy. Commitment thus serves as an anchor, making the first judgment more difficult to dislodge when contradicted by new information.[5]

I have already reviewed the role of ambiguity in Trope's theory of dispositional attribution.[6] When two pieces of information point in different directions, we obviously expect that the more ambiguous piece of information will be shaped by the less ambiguous piece. Putting the factor of commitment aside, it is certainly possible that an ambiguous expectancy will be reinterpreted or even cast aside in the face of less ambiguous subsequent information about a target person. Ambiguous actions that conflict with unambiguous expectancies can just as easily be assimilated or reinterpreted. It is important to keep the two variables of commitment and ambiguity in mind as we think about the variety of expectancy effects in person perception. They are obviously of crucial importance in predicting the fate of informational conflict.

Expectancy effects, by definition, involve a time or order dimension. Expectancies point to and concern the future. For obvious reasons, the case in which most psychologists are interested is that in which early information is disconfirmed by later information, or at least the case in which later information is not completely redundant with an earlier expectancy. In Asch's study of first impressions, discussed briefly in Chapter 2, subjects were asked to form an impression based on a string of adjectives presented in a particular order.[7] In some cases Asch presented a set of positive adjectives followed by a set of negative ones; in other cases these same adjectives were presented in reverse order. Asch found that there was generally a *primacy effect* such that the early adjectives had more influence than the later adjectives on the final impression. In dozens of follow-up studies, Norman Anderson also generally found that primacy effects occurred after the sequential presentation of a short list of adjectives describing a person.[8] Anderson also found, however, that this tendency toward primacy effects could be overcome if subjects were asked to engage in any activity that made the later activities more salient or more difficult to discount. For example, primacy was inhibited when subjects were asked to pronounce each adjective as it appeared.[9] Primacy effects can also be minimized if subjects are forewarned that they will be asked to justify their impression of a target person.[10] Other studies have shown, not surprisingly, that the length of the time interval involved in the study of order effects is important. Thus, if I am told that Mary is generous and learn nothing about her until I am told several months later that she is stingy, the chances are that I will have forgotten the earlier information or at least that I will pay more attention to the information more recently received. We might expect *recency effects* to occur under any conditions that make temporally remote events more difficult to remember. When subjects are asked to form an impression based on inconsistent actions of a target person, the time interval between the two observed actions can be important. If, for example, one action occurred in high school and another in college, an observer will readily infer that the target person has changed.[11]

To make a long story and a voluminous literature short, the effects of order can be summarized as follows. Primacy effects are more likely when:

1. Subjects are induced to commit themselves in any way to a judgment or evaluation based on the early information before being exposed to the later information.

2. The expectancy is less ambiguous than is the subsequent information or more directly relevant to the judgment called for.

3. The expectancy is target-based and not category-based.

4. The information is about an entity that is not expected to change over time (where there is little likelihood that a particular personal characteristic would change through experience, practice, or education).

Recency effects, on the other hand, will be favored to the extent that any of the above conditions is absent. In particular, recency effects will be most likely when the recent information is more memorable and/or vivid than the earlier information on which the expectancy is based.

As a general, actuarial conclusion, I would propose that primacy wins out over recency more often than not. There are a variety of plausible reasons for this, but perhaps the most important general reason is that our initial impressions (i.e., expectancies to which there is some degree of commitment) are important in determining how subsequent information will be selected, retained, and interpreted. These shaping properties give first impressions a typical advantage in the integration of inconsistent information that is presented over an interval of time. This is but an instance of the notorious *conservatism* in people's judgments about others that cognitive psychologists and decision theorists have emphasized. Primacy is also undoubtedly favored by the human tendency to be satisfied with the "closure" provided by initial impressions, causing the performer to discount or withdraw attention from new information that challenges the impression's validity.[12]

Expectancies, Theories, and Knowledge Structures

If we want to understand how impressions develop and change over time, it is certainly important to learn what we can about the effects of order in processing or integrating inconsistent information. It is also important to recognize the complexity and framing power of many of our expectancies. Though I have hidden many of these complexities by using a generic expectancy label, I must now say a few words about the various "brands" to which the label refers. Expectancies can reflect highly articulated knowledge structures, which have been variously designated social schemas, prototypes, scripts, and implicit theories. A social schema, for example, is defined as organized knowledge about a concept or stimulus that is somewhat abstract, contains a number of attributes, and involves some implicit set of hypotheses about how they relate to each other.[13] Most of us have social schemas that contain organized knowledge concerning the interrelated attributes of professors, addicts, basketball players, police officers, paraplegics, and cowboys. In considering such knowledge structures, it is important to emphasize their enormous importance when we encounter specific instances of such categories. Our knowledge structures help us to fill in the gaps, to go beyond the information given, and to make certain bridging assumptions about what we do not see, based on the actions and appearances we do see.

Target persons do not, of course, fall conveniently into a single category. A particular professor may be female, nearsighted, elderly, and dogmatic. These attributes may make accessible a whole network of both overlapping and distinct subcategories. Marilyn Brewer proposes that perceivers begin with crude or primitive categories, centering around such "pictoliteral" features as gender, age, or social role.[14] Behavioral data then lead to individuation and subcategorization that proceeds "from the top down" until the highest level of useful abstraction is reached. In other words, people do not particularize or differentiate any more than they have to when they go from the top down. Also, all of a perceiver's categories are not equally accessible at a given time. The context, or new information, may determine which categories and subcategories are considered relevant. George Quattrone refers to *taxonomic shifts* to help us understand instances where there is a change in category accessibility.[15] For example, a peer may initially categorize a Mormon who belongs to the Sigma Xi fraternity as a "fraternity type" until observing that he is a teetotaler. At this point there may be a taxonomic shift such that the peer now "sees" the person as a typical Mormon rather than as a typical fraternity member.

The various kinds of knowledge structures — whether social schemas, prototypes, category systems, or implicit personality theories — are more than repositories that reflect our experience and change to accommodate our growing wisdom about others. They are active and influential, imposing meaning and stability on what we observe. Our impressions of others are driven both by the data of their behavior and by our theories of covariation and causal attribution. Contemporary scholars of social cognition have been particularly interested in characterizing these theories and identifying their consequences in processing information about persons.

Such scholars have argued that attributional models do not tell anything like the whole story of person perception — or even the whole story of causal attribution. As I noted in the previous chapter, newer treatments of the attribution process have tried to amend traditional attribution models to include ways of handling experience-based knowledge.[16] Thus, Kelley emphasized the importance of perceived covariation in assigning causation,[17] but our individual and cultural experience tells us what normally covaries with what. It turns out that we think we know much more than we do. In the discussion of stereotypes I shall have much to say about *illusory correlations*, one form of biased covariation perception. Richard Nisbett and Lee Ross make the general point that many of our assessments of covariation are "theory driven" and unfortunately can depart seriously from objective assessments of real-world covariation.[18] For example, subjects have theories about the relationship between a child's capacity to delay gratification and his or her ability to resist the temptation to cheat. Such a relationship seems psychologically reasonable, and subjects in fact think these two tendencies will be highly related. They are not. At least, in one study[19] the empirical relationship was negligible.

In summary, our expectancies often reflect complex knowledge structures, structures that influence how we select and interpret information about a specific person. As we shall see, individuating behavioral data are very important in shaping our impressions of the actor (we do engage in "data-driven" processing to some extent and in some circumstances), but social cognition scholars have been more impressed with "theory-driven" contributions to impression formation.

Stereotypes as Expectancies

Our understanding of expectancy effects has been advanced through the years by the attempts of social psychologists to analyze the most extreme (and often socially dangerous) form

of expectancy: the social stereotype. Since the study of stereotypes throws into sharp relief many of the most interesting
features of social information integration, I think it is useful to
review some of the major functions and consequences of stereotype formation.

Characterizing Stereotypes

Everyone knows what stereotypes are, and yet no two people
are in agreement about a precise definition. Stereotypes
clearly fit my definition of a category-based expectancy; what
does the stereotype concept add? Most textbooks emphasize
that stereotypes involve distortion and oversimplification and
usually suggest that they are tenaciously held and quite resistant to the implications for change of any new information.
Some writers speak of positive as well as negative stereotypes,
but certainly the emphasis has been on negative or invidious
conceptions. There are undoubtedly category-based expectancies that involve positive oversimplifications, and perhaps
some of these are even very resistant to change, but negative
stereotypes have been the focus of considerably more attention because of their disruptive social significance as a central
feature of racism, ethnocentricism, nationalism, and invidious
discrimination in general.[20]

I don't know whether it deserves to be part of the definition, but one very common feature of stereotypes is that they
are based on salient or readily available cues that are used as
identifiers of underlying attributes. Clearly, the stereotyping
process is facilitated when groups or categories of people can
be easily identified because most or all of them share a particular physical or behavioral characteristic. Quattrone's recent
work emphasizes the importance of physical similarity in
forming generalizations about group members.[21] I suggest that
people are more likely to have stereotypes about blonds,
Shriners, priests, marines, and blacks than they are about
Hoosiers or Democrats. In fact, it is the loose and often arbitrary connection between physical characteristics underlying
personality features that leads us to indict many stereotypes as
unfair and inappropriate.

Many of the more vicious stereotypes share a further characteristic: The underlying negative attributes are believed to be genetic or at least fairly immutable. We may note that black high school students have lower scores than white students on standardized aptitude tests. How this information fits into a stereotype about blacks largely depends on the extent to which the differences between blacks and whites are seen as genetic in origin, rather than the product of particular kinds of childhood experiences. Certainly, I would not argue that all stereotypes involve genetic attributes, but to the extent that one believes that distasteful traits or annoying actions are culturally, historically, or contextually determined, one has more difficulty forming a rigid and unyielding stereotype. We can, of course, have very negative attitudes toward groups of persons who deliberately traduce our values, but I question whether this necessarily involves stereotype formation. After all, our hostility toward some groups and persons can have a very legitimate basis in the threat they pose to our own cherished values.

Why Do People Form Stereotypes? A Historical Digression

It is probably fair to say that all who study cognitive processes begin with the assumption that the informational complexity of the real world must be reduced to manageable terms. The goal of cognition is to extract or impose meaning on the stimulus world in such a way as to prepare us for adaptive action. Perception psychologists have believed for many decades that any analogy that compares the perceiver to a camera is extremely misleading. A camera is an unselective recording device, whereas perceivers are highly selective and attempt to get by with the simplest view of the world that is compatible with adaptive action. In fact, many contemporary cognitive psychologists speak of the perceiver as a cognitive miser,[22] intent on spending as little cognitive energy as possible.

The cognitive miser view seems particularly appropriate when we focus on perceptions of the social world, a dynamic mix of interconnected and temporarily extended events. We do not perceive persons in all their multifaceted complexity; we inevitably simplify and categorize to avoid being overwhelmed by informational excess. Stereotypes can be viewed as unfortunate, socially disruptive extremes of this simplification process.

The journalist Walter Lippman introduced the term *stereotype* in his 1922 book, *Public Opinion*. For him stereotypes were "pictures in our head," renditions of the social world compatible with our values and beliefs. They are thus pictures charged with feelings and infused with evaluation. Lippman agreed that stereotypes might have negative consequences, but he believed that they were also an inevitable feature of normal cognitive processing. This emphasis on the "normality of prejudgment" was many years later (1954) promoted by Gordon Allport, whose influence did much to rescue the term from those who emphasized that stereotypes were merely rationalizations constructed to justify unconsciously determined prejudicial feelings.

In the years intervening between Lippman's and Allport's contributions, the conventional view of prejudice in general, and ethnic prejudice in particular, was anchored in the crucial concept of *displacement*. Psychoanalysis paved the way for the use of displacement concepts through its hydraulic view of human motivation (libido theory) and the particular assumption that unconscious motives will always press for gratification, even when forced into disguised and socially sanctioned channels.

A group of Yale psychologists took the psychoanalytic assumptions and dressed them in more behavioristic terms as "frustration–aggression theory," publishing their manifesto in 1939.[23] The essence of this theory was that frustration always leads to the tendency to aggress, but this initial tendency may be displaced toward those who bear little or no responsibility for the frustration. One of the authors of this manifesto, Neal Miller, later gave a more precise formulation of the displacement notion in terms of approach/avoidance theory.[24] Miller treated frustration as an instigation to respond (approach), but one that might be inhibited (avoidance) in its actual expression. Both instigation and inhibition tendencies were expressed as gradients along a dimension of similarity to the original frustration. Thus, the greatest instigation to aggress is toward the actual source of frustration, and the tendency to aggress toward others declines as these others become more dissimilar to the original instigator. Of course, there are instances where the aggression is simply directed at the instigator. Often, however, the agent of frustration is more powerful than the frustrated person, so a direct aggressive reaction will be inhibited. Just as classic approach/avoidance theory typically assumes that avoidance gradients are steeper than approach gradients, Miller assumed that there would be some point on the dimension of similarity where the instigation to aggress (approach) would be greater than the tendency to inhibit (avoid) aggression. At this point, then, there would be a displacement of the original aggressive tendency toward some less powerful but nevertheless somewhat similar target person. Thus, I may come home from a frustrating day at work, having been chewed out by my boss, and blow up at my son or kick my dog. The general notion of displacement has some intuitive appeal, since we all have had moments where we find ourselves being unusually harsh toward someone who has done nothing to deserve our hostility. An example in the spirit of Miller's model is diagrammed in Figure 4-1.

The elegance of Miller's formulation seemed to have great promise for developing a testable theory of displacement. Unfortunately, no one has ever found a way to plot the instigation and inhibition gradients with enough precision to predict accurately the displacement outcome. Perhaps the biggest obstacle is the determination of the perceived similarity dimension itself.

Because of the appeal of the displacement notion, an earlier generation of psychologists and sociologists looked for correlations between events like a bad cotton crop (frustration for the Southern farmer) and the number of lynchings (displaced aggression). The resulting correlations were usually low at best and often explicable in other terms. Nevertheless, although the displacement notion cannot be used with the elegant precision suggested by Miller's theory, it later found a home as the centerpiece of authoritarian personality theory.

The authors of *The Authoritarian Personality* (Adorno, Frenkel-Brunswik, Levinson, and Sanford) set out shortly after World War II to determine whether certain personalities were prone to be ethnocentric and especially anti-Semitic. Could

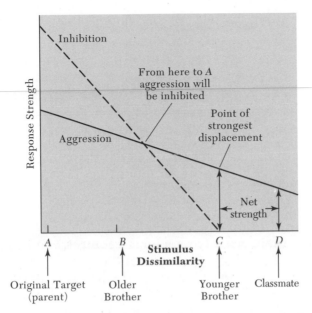

FIGURE 4-1 Displacement produced by greater steepness of inhibition than elicitation gradients. Example: A child is angered by his father. (Adapted from Miller, 1944, in Jones and Gerard, 1967, p. 94.)

the Nazi tragedy of the Holocaust be based in part on the political ascendance of particular Germans with fascistic personalities? Are there, in other words, individual differences along a general dimension of authoritarianism? Are there prefascistic personalities in the Unites States, and can such tendencies be measured? Empirically, Adorno and his colleagues were able to show an interconnectedness between different forms of prejudice, various political attitudes, and certain beliefs about conventionality and impulse expression.[25] Through interviews with extreme scorers and inferences from projective techniques, the authors were able to develop a plausible developmental account of the authoritarian (prefascistic) personality. In brief, the account featured a kind of suppressed rage toward the father accompanied by conscious idolization and an unwillingness to say anything negative about him or, by extension, about members of the in-group. Ethnic prejudice and anti-Semitism were viewed as the displacement to convenient out-group targets of this ambivalence toward crucial in-group figures.

The Cognitive Basis of Stereotypes

Throughout the era briefly surveyed above, an era featuring a motivational displacement account of ethnic or outgroup prejudice, stereotypes were generally seen as the rationalized justification for prejudice. People were prejudiced toward blacks or Jews or Chicanos as a function of the irrational displacement of frustrations imposed by unassailable in-group members. But their negative feelings required explanations (to themselves as well as to others), and it was out of this need to justify the irrational negative feelings that stereotypes emerged. A further step was not fully covered: How does one get from the rationalization of displacement to the idea of stereotypes concerning entire groups of people? Perhaps, if in-group members are idolized and seen as always correct and always superior, it may be natural to assume that all out-group members are in various ways inferior and threatening.

I am quite prepared to believe that some stereotypes do have their origin in the justification of displaced aggression, even though this may be very difficult to document in any convincing way. The various displacement models of prejudice have at least a kernel of plausibility, and we know enough about human nature to know that people will usually seek some set of reasons (rationalizations?) to support their affective judgments about other groups or categories of persons. The recent thrust, however, has been to try to understand those features of normal cognitive processing that can underlie stereotype formation — quite independent of the psychodynamics of displaced affect.

The most important distinguishing feature of the cognitive approach to stereotyping is the intent to ignore any degree of emotional investment in the validity of particular stereotypes. Instead, those who champion the cognitive approach want to see how much they can explain by identifying stereotype formation mechanisms that have nothing to do with motivation or emotion — or, in general, the psychodynamic position. Any explanation of stereotype formation, of course, has to deal not only with the emergence of stereotypes in general, but also with the reasons that particular stereotypes (and particular forms of prejudice) are so prevalent. The following is a sampling of the major cognitive contributions to our understanding of why stereotypes are formed.

- **Illusory Correlations**   David Hamilton has provided some reasonable empirical support for the idea that we tend to see rare or distinctive events as somehow related, even though there is no logical or realistic basis for perceiving this relationship.[26] People have both positive and negative characteristics, but negative characteristics tend to be more unusual and more distinctive — or at least more memorable. Minority group members are also more unusual and distinctive, by definition, than majority group members. Could it be that people are therefore more inclined to associate distinctive negative characteristics with distinctive minority groups simply because both are relatively uncommon? In order to explore this possibility, Hamilton and Gifford devised an experimental design in which two fictitious groups (A and B) were associated with several characterizing statements.[27] The information was so constructed that statements about A were twice as numerous as statements about B, and positive statements were twice as numerous as negative ones. Even though the actual association of positive and negative statements with A and B were proportional to their total, however, subjects tended to identify more of the negative characteristics of group B members.

Other experimental variations showed that the same "illusory correlations" existed if positive characteristics, rather than negative ones, were more unusual. In such circumstances positive characteristics were also associated with the group that was less frequently mentioned. Thus, we tend to see infrequent events as related even when they aren't and even when there is nothing about the content of the events that says they should be. Some quirk of the cognitive apparatus (or perhaps some subtle effect of Western culture) can thus operate to promote a "thoughtless" tendency to associate negative events with minority membership. In the everyday world, presumably, this provides one reason why we might associate crime with minority membership more than the actual covariation of these two would suggest.

• **From Acts to Dispositions** Converting the possibility of illusory correlation into damaging stereotypes, however, requires more than the association of particular actions with particular groups of people. It requires that these actions be attributed to underlying dispositions defining the basic identity or nature of group members. The fact that minority children are perceived as having lower scores on aptitude tests (a perception that may be bolstered by the illusory correlation tendency) is not in and of itself a central feature of a discriminating stereotype. It becomes so when this perception is linked to a presumably stable dispositional cause like "intelligence," and especially when the disposition is judged to be genetic in origin.

This tendency to jump to dispositional conclusions is by no means restricted to the domain of stereotypes about groups or categories of people. As we shall see in Chapter 6, there is a pervasive tendency to exaggerate or overestimate the correspondence between acts and explanatory dispositions. This tendency toward "correspondence bias" is undoubtedly a crucial link in the formation of discriminatory stereotypes. Thus, instead of attributing negative actions to understandable cultural differences, childhood training, or economic circumstances, we are overly inclined to attribute such actions to underlying dispositions that are so stable as to be irremediable if not actually genetic.

A special instance of this correspondence bias tendency may be seen in the all-too-common confusion of roles with personalities. A number of social scientists have suggested that stereotypes are formed and sustained by the association of certain categories of people with certain roles in society. In the history of the Jewish people, for example, when the Jews were forced to flee from their homeland in the great diaspora, they found it difficult or impossible to own land and often ended up in the position of usurous moneylender. Thus, circumstances forced them into an inevitably unpopular social role, one that made them seem parasites living off the labor of others (as immortalized in Shakespeare's Shylock) — and one wonders how much this role contributed to the development of anti-Semitism in Europe.

Alice Eagly and Valerie Steffen raised the same kind of issue concerning gender stereotypes.[28] Perhaps women are seen as genetically less assertive and more nurturant because of the homemaker role to which they have traditionally been assigned. What would happen to this gender stereotype if the homemaker role became independent of gender—if women were as likely to be employed as men, and men were as likely to be homemakers? One of their experiments demonstrates that such changes in role information indeed erode the tendency to attribute nurturance and passivity to females in general.

A widely cited experiment by Lee Ross and his colleagues emphasized the contributions of correspondence bias to attributions concerning "general knowledge."[29] This experiment featured a quiz game with certain special features. Three subjects participated in each experimental session. One was randomly assigned the role of Contestant, another was assigned the role of Questioner, and the third was an Observer. The Questioner was told to make up a series of questions that would be extremely difficult to answer but were not unfairly based on private information (such as the Questioner's brother's birthdate). Naturally, the typical contestant trying to answer such questions missed the vast majority of them. After these episodes of inadequate performance, Contestants subsequently rated themselves as lacking in general knowledge, and so did the Observers. Only the Questioners were able to resist this confusion of role assignment with dispositional attribution. In recording their attributions of general knowledge, neither the Contestant nor the Observer made sufficient allowances for the enormous advantages given to the Questioner by the role assignment. Almost anyone given the Questioner's role of devising very difficult questions could be expected to develop a list that almost anyone else would be unable to answer.

Thus, there is solid experimental evidence supporting a tendency to make dispositional attributions to explain actions that are in fact constrained by assigned roles. I shall have more to say about why this might be the case in Chapter 6; here, I would like to emphasize the consequences of this for stereotype formation and maintenance. We hardly need experimental evidence to help us imagine a vicious cycle flowing from the confusion of roles and dispositions as we think about the "underclass" in contemporary society. Minority group members, when they are offered steady employment, are often assigned the most menial and least prestigious jobs in the occupational hierarchy. Advancement is made difficult by the documented tendency to assume that the qualifications for performing the low-level jobs are indeed the only qualifications that the job holders possess. If a minority job holder does well on a job, he or she confirms that this is where he or she should be functioning, along with supporting the stereotype of limited capacity. If the job holder does poorly, of course, things become even worse. A specific example might be helpful here. As recently as the 1960s, black employees in the American South were not allowed to handle money in most commercial establishments that were run by whites. I can recall driving into many a North Carolina gas station in that era and being served by a black attendant who had to signal to a white attendant to arrange for payment. One can only imagine how such a practice helped cement the stereotype that "because blacks did not enter in to the monetary transactions, they *could not*, for reasons of ignorance (not being able to count money?) or untrustworthiness (they would pocket some of the cash?)." Although this example may be more blatant than most instances of unfairly restricted employment, there still exist many structural impediments to occupational mobility, impediments that cannot help but feed stereotypes concerning ability, motivation, or trustworthiness. As these stereotypes develop, furthermore, they serve to justify the structural arrangements that led to them in the first place.

• **Salience and Tokenism**   When several people sit around the table, not everyone is equally salient. Setting aside relevant differences in the behavior or individuals, such as speaking a lot, speaking well, or telling tension-relieving jokes, there are more subtle cues that enhance distinctiveness and capture our attention. Shelly Taylor and Susan Fiske have shown, for example, that a person sitting across from us is more salient to us

than one sitting off to the side.[30] Whether the contributions to
a discussion are experimentally controlled or merely allowed
to vary randomly, we tend to think that the "salient" person
across from us had a great influence than others had over the
discussion. Other research shows that when we attend to some
members of a group more than others, we become more consistent and extreme in our evaluations of the vivid or salient
group members.[31] If the target persons say something we
don't like, for example, we will dislike them more if they are
salient. We will also like salient target persons more if they say
things with which we agree.

Differential salience can occur for many reasons. Which
stimulus properties become salient can obviously depend on
the various characteristics of the group serving as a context.
One female in a group of six males will be salient, whereas the
same female would not stand out in an all-female gathering.
The same would be true of an older person among youngsters,
a youngster among elders, and so on. Distinctive physical
characteristics can contribute to salience. Bright red hair, a
loud plaid shirt, and movement (e.g., the only person sitting in
a rocking chair) have been shown to attract disproportionate
attention, with at least some of the consequences suggested
above: increased causal attribution and greater evaluative
consistency.[32]

It is an easy step to the consideration of what might happen when a minority group member participates in a group
otherwise composed of majority members. The issues raised
by such considerations have led to a small but intriguing body
of research into the effects of "tokenism," the practice of
hiring or admitting a few minority members as tokens of integration efforts. An important question is whether tokens, because of their salience, are more likely to be treated in a
stereotyped way. If we enter a group situation with a stereotype that includes the attribution that most blacks are inarticulate, for example, are we more likely to judge a black token as
inarticulate than we would judge the same black who says the
same things in a group consisting of other blacks?

Taylor and her colleagues conducted a series of experiments to explore this and related questions.[33] In their most
elaborate (and relevant) study, an audio tape was made by

three males and three females instructed to improvise a teachers' lounge conversation. From this master tape, several versions were constructed, varying the number of male versus female voices playing the same roles and saying precisely the same things at the same cadence. These alternative versions ranged from six males and no females to six females and no males. There were also versions containing one male in a group of five females and one female in a group of five males. A given subject listened to one version of these tapes and then made a number of judgmental ratings.

In keeping with the salience results mentioned above, both males and females were seen as having more impact, the fewer their numbers. There was a tendency for more sex-typed roles to be assigned to members, the fewer their numbers. Thus, token males were more likely to be seen as macho leaders or father figures than were males in an all-male group; female tokens were seen as nurturant or secretarial types to a greater extent than were females in an all-female group.

Studies of tokenism can hardly explain stereotype formation and certainly don't carry us very far down the path of understanding ethnic prejudice and other kinds of social discrimination. What such studies do suggest, to me at least, is that token status can elevate the importance of certain dimensions of categorization, and the elevated dimension in turn can evoke a stereotype that otherwise might have lain dormant. The possibility of such "taxonomic shifts" was discussed earlier in this chapter. Let us imagine as a target person, Wilma, a black female Harvard student from Jamaica who is the star of the women's track team. Let us also imagine a perceiver well endowed with stereotypes about blacks, Third World countries, females, Harvard, and athletes. Let us further assume that many of these stereotypes have features that contradict one another. Tokenism research suggests that the stereotype that predominates may depend in a crucial way on the surrounding social contexts. If we see Wilma in the context of other black athletes, the fact that she is a Jamaican or a Harvard student may be the most salient feature governing our impression. If we see Wilma among other Harvard students, on the other hand, her color and her accent may be the most salient features, evoking whatever stereotypes or expectancies we may have about such features.

• **Out-Group Homogeneity**   A key feature of ethnic and other category-based stereotypes is the tendency to overemphasize the similarity of category members to each other. All categories tend to be represented in our minds by prototypes, or typical instances, and one reason stereotypes are false and misleading is that they are prevalent when information is meager: We are more likely to stereotype groups of people remote from us than groups to which we belong. Is there evidence that we perceive out-groups as less variable, or more homogeneous, than in-groups? Indeed there is, but it is important to frame carefully the hypothesized in-group/out-group comparison. The actual level of homogeneity in the two types of groups is obviously a crucial variable. There is nothing surprising about the fact that an American Protestant thinks his fellow Protestants are more variable in their personalities and actions than are out-group Hassidic Jews. The proposition only makes general sense as a two-way street; that is, group A members see group A as more heterogeneous than group B members do, and B members see group A as more homogeneous than A members do: Protestants believe Hassidic Jews are more similar to each other than Hassidic Jews do; Hassidic Jews, on the other hand, see greater Protestant homogeneity than Protestants do.

George Quattrone and I put this general proposition to the test by doing an experiment that involved volunteer subjects from two rival colleges (Princeton and Rutgers).[34] At Princeton, subjects viewed a videotape of a college student allegedly participating in another experiment, faced with a choice of waiting alone or with other subjects. Half of the Princeton subjects were led to believe that the student in this tape was from Princeton; the other half believed that he was from Rutgers. The same experiment was run at Rutgers, again with subjects led to believe that the target person on the videotape was either from their own school or from Princeton.

After watching the videotaped target person decide whether he wanted to wait alone or with other subjects, each subject was asked to estimate what the average person from the same institution would have decided to do in the same situation. As predicted, subjects in the out-group conditions generally assumed that the subjects would make the same choice, though the tendency was stronger with Princeton target persons than with Rutgers target persons. Subjects who believed that the videotaped person was from their own school were less likely to generalize from his decision to the likely decision made by the average member of their own group. Interestingly enough, this out-group homogeneity effect does not hold for behavioral decisions that are part of one group's stereotypes (i.e., priors) concerning another. When the purported choice was between classical and rock music, all subjects tended to agree that Rutgers students were more likely than Princeton students to prefer rock music, regardless of the actual choice made by the taped target person. So from this experiment, at least, we must restrict confirmation of the homogeneity proposition to cases where there is no clear a priori expectancy to be overcome—the choice between waiting alone or with others was deliberately selected in the experimental design as a choice uncontaminated by any such expectancy.

To follow up on the implications of this study, George Wood, George Quattrone, and I conducted a straightforward test among male members of several Princeton eating clubs asking them to rate the average member of their club and each of several other clubs on a list of trait antonyms we thought would be relevant in differentiating prototypical members.[35] After rating the average club member, each participant in the study was also asked to draw brackets on each antonym scale within which he thought 50 percent of the other members of the target club would be rated. Simply stated, the results showed that the bracketed intervals were wider for in-group ratings (summed across the various traits) than were ratings of out-group members. This, then, provides a straightforward confirmation of the out-group homogeneity hypothesis.

Why should this happen? One simple explanation is that we have more experience with in-group than with out-group members. Almost by definition we know more members of the in-group than of the out-group and therefore are in a better position to appreciate their variety. Surprisingly, there is little direct evidence that degree of acquaintance plays such a role. In the eating club study just described, sophomores were no less likely than juniors or seniors to show the out-group homogeneity effect, even though the degree of actual acquaintance with fellow in-group members was much lower for those who had just joined the club, and the differential knowledge of out-group versus in-group members was more discrepant for juniors and seniors than for sophomores. A more subtle variation of the experience hypothesis takes into account the probable quality or variety of interactions that we have with in-group versus out-group members. We are likely to see in-group members in more diverse settings, playing a greater variety of roles, than would be the case with out-group members. At least, it is often the case that our only contact with members of an out-group are brief and role constrained. We see hatted and bearded Hassidic Jews walking down Forty-seventh Street in Manhattan, and we may buy jewelry from them, but we do not enter into their lives to see them laugh and cry and get angry in a variety of different circumstances.

Bernadette Park and Michael Rothbart provide additional evidence for the out-group homogeneity effect.[36] They found that males are less likely than females to stereotype fellow males, and that females are less likely than males to stereotype fellow females. In another study, members of one sorority tended to see members of other sororities as more similar to each other than members of their own sorority on a variety of relevant characteristics. In a final study Park and Rothbart were able to show that people use higher-order, superordinate classifications when dealing with actions of an out-group member, whereas they characterize in-group members acting in the same way with a more differentiated schema. Thus, after being exposed to a vignette about a male or a female grocery store cashier, males remember that a male was cashier more reliably than females do, whereas females remember that the female was a cashier better than male subjects do.

We are all members of multiple categories, and the Park and Rothbart experiment seems to suggest that the in-group category label is not very salient when we are looking at other in-group members. Relatively speaking, other more subordinate labels become salient and are remembered better. A related possibility also seems to follow from the assumption that our experiences with in-group members are richer and more diverse than our experiences with out-group members. To the extent that this assumption is true, there may be interesting consequences for our cognitive representations of the two categories. It would seem to follow from the greater richness of in-group experience that our category-based expectancies for in-group members are probably more complex and multidimensional. If we see category members in a variety of different settings confronting different kinds of decisions, it seems likely that we have developed a larger set of attributional dimensions to make sense out of their actions. To summarize this suggestion, when we think about in-group members, our categories should be more complex and multidimensional than when we think about out-group members.

And if, indeed, we use more dimensions in thinking about the in-group, it should follow that our evaluations of particular in-group members should be more tempered or less polarized than our evaluations of out-group members. This is hardly a behavioral law, but it can be shown mathematically that the chances of a mixed review become greater, the greater number of features or dimensions of assessment taken into account.

Patricia Linville and I tried to exploit this reasoning in an experiment asking subjects to evaluate the credentials of a law school applicant.[37] The (actually contrived) applicant was presented as either white or black and either male or female. All subjects were white males or females. Materials on the applicants included a résumé, a personal statement of goals and interests, and letters of recommendation. These credentials were either very positively slanted or presented with several reservations. As we predicted, when the applicant was an out-group member (that is, either black or of the opposite gender), there was a greater tendency toward polarized appraisals. Thus, the outstanding black applicant was seen as more talented than the outstanding white applicant; similarly, an outstanding applicant of the opposite gender was rated more positively. The opposite was true when the applicant was weak. Opposite-sex applicants were seen as weaker than same-sex applicants, and blacks were seen as weaker than whites. These results were not terribly strong, but the logic has been pursued by Linville in a succession of experiments that add greater validity to the connection between cognitive "simplicity" and polarized evaluations.[38] Her results are at least consistent with the somewhat tenuous chain of assumptions and implications leading from out-group homogeneity through reduced cognitive complexity to polarized evaluations.

Linville has also been able to produce evidence for the assumption that our in-group categories have more cognitive complexity than our out-group categories. One technique for demonstrating this involves a card-sorting task. Subjects are given cards with a different trait adjective on each and ask to sort them into similar clusters. That is, each cluster was to contain traits that seemed to belong together. The underlying assumption of this technique is that the greater the cognitive complexity, the greater the number of separate trait clusters and the less the overlap between them. It turns out that when subjects are thinking of out-group members as they engage in this sorting task (for example, when college students think of retirees) they tend to use fewer categories, to differentiate less thoroughly among the possible characteristics, than when they are thinking of the in-group.

Charles Perdue used a variation of this technique in his study in which he created what we might call minimal in-groups and out-groups on the spot.[39] This was done by having subjects sort pictures of two groups of faces into clusters of meaningful similarity. One group of faces included a Polaroid photo of the subject's own face. Arbitrary in-groups and out-groups were created by having each subject shuffle the pictures, divide them into two groups (one including his own picture), and then, for each group separately, sort the pictures into similarity groupings — as many as judged meaningful. Quite remarkably, subjects showed greater complexity (by this measure) when sorting the group of faces that included their own than when sorting the group of faces that did not. What is remarkable about this, of course, is that the assignment of faces to groupings was completely arbitrary and the subjects who shuffled them were obviously aware of this. The complex sorting tendency was no greater when subjects, in one condition, were led to believe that there was some psychological basis for the division into the two groupings.

The theoretical meaning of these findings is not at all clear, but Perdue was also able to show the same tendency when cards containing clusters of traits instead of pictures were sorted. The group of cards containing the subject's own trait cluster (i.e., traits he thought characterized himself) were sorted into more complex groupings. These minimal group findings suggest that the related phenomena of group homogeneity and group similarity do not require differential experience. Subjects are prone to differentiate among in-group members more than among out-group members solely because they are among those being considered in the former case. Perhaps, when thinking of the in-group, we use ourselves as comparison anchors, and the richness of our self-knowledge is enough to generate a variety of dimensions in the categorization of others associated with us.

Stereotypes and Expectancies: A Brief Summary

The basic theme of the preceding section is that stereotypes are a form of category-based expectancy distinguished from "ordinary" expectancies by their invidiousness, the fact that they coalesce around salient physical and behavioral characteristics, and their relative resistance to change in the face of inconsistent information. Ethnic stereotypes in particular involve the further feature of a distinction between in-groups and out-groups. Thus, we have stereotypes about out-groups but not about in-groups.

I have tried to show that stereotypes can emerge from various cognitive processes, some of them newly discovered, and do not require the psychodynamic underpinnings of a concept like hostility displacement coupled with cognitive justification. It is obvious that categorization is a routine and essential cognitive activity. It is also obvious that stereotypes can misrepresent reality and can be socially destructive. The line between a useful category and a misleading stereotype is not an easy one to draw, but I have pointed to some special characteristics of cognitive functioning that seem to create such a line when people think about out-groups. Because we tend to see out-group members in highly restricted roles, we therefore tend to look upon them with relatively uncomplicated expectancy structures and exaggerate their similarity to each other. Because of the nature of our exposure to out-group members, then, a process is set in motion to create and sustain ethnic stereotypes. In addition, we can point to the illusory correlation phenomenon, as well as to those phenomena associated with salience and tokenism.

When we try to understand why particular target groups are singled out for distorted and evaluatively polarized stereotypes, however, this otherwise useful cognitive approach seems limited. We do not have distorted, polarized stereotypes toward all out-groups. An exclusive cognitive approach does not explain anti-Semitism, racism, or the more virulent forms of anticommunism. So much passion seems to animate some of our more unfortunate stereotypes that a purely cognitive characterization seems quite inadequate. While we should give a number of relevant cognitive principles their due, therefore, I think we must return to some form of displaced affect plus justification as an important motive for contributing to our perceptions of homogeneity, our affective polarization, and stereotypic resistance to change. I believe there is at least some empirical (and certainly some anecdotal) support for the classic psychodynamic formulations of frustration – aggression theory and authoritarianism theory, and I am not prepared to relinquish this part of our cultural wisdom until someone comes up with cognitive explanations that are not only consistent with what we know about stereotypes, but can tell us why we are especially prone to stereotype certain out-groups more than others. Cognitive processes may provide a pretext, but something else seems to be necessary to drive this tendency toward socially dysfunctional extremes. The particular historical relations between specific in-groups and out-groups is obviously an important determinant. In addition, the maintenance of stereotypes can serve important social functions of contributing to in-group solidarity and at least the illusion of moral or intellectual superiority.

When Behavior Violates
Category-based Expectancies

Consider the case when our stereotype of an out-group is clearly violated by the actions or appearance of an out-group member. There are at least two major things that an analyst trying to understand the nature of stereotypes would want to know:

1. Does the stereotype affect our perception and interpretation of the violation and the violator?

2. Does the violation bring about or initiate any change in the stereotype itself?

Do Stereotypes Affect Perceptions and Attributions?

Until fairly recently, the conventional wisdom among social scientists was that out-group stereotypes are very prevalent in society and strongly influence perceptions and interpretations of personal actions. However, in 1971 Jack Brigham reviewed the stereotype literature and could find little evidence that stereotypes actually affect our perceptions of individual out-group members. Subsequently, Ann Locksley and her associates raised the issue more sharply, suggesting that out-group stereotypes are rather easily cast aside and have little or no influence when one judges an individual who violates the stereotype.[40] Thus, though most of us would be more likely to include "assertiveness" in our male stereotype than in our female stereotype, a female who engages in an assertive act is judged to be just as assertive as a male engaged in the same act. According to Locksley, individuating diagnostic information tends to overwhelm normative expectations about members of a category or group. Kenneth Rasinski and his colleagues have challenged Locksley's particular findings, claiming that her estimate of the normative base rate was inappropriate.[41] They argue that people do make appropriate adjustments, integrating individuating information with beliefs about relevant group norms.

One fruitful way to think about the role of stereotypes may be to consider them as provisional hypotheses, starting points for processing information about individual category members. A striking study by John Darley and Paget Gross provides a clear example of how such hypotheses might function.[42] College student subjects observed a videotape of a young school girl, Hannah, filmed against alternative pictorial backdrops—either an affluent or a disadvantaged neighborhood. The intention was to convey a subtle "demographic expectancy," with subjects led to believe that Hannah's family background was either of high or of low socioeconomic status. When subjects who merely observed this videotape were asked to estimate Hannah's aptitude and most probable grade level in several achievement areas, there was no evidence that the demographic clue was relevant for their assessment. Subjects placed the low-status Hannah at approximately the same grade level in each area as they estimated for the high-status Hannah.

However, when other subjects saw the same videotape and also subsequently saw a tape of Hannah performing quite inconsistently on twenty-five achievement test problems, the demographic expectancy had powerful effects. Those subjects who viewed upper-class Hannah's performance placed her at a higher grade level in mathematics, reading, and liberal arts than did those who assumed Hannah was from a lower socioeconomic class.

These findings support the idea that at least some stereotypes are carried around as working hypotheses. They prime us to be alert and selectively responsive to confirming data, but they do not directly affect our impressions in the absence of such confirming data. When ambiguous, inconsistent performance data were provided for some subjects but not for others, only the former subjects showed the effects of the manipulated demographic expectancy. We can reasonably infer that they perceived the performance data in a biased way to confirm the stereotype.

Stereotypes, along with other types of "knowledge structures" considered earlier in this chapter, undoubtedly have shaping effects when it comes to the interpretation of ambiguous behavioral information. What is not so clear is the role they play when the behavioral information seems clearly disconfirming. I suspect that the issue of what happens when we see a group stereotype violated by a group member is actually a complex of issues. Surely the results for interpersonal perception depend greatly on (1) the strength of the stereotype, including the degree of perceived homogeneity of persons in the stereotyped category, (2) the severity of the violation, and (3) the constraining nature of the situation. According to my earlier characterization of category-based expectancies (of which stereotypes are an extreme example) people should not be unduly troubled by stereotype violations due to the probabilistic nature of such expectancies. I would certainly expect some assimilation to the stereotype in those instances where the violation is not extreme, but I also think that one can temporarily set aside even a strong stereotype and merely treat the stereotype violator as an exception to which the stereotype simply does not apply.[43] Although the phrase "the exception proves the rule" was originally intended to mean that exceptions *test* whether the rule is correct, we hear the phrase more often than not as a justification for maintaining a generalization that has been threatened.

Do Stereotypes Change When They are Violated?

It should follow from the above discussion that members who violate stereotypes about their group do not necessarily undermine the stereotype itself. In fact, the rigid information-resistant nature of stereotypes (as they are usually defined) must preclude the erosion of stereotypes in the face of individual exceptions. The issue becomes one of how many exceptions will be necessary before such changes begin to be reflected in the stereotype itself.

Even if we are left with a pattern in which we have group stereotypes but perceive individual members without being affected by these stereotypes, this hardly means that stereotypes are socially benign. Group stereotypes can obviously lead to negative actions that affect each member of a group adversely, even if the stereotyper ignores or discounts the stereotype each time he or she makes a judgment of a specific group member. Explicit or implicit minority quota systems in hiring, education, or housing, for example, may place minority group members at an obvious disadvantage even though our experience with individual minority members leads us to see each person as an exception to the stereotype.

The Naive

Assessment of Situational

Constraint

The scientific psychologists that some of us are and the naive psychologists that all of us are share an interest in predicting and understanding the causes of behavior. A central problem that confronts both kinds of psychologists is how best to conceptualize the situations in which behavior occurs. We must understand the role that situations play in eliciting and shaping behavior if we want to characterize its social meaning or understand its causal roots. In this chapter I shall discuss how scientific psychologists have construed the stimulus world for *their* purposes, but I shall do this mainly in the hope of developing a clearer picture of how naive psychologists conceive and utilize the role of situations in their perceptions of other persons.

Kurt Lewin's truism that behavior is a function of the person (P) and the environment (E) secured an honored and important place for the causal role of situational events. To a rough and fuzzy extent, the formula $B = f(P,E)$ might also suggest a division of labor between personality and social psychologists.[1] While not denying the obvious fact that the personal and situational determinants of behavior are interactive, personality psychologists have typically tried to conceptualize and study individual differences in response to standard situations; social psychologists have for the most part tried to conceptualize and to study the impact of systematic situational variations on the responses of the average or prototypical person. Experimental social psychologists, in particular, have essentially concerned themselves with the subtle and normally unrecognized influence of social situations on behavior. No one would deny that different kinds of people react differently to different kinds of settings, but the primary situational focus of the experimental social psychologist has been especially valuable in leading to theories of attitude change, cognitive dissonance reduction, conformity, and social influence in general. And yet psychologists have focused on the role of social situations without coming to much agreement about what a situation actually is.

For generations, the introductory psychology student has been exposed early and often to the concepts of stimulus and response, those observable independent and dependent variables that are the building blocks of the science. A typical approach in such courses is to move from simple S–R connections, such as those involved in reflexes and sensations, to an understanding of more complex molar behavior. When psychologists attempt to analyze complex behavior in the everyday world, their normal tendency is to relate S to R by construing various features or tendencies in the organism that mediate between the two. Thus, the S–R formula becomes an S–O–R formula, where the O stands for "organism." The hypothesized mediating factors in O can range from more or less elaborate cognitive processes to personality variables.[2] It is easy to convey the notion that there is a standard stimulus world that is selectively perceived and acted upon by an organism with a particular set of motives and expectancies and that out of this subjective view of the stimulus world comes a response that we can observe whether we are in our role as naive or as scientific psychologists. The S–O–R formula, with its provision for experienced-based and gene-based individual differences in O's, fits rather nicely into the naive psychology of our man-on-the-street. In my own experience as a teacher of social psychology, however, there is typically a certain amount of resistance to any emphasis on the S factor, on complex situational patterns that can be shown to influence the behavior of the average person in theoretically predictable ways. Students want to include in the O term all those factors that convert the physical energy that comprises the stimulus into stimulus patterns that have particular meaning for particular people.

In previous chapters I have referred many times to the great trade-off between person and situations — a trade-off offered by Heider as a core feature of naive psychology.[3] People certainly do make use of this trade-off in organizing and responding to their interpersonal world, but they also carry with them an obstinate, irreducible belief in the overwhelming importance of individual differences. People are unique; people differ from each other — these are such readily accepted and dominating truisms that it is sometimes difficult for social psychologists to get their students to recognize that the E part of the Lewinian equation is just as important as P. Part of the problem, as Skinner noted, is that "We can see what organisms do to the world around them, as they take from it what they need and ward off its dangers, but it is much harder to see what the world does to them."[4]

The major gift of social psychologists has been to inform us that we are influenced by situations in unexpected ways, in ways that actors themselves do not always acknowledge. Indeed, if people did think about situational influences in a more sophisticated way, social psychology would be a less important and a less interesting discipline.

I shall turn then to consider the various phenomena of social constraint — both the subtle and the obvious kinds of cases — in an effort to redress the imbalance of naive psychology. In the next chapter I shall have more to say about the imbalance itself and about why situational influences are so often underestimated. The justification for focusing on situational constraint should be obvious: Interpersonal perception always involves an integration of information relating behavior to its setting. Though we may sometimes fail to recognize the fact, behavior has meaning for the perceiver only in relation to the context in which it is embedded. That context is the situation to which the behavior is a response.

To put it another way, it is obvious that most, if not all, personal dispositions are variably expressed; their expression depends on the situation, on what is appropriate, on what response options are generally available and salient. Although we are convinced that Marilyn is a hostile person, a malicious gossip, we are nevertheless not surprised to see her behave in a warm and friendly manner toward a new acquaintance. Nor are we all that surprised when sweet, gentle Ben erupts in blasphemy when he tears his pants on a protruding nail. Bowers makes the same point more dramatically when he suggests that we should not be surprised to learn that a "usually honest man lies to a rapist concerning the whereabouts of his wife."[5] We generally carry around with us a sense of what many different situations call for, and we use this sense of situational norms to evaluate the actions of target persons. Situations are the (often silent) backdrop without which no action can be assessed or interpreted. When theorists treat behavior as if it were intrinsically informative, we may charitably assume that in some way they are taking the role of situational contexts for granted.

Grappling with the Situation Concept

Although we may have our solipsistic moments when we wonder if anything exists independently of our perceptions, most of us most of the time believe that there is an objective environment out there, a physical world of light and noises and weights and temperatures. The field of psychophysics is concerned with how people translate various physical energies into sensory and perceptual experiences. That is pretty straightforward stuff, even though the resulting translations can get fairly technical. Unless we are in a highly artificial and constraining psychophysical experiment, it is obvious that we act on the environment *that we perceive*. We construe or interpret the objective physical environment in ways that help to prepare us for adaptive action in that environment. To quote Nancy Cantor and John Kihlstrom, "A dinner party is a recreational situation for most guests, an achievement exercise for the nervous host, and a forum for self-promotion for the ingratiating local politician."[6]

How can this "subjective environment" be characterized in terms other than, or independent of, the actor's response to it? This has been the major challenge of psychology in general, and of social psychology in particular.[7] One obvious solution is to embrace phenomenology: to ask people about their environments, about what their stimulus world looks like to them. But there is abundant evidence that the answers to such questions are not always helpful. If we ask people about the stimulus before they respond, their subsequent response is hardly independent of the "interpretation" we have forced them to come up with. If we ask them after they have responded, we will normally get a perception or an interpretation that will justify or make good sense out of the response. Aside from these reactive measurement problems, there is abundant evidence that we often respond to features of the situation of which we are unaware, both at the time and later when asked. How do we psychologists know this? Because of inferences that we can draw from the logic of the experimental method. If most subjects in a given experimental condition are influenced to respond in a similar distinctive way and later cannot identify the variable that caused them to have a particular response, we can assume that they were unaware of what made them respond the way they did.

There are many examples of this in the experimental literature, especially in the literature of cognitive dissonance research. A large portion of this literature deals with cases in which persons are subtly induced to engage in actions that they would normally want to avoid. This inconsistency between action and beliefs or values can lead to dissonance arousal and subsequent changes in beliefs or values. The underlying cause of such changes, built into the very logic of dissonance theory, is the actor's failure to recognize the full force of those situational pressures inducing an "uncharacteristic" action. Dissonance theory works precisely because people underestimate or misperceive the power of the situation they are in and yet are strongly influenced by it. Nisbett and Ross provide numerous further examples of systematic situational influence, the sources of which are unrecognized by the subjects who are targets of influence.[8] For example, women faced with four identical sets of pantyhose arranged on a table in front of them have a strong tendency to evaluate the right-hand set as the most attractive. When asked whether their ratings were affected by the positions of the pantyhose, virtually all subjects denied such influence and were often annoyed with the experimenter for even suggesting such a factor.[9]

Kurt Lewin thought long and hard about how to conceptualize the situation as it impinges on the individual actor. He had various solutions to the problem, the most prominent of which was the concept of the "life space" or the psychological environment as it confronts the subject. The life space contains all those situational forces combining to determine the behavior of a given actor. But Lewin did not equate the life space with "the environment as perceived by the actor." He apparently realized that there are features of the life space — situational determinants of behavior — that are not represented in the phenomenal awareness of the actor. The same reluctance to embrace a complete phenomenology was apparent in Heider's naive psychology. He, too, wanted to reserve some place for situational determinants of which the actor was not specifically aware.

Perhaps it is the case that such hidden determinants are actually quite rare, that most of the time our actions follow directly from our perceptions of the situation. Nevertheless, the lack of fit between the phenomenal or subjective environment and situational determinants of action presents conceptual and methodological problems. There is an objective situation, there is the situation as perceived, and then there is something like "the life space" or the psychological environment, which overlaps with both but is not the same as either. Well, perhaps it is not too surprising to reach the conclusion that our awareness of what determines our own behavior is less than complete. After all, unconscious motivation has been a centerpiece of Freudian psychoanalysis for decades. All we are asked to do now is to recognize that there are stimulus determinants—things out there—that are affecting us without our being aware of their causal significance. If this seems bizarre or unlikely on the face of it, perhaps it will help to think of all those activities that have become automatic, like driving an automobile or brushing our teeth. A classic example of "unconscious inference" is the perception of size constancy. Clearly, our ability to perceive objects at different distances as relatively constant in size, along with many other integrative perceptual achievements, involves complicated responses to intervening stimuli of which we may be unaware until something happens to make them specifically salient to us. I agree with Skinner that "one need not be aware of one's behavior or the conditions controlling it in order to behave effectively—or ineffectively."[10]

A Taxonomy of Constraints

It may help to descend a little from this plateau of abstraction to consider the various sources of constraint that in fact shape our behavior.

Physical Constraints

An obvious place to start our analysis is with the constraining features of the physical environment in combination with our abilities to deal with them. Our concern here has its parallels in Heider's inclusion of "task difficulty" and "ability" among the determinants of action in naive psychology. Setting aside, for the moment, individual differences in ability, there are obvious physical constraints imposed by gravity (weight), time, and distance: We cannot spontaneously levitate, we cannot be in two places at once, and we cannot lift buildings or elephants. As for cognitive abilities, we cannot remember everything we ever knew or calculate with the speed of even the most modest electronic calculator. As we leave these clear-cut boundary conditions of general human capacity and imagine somewhat more modest physical and intellectual barriers, individual differences obviously become relevant. Some people can move faster or lift more or solve more calculus problems than others. Thus, we may speak of *ability constraints* to summarize all those performances that are beyond the capacity of a particular actor at a particular moment. The actor could not execute the performance even if he or she wanted to.

A moment's reflection suggests that the "particular moment" notion is of critical significance here. It is not just that some of us could never run 100 meters in eleven seconds, while others can; it is also the case that our ultimate capacities may not be expressible, given the opportunities afforded by the present situation. We cannot write without an implement, swim without water, or make love without a partner. Thus, ability constraints include both *capacity limitations* and *opportunity limitations*. The case may be that either we are incapable of a particular performance or, whatever they might be, our capabilities cannot be manifested without appropriate environmental resources.

I assume that some general conception of ability constraints comes very early in life for all of us. It might be argued that ability constraints form the basic metaphor for all other forms of situational constraint. Often when we say "I cannot do *x*," we really mean that we do not want to, that we consider doing *x* immoral, a waste of time, or too low in our scheme of priorities. When people engage in attributing causes for observed behavior, it may be that their view of the vast and diverse array of psychological constraints on behavior borrows meaning from developmentally prior notions of ability constraints. If and when this happens, such constraints may be attributed more imperative quality, more finality than the actual case merits.

On the other hand, ability constraints may often stand as an anchor to contrast with psychological (i.e., nonability) constraints. While a learning theorist might argue that one's reinforcement history is just as constraining as one's physical limitations, most naive psychologists probably tend to attribute greater choice when someone is constrained by incentives rather than by physical barriers. Since there is considerable evidence that people do, in fact, overestimate others' freedom to ignore incentive structures in the environment, we favor the anchor-contrast alternative when considering the impact of ability constraint notions on other forms of attributed constraint. At least this is the case if we define *constraint* by using consensus as an index—if everybody does it, it must have been constrained. In attitude attribution research, in which subjects are asked by an experimenter to defend attitudinal positions with which they may in fact disagree, all subjects invariably comply. The same subjects—or observers apprised of the experimenter's instructions—will nevertheless conclude that there was considerable freedom to choose in the situation.[11] We shall return to the consensus criterion later. For the moment we shall simply suggest that the consensus criterion is an extremely important tool for attributors to use in their efforts to dichotomize persons and situations. Perceived consensus provides the most convenient operational definition of a situation, one that gives the bystander confidence that he or she has indeed identified a constraining, or even a "demanding" setting.

• **Socially Induced Ability Constraints** In view of the constraining significance of opportunity limitations, it is hardly surprising that one actor can have considerable influence over the performances of another. In various ways an actor can, in effect, disable another actor. Interviewers may bring out the best or the worst in a political candidate by manipulating the candidate's opportunity to respond; thus, there are *socially induced opportunity constraints*. Many readers will remember Bernard Shaw's question to Michael Dukakis during the 1989 presidential debate: "Governor, if Kitty Dukakis were raped and murdered, would you [still] not favor an irrevocable death penalty for the killer?" Dukakis seemed clearly disabled by this question—although it is difficult to imagine how anyone could have answered it appropriately.

There are undoubtedly many forms of "conversational disabling" in which the actor is subtly deprived of the opportunity to talk about the things he or she knows best. Similarly, many athletic competitions turn on one actor's success in limiting the opportunities of another actor to express his or her abilities. The tennis player who repeatedly hits to an opponent's backhand may be doing so to limit the opponent's opportunity to display a murderous forehand.

In addition to controlling opportunities, one person can sometimes find ways to control the current performance capacity of another. There are many examples from the sports world where a player induces an opponent to perform well below his or her potential by "psyching the opponent out" or "messing with the opponent's head."

Psychological Constraints

I use this ambiguous label to capture all those forces of situational constraint besides those that are physically limiting. Psychological constraints may be just as compelling as physical ones, but as already noted, they are perceived differently. Naive conceptions of human nature invariably distinguish between not being able to do something and not wanting to do it, being "deterred" from doing it, or not recognizing the alternatives when most people would. The difference lies in the perception of potential control, even though the attributor may realize that no one would ever try to overcome psychological constraints in many cases of high incentives.

Whereas the world of physical constraints is fairly straightforward and easily understood, the world of psychological constraints is baffling in its complexity. Indeed, almost the entire field of psychology is concerned in one way or another with the analysis of psychological constraint, whether in the form of reinforcement theory, social influence and comparison theory, socialization and education theories, or even studies of perception and memory, so it is hardly surprising that attributors are typically forced to adopt simplifying strategies to deal with the complexities involved in assessing such things as the role of incentives and expectancies in "explaining" the behavior of others. Here, we provide an overview of various types of psychological constraint and briefly consider their attributional implications.

• **Motivational Constraints**   People reveal their nature by expressing or acting on their desires and aspirations, and to the extent that these actions are unique or distinctive, important dispositional inferences are likely to be drawn. But when individual motives are widely shared and a particular situation provides positive or negative incentives that are relevant to those shared motives, we think of the situation itself as constraining. We are not likely to attribute generosity to a holdup victim. A psychologist might think of the "approach or avoidance gradients" of the situation, visualize a "payoff matrix," or speak in terms of a situational "press" or "valence."[12] Once again, perceived consensus is likely to be extremely important as the attributor attempts to locate the wellsprings of behavior in the commonly desired incentive out there or the revealing "need" in the person.

The psychologist's general task is to analyze the determinants of behavior in the most empirically fruitful way. The task of attribution students, of course, is somewhat different. Never mind what actually causes behavior; what do people perceive or infer as behavioral causes in particular instances, and how can we generalize about these inference processes? It may be, for example, that a gentle request in a particular setting is just as constraining, as "motivating," as a large bribe. It may also be that few subjects will see it that way, and it is up to the attribution student to try to figure out why. It is just as likely, a priori, that truly different constraint conditions are treated as equivalent by most attributors, and again we need to understand why this is the case. A third possibility is that incentives that are logically or economically equivalent elicit different responses from those affected and are treated as different by attributors as well. Examples of each of these possibilities may be found in the literature comparing positive and negative incentives.

POSITIVE VERSUS NEGATIVE INCENTIVES.   The maxim goes, "A bird in the hand is worth two in the bush." This may be interpreted either as a psychological truth or as a moral admonition (take what is at hand and don't wait for "pie in the sky"). The former reading is consistent with the widely acknowledged general human tendency toward risk aversion.[13] It turns out that people do not always prefer the sure thing; there are specifiable conditions when they will seek rather than avoid risk.[14] Nevertheless, the more general expectation is that people avoid risks because the prospect of a loss hurts more than the prospect of an objectively equivalent gain.

The implications of this general tendency for my present discussion are several. The motivation to avoid loss or pain (i.e., negative consequences) is generally stronger than the motivation to achieve positive incentives. Therefore, situations containing threats of negative incentives will be seen as more powerfully constraining than those involving potential rewards. Perhaps this is why, as I have previously noted,[15] perceivers attribute dispositions to explain "effects obtained" more readily than they attributed dispositions for "effects forgone." The forgone effects may be seen as more compelling or constraining (i.e., everyone would avoid them), whereas positive effects or incentives more typically involve choice. People "prefer" certain positive effects to others. Their escape from negative effects is so "obvious" that it is not so informative about their nature.

OUTCOME CONTROL VERSUS CUE CONTROL.   Harold Gerard and I distinguish between responses explicitly directed toward the attainment of rewards or the avoidance of punishments and those elicited or shaped by cues that tap into preestablished habit patterns.[16] B. F. Skinner distinguished among the elicitation, discrimination, emotional, and reinforcing functions of stimuli,[17] though his major interest was in showing the importance of reinforcement in establishing new stimulus–response connections. John Thibaut and Harold Kelley distinguished between "instigations" and reinforcements.[18] There are many similar distinctions drawn in the learning and conditioning literature. For present purposes *cue control* comes about when the controller provides stimulus information that affects the controlled person's behavior by triggering that person's dispositions rather than providing reinforcements. The better one person knows another, the more power that person presumably has to move the other into a psychological position in which the stimuli for well-established propensities become enhanced or salient. *Outcome control* involves the direct provision of rewards, promises, or threats in order to increase the likelihood of actions desired by the provider. Only a general knowledge of preferred and aversive incentives (plus the repertory to provide them) is necessary to exert outcome control.

A dimension correlated with the outcome – cue distinction is the extent to which the response in question is a thoughtful decision or an automatic response. Actors are usually more aware of their efforts to make rewarding decisions or even of their operant responses to reinforcement contingencies than they are of the fact that a disposition has been triggered by a relevant item of information. It is probably the case that the majority of social role playing falls at the more automatic end of this dimension. Social roles are typically overlearned patterns of response to particular settings: We follow the leader; we flirt; we comply with red lights and the police in a relatively mindless manner.[19] Huge chunks of our situation-specific behavior have thus been automatized to make room for responses to novelty and for more elaborate, conscious, decision making.

Although each of us may use different terms to think about something similar to the distinction here proposed between outcome and cue control, we would probably all agree that some such distinction is useful in describing different forms of situational influence. But the present question is whether attributors respond differently to these different forms in deciding about the causes of behavior. Is a cue-controlled response more "situational" than an outcome-controlled response, or vice versa? Do we learn more about a person by observing what he or she is willing to work for or by noting the cues that trigger automatic behavior? In both cases, consensus is presumably relevant once again: How much does the behavior in either case depart from our expectations of "everyman"? There are games like "Simon Says" in which almost everyone can be tricked into responding under the cue control of repetition and we gain little information about a cue control victim in such a game. However, since dispositions (the ultimate interest of the attributor) can be fairly easily mapped into "past learnings," there are two special reasons why observations of cue control might be more informative than observations of outcome control:

1. There is probably greater agreement about what constitutes an incentive than about what paths have led to incentives in the individual's past history. We are, perhaps, more

similar in our likes and dislikes than in our habits, our built-in conceptions of instrumentality.

2. Since people are probably more aware of being controlled by outcomes than by cues, they can shape their own behavior in a self-conscious way to manage a favorable (and therefore not terribly informative) impression.

- **Cognitive Constraints**   There is a final form of situational constraint that lies ambiguously between ability constraints, on the one hand, and motivational constraints, on the other. This is the constraint inherent in the actor's perception of the options available in a particular setting. There are a variety of reasons why the perception of options may include less than the full range available or at least be more restricted for one individual than for another in the same situation. The most obvious reason is *intellectual limitations*. Some of us are simply not as smart as others in perceiving relevant options, much less in choosing the right one, whether in chess or in major life decisions. Lack of smartness in this case may include a variety of deficits, ranging from expert knowledge to creative imagination. Smart people may know more about the potential availability of other settings in other places at other times and thus feel less constrained by their present circumstances.

  Then there are priming, or setting, factors. Immediate prior experience may have oriented us to recognize certain solutions but not more efficient alternatives.[20] Such *priming, or setting, deficiencies* can be overcome presumably by training or instructions (counterpriming), but they nevertheless can play an important role as determinants of decision making. More generally, something in our past history may have decreased the likelihood that certain options will ever be noticed in particular situations. This is in many ways the essence of socialization: One end result of the internalization of values and beliefs is the ruling out of perceived alternatives. We learn to behave the way we do because our socialization functionally limits the range of behavioral alternatives in almost all the situations in which we find ourselves.

  In addition to experience-based blind spots, alternatives may not be perceived because an actor's perceptions may be constrained by his or her current motives. Examples of such *motivated selectivity* are not hard to enumerate. Hungry people seldom consider all the things they might do with the dollars in their pockets. Our pride during a bitter negotiation session may blind us to a conciliation alternative that would be obvious to a negotiator who was less ego involved.

Again, the question is, what are the attributional implications of this category of perceived constraint? Here would seem to be a class of cases in which the perceived situation "causes" behavior but something about the person causes the situation to be perceived in a limited or special way. If somehow aware of this, the attributor may attempt to decide whether the cognitive constraint is capacity related or tied to personal motives and values. Such a distinction might be very consequential, causing the attributor to conclude, for example, that the actor is stupid but not venal or self-serving. It is more likely, however, that instances of cognitive constraint will go undetected by the attributor. Thus, he or she is more likely to conclude that the actor considered and discarded the option than to conclude that the option was never even perceived. Presumably this will be more probable to the extent that the options appear salient to the attributor and therefore difficult to ignore.

The preceding taxonomy of situational constraint is summarized in Table 5-1.

Some Further Complexities

Alternatives, Goals, and Incentives

The preceding discussion states that situations can be both physically and psychologically constraining. The attribution of abilities is directly tied to assessments of physical constraint (represented by Heider as task difficulty or effective environmental force acting against the actor[21]). The attribution of motives or goals depends in a similar way on the perceiver's

---

TABLE 5-1   A Taxonomy of Situational Constraint

Physical constraint

Physical ability constraints
   Capacity limitations
   Opportunity limitations

Socially induced ability constraints
   Controlling opportunities
   Controlling current capacity

Psychological constraint

Motivational constraints
   Incentives: positive versus negative
   Outcome versus cue control

Cognitive constraints
   Intellectual limitations
   Priming or setting deficiencies
   Motivated selectivity

---

assessment of the choices confronting the target person and the incentives they represent. A basic assumption of the attribution approach is that the attributor, in one way or another, has to try to take into account the world as it looks to the target person. Harking back to our discussion of correspondent inference theory, we observe a target person in action, but what that action tells us about the target person depends on further assumptions we make about the alternatives that he or she confronted. In other words, the meaning of an action is understood only against the backdrop of alternative actions forgone.

The task of the person perceiver is made even more difficult by some additional complexities:

1. There is initially, of course, the problem of trying to determine what alternatives the target person is considering

among the conceivable alternatives. How do we know, for example, what exists in the perceptual field of the target person?

2. Target persons do not typically simply find themselves confronting a situation. In the large majority of cases in the real world, the fact that they are confronting one set of alternatives rather than another is a function of certain prior choices, and these prior choices themselves are informative about the person. Thus, the perceiver needs to answer the question, how did the target person get him- or herself into this situation? The range of available alternatives confronting the target person might be a function of immediate prior choices, might be the end result of a long sequence of past experiences, might reflect the individual's current emotional state, might be determined by certain limitations in cognitive capacity, and so on.

3. What are the incentives involved in each alternative? In other words, what is the pattern of outcomes that is most likely being perceived by the target person standing at the threshold of action? To begin to answer this question, the perceiver must not only know what alternatives are being considered, but must make certain inferences about how appealing each of these alternatives is to the target person. The perceiver must also try to determine how *legible* the incentives are in the situation confronting the target person. The alternatives can involve different goals or different paths to the same goal. Unfortunately for the perceiver, target persons may misjudge the probability that certain actions will lead to certain goals, and their choices of action can therefore mislead the perceiver concerning the target person's motives.

4. In addition to the incentive legibility of a course of action, perceivers might also consider the extent to which action choices have a ballistic property; that is, to what extent does a behavior choice involve an irrevocable commitment, like a struck golfball whose flight cannot be altered by any further actions? Choices that are subject to further guidance may in the long run provide more information to the perceiver, who may observe the extent to which the target person

persists when there is an alternative to stop or to reverse the decision that has been made.

Answers to each of these questions may be crucial in shaping the perceiver's explanations of observed action. It is of extreme importance to know, for example, the extent to which the target person is trapped in a stream of uncontrollable events or whether the target person has a range of alternative choices. In the latter case, obviously, the incentive quality of the chosen and forgone alternatives conveys useful information about the motives, goals, or traits of the target person. These complexities make us realize that our earlier statement of correspondent inference theory is very sketchy and incomplete.

Even further complexities become apparent when we seriously consider the dynamic nature of interpersonal events. In the typical interaction sequence, the alternatives do not stay put; they do not array themselves in an obvious manner for our reflective behavioral decisions. The available alternatives are governed by a rapidly changing social context. A set of alternatives may be available only for a fleeting instant as one person attempts to respond to the behavior of another. Furthermore (and I shall have much more to say about this later), the ongoing social situation is one that is partially controlled or elicited by our own actions.[22] The consequences of this are intriguing; they point up the uniquely social aspect of interpersonal perception, and they certainly add another dimension of complexity to the entire process of interpreting behavior.

The Varieties of Constraint:
A Summary

In the preceding discussion I have tried to suggest some of the complexities that should be considered when we attempt to analyze the various ways that situations can constrain behavior. I have also referred, from time to time, to the task of a perceiver who is trying to determine whether and what constraints were involved in a target person's actions. Since the problem of reading situations is so complex, it is not surprising perhaps that perceivers are sometimes inept at deciding what to attribute to a situation and what to attribute to some idiosyncratic disposition of the target person. If we had better theories of situational constraint, we would be in a better position to determine and analyze the particular shortcomings of the attributor. As it stands, the question of how naive attributors perceive situational constraint is one of the most important but least understood aspects of interpersonal perception.[23] The preceding considerations of the varieties of physical and psychological constraint give us some insight into the magnitude of the perceiver's task, but the naive psychology of situational constraint is still poorly understood by students of the person perception process. The following section represents a brief and preliminary attempt to get inside the head of the attributor and to speculate on how information about a target person's situation is used in understanding how his or her motives, abilities, and other dispositional characteristics are perceived.

Situation as Expectancies

The attributional approach alerts us to the naive psychologist's ever-present trade-off between persons and situations. If everyone behaved the same as Virginia in the same setting or circumstance, we might say that Virginia's actions are "caused" by the situation and tell us nothing about Virginia herself. A high consensus response generally means that everyone sees the situation in the same way and, furthermore, that everyone reacts the same way because it is the sensible thing to do. It is this shared agreement about situationally contingent appropriate behavior that underlies convenient, loose references to situational causation.

The "situation" generally plays the role of a default position in the attributional scheme. We infer or attribute causation to the situation when we think that a person's actions are uninformative, but we may not know exactly why the situation led to the action. Our language is rich in terms that refer to personal traits and dispositions; it is impoverished in providing situational labels.[24] In fact, most recent efforts to develop a taxonomy of situations end up describing the behavior of prototypical persons in the situation rather than the situation itself.[25] In spite of our verbal impoverishment, however, situational attributions play an important role in dealing with actions that violate our expectancies about persons. If a person behaves in an unexpected way, one reason that must be considered is that "something about the situation" prompted the person to go against his or her nature. Again, we need only recall the honest man and the rapist.

But how do we determine when an action is idiosyncratic and when it is "called for" by the situation? Where do our ideas about consensus come from? An obvious source is empathetic role playing, taking the role of the actor that we, as perceivers, are trying to understand. Many situational norms are inferred from our own actual or imagined actions in the settings involved. If subjects in an experiment, for example, are confronted with a new behavioral decision ("Will you carry this 'repent' signboard around the campus?"), they will make their decision along with a strong assumption that most other people would have decided the same way. This has been called the "false consensus effect" by Lee Ross and his colleagues,[26] who have shown that we tend to assume our reactions are more in tune with the consensus than, in fact, they really are.

Richard Nisbett and I have tried to suggest why this might be with our proposal concerning actor–observer differences in attributional tendencies.[27] The actual proposal is that "there is a pervasive tendency for actors to attribute their actions to situational requirements, whereas observers tend to attribute the same actions to stable personal dispositions."[28] An obvious implication is that you and I as actors generally consider ourselves alert and responsive to the stimulus conditions confronting us. On some occasions we feel that the situation requires us to behave in a particular way; on other occasions we see the situation in terms of opportunities for motive fulfillment. We usually see ourselves as rational and realistic and therefore consider our acts adaptive and defensible — generally, what anyone who is intelligent and perceptive would do in the same setting. (There are exceptions, of course, as we may recognize the relative distinctiveness of our individual tastes and values, but even here we probably overestimate the consensus, assuming that anyone with the same tastes and values would behave the same way.) I suggest that the false consensus effect follows from this tendency of actors to explain their own actions as eminently reasonable responses to situational stimuli. After all, unless we endow ourselves with unique perceptiveness, we should find solace in the confirming belief that other intelligent and well-adjusted people would have done the same thing we did.

So I argue that there is a strong tendency for us to substitute consensus for our personal (and perhaps quite idiosyncratic) reading of a situation. Our own actual or imagined actions become the norm and have a lot to do with setting up situational expectations for others. Norms can also be defined in other ways, of course. There are certainly legal norms, and we expect most people to obey most laws. Then there are norms that we learn through endless observations of the social scene. Our ideas of consensus are partly projected (see above) but also observed and remembered. Through social comparison we learn how most people react to the theft of their personal property, to passing or failing a crucial examination, to the death of a grandfather, to the receipt of compliments or gestures of support, to the prospects of surgery, to a hometown victory. We trade on such knowledge when we observe actions that we define as conformity and deviation. These situational norms become a crucial part of the relevant mixture of information shaping our inferences and attributions.

Finally, we must remember the crucial feature of Trope's theory of dispositional attribution.[29] When situational norms are ambiguous and a target person's actions are unequivocal, our perceptions of situational requirements will be shaped by that observed action. The freshman in her first college class may immediately learn whether college classes are to be informal rap sessions or settings with lectures delivered by professors, from which everyone is expected to take careful notes. In the discussion of attributional approaches in Chapter 3 I acknowledged that one weakness of correspondent inference theory was our failure to realize the likelihood that expectancy violations will be attributed to the situation. This follows from

Trope's point of situational malleability and is illustrated by some recent experimental findings: James Kulik showed that a setting contrived to be quite ambiguous in its normative pressure for extroverted or introverted behavior will be readily redefined to "explain" the actions of a target person that are inconsistent with a perceiver's knowledge of that person's dispositions.[30] Thus, for example, if an extrovert is not outgoing and sociable in a particular setting, the subject's tendency is to see that setting as one with norms favoring aloof or unresponsive behavior. The same tendency was observed in an experiment by Carolyn Weisz and myself, in which an unaggressive child who behaved in an aggressive way was seen as provoked.[31]

Choosing Situations and Responding in Them

Situational attributions can thus serve as a refuge to allow us to perpetuate our impressions about a person whose actions violate our expectations. But certain kinds of situational attributions can also *facilitate* dispositional attributions. An important distinction needs to be drawn between how a person behaves once in a constraining situation and how a person chooses to enter one situation among many. Thus, situations can be determined by persons, just as a person's actions can be determined by situations. Paul Wachtel has accused social psychologists of ignoring the personal diagnostic value of situational choices because our experiments assign heterogeneous subjects to powerful situations that mask their individual differences.[32] In the "real world," he argues, people choose their situations and in doing so reveal much about the kinds of people they are. It probably won't surprise you to learn that I find this attack on experimental social psychologists overdrawn. There is no intrinsic reason why we cannot do experiments on how people choose to enter one versus another situation. Nevertheless, the general point is well taken. The situations people choose can be very revealing; such choices lend themselves to target-based expectancies. After all, someone who seeks out horror films, spends his or her income on night school courses, or quits a job in California to move to Brooklyn is conveying very relevant information about values, attitudes, and life-style by putting him- or herself in these different situations.

What is the most fruitful way to treat this distinction between choosing situations and behaving in them? Actually, this is but an old and familiar problem appearing in a slightly different form. It is really the problem of priors, in Trope's terms,[33] or the problem of prior choices confronted in our earlier discussion of correspondent inference theory. When we learn that Mary chooses to accept a position in the Tulane rather than the Vanderbilt economics department, we not only learn something about her immediate preferences (the non-common effects associated with this particular choice), we obviously can speculate meaningfully about a set of prior decisions that led her into the position of being able to make the choice about which we are informed. These prior decisions, creating the "situation" Mary has just confronted in making her choice among economics departments, are obviously very informative. In this sense, situations that reflect prior choices by a person can hardly fit the simple attributional logic of the discounting principle, which refers to the great trade-off between situation and person and specifies that dispositional causes will be "discounted" to the extent that powerful situational constraints are at work. There is no trade-off when the more we learn about the situations an actor confronts, the more we learn about the actor confronting them.

It is important to realize that every act is in one sense a situational choice. If I choose pepperoni rather than anchovy pizza, I put myself in the situation of eating (or not eating) a pepperoni pizza. If I am induced by a subtle cognitive dissonance manipulation ("It is entirely up to you, but do you suppose you could . . .") to write an essay counter to a cherished attitude, I put myself in an essay-writing situation and also in a broader setting of realizing that I believe x but am espousing not-x. Certainly, if I act to take a drug, I put myself in a new situation with more or less predictable consequences. And so on. It is therefore difficult to maintain a strict dichotomy between choosing a situation and behaving in a situation. To the extent that such a dichotomy makes sense, we are really talking about three overlapping phenomena: (1) the range and distinctiveness of the options available, (2) whether an act is obviously instrumental (on the path to some goal) or consummatory (enjoying the fruits of reaching the goal), and (3) a temporal dimension reflecting the fact that acts occur in a sequence over time. An act just observed may appear to be more vivid and easily remembered than actions that must logically have preceded it. It is quite possible that the recency of a terminal act results in attributing greater diagnostic significance to it than it deserves, whereas more meaningfully informative behavioral precursors (prior choices) may be ignored or assigned too little attributional weight.

It is always tempting and almost conventional to end a speculative discussion with a plea for more research, but in this case such a plea seems amply justified. We have hardly scratched the surface in our efforts to discover what perceivers make of terminal versus instrumental responses, of prior versus current choices, and of choices among multiple versus restricted alternatives. In the next chapter I shall mention a few attempts to "scratch the surface," but there remain many questions for which we don't even begin to have firm answers. It seems reasonable to conclude that the research process would be helped by a more sophisticated theory of situations, one that includes the idea that situations are both a cause and a result of action.

Concluding Remarks

What can we say about situational constraint at this point that will help us better understand the phenomena of interpersonal perception? My first bit of advice is to avoid panic. The social world is indeed a complicated place, but we have a lot of commonsense wisdom about how it all works. Trying to conceptualize "situational constraint" has proved frustrating, but largely because we have taken the rigorous perspective of a perceiver who is determined to reach some conclusions about what a target person is "really like." In that role difficulties in assessing the degree and quality of situational constraint contribute to our frustration.

From another perspective, however, our use and mastery of situational concepts is both remarkable and invaluable. It is precisely because situations are so powerful, and so often clear in their normative implications, that we don't need to figure out what most of our interaction partners are "really like." To use a nautical metaphor, we can navigate in all but the most turbulent interpersonal seas with the comforting aid of normative pilot lights. We are constrained by norms, and so are others. Typically they are the same norms. The social structures that ultimately constrain us vastly simplify our tasks as person perceivers. Most of the time the behavior of others is not problematic. Even when actors are not entirely under normative control, their deviations do not always require us to get involved in the higher-order cognitive challenges of dispositional attribution. Serious collisions can usually be avoided by a little extra vigilance in monitoring the deviant courses of action themselves.

Perhaps it is not too fanciful to say that one of the reasons we don't think a lot about situational constraint is that most such constraints are so blatant. People are fascinating in their uniqueness, their capricious complexity, their private aura of inaccessible mystery. Situations, on the other hand, are routinely powerful in governing many of our moment-to-moment actions. Many situations are covered by scripts that define in general terms the sequence of actions expected in them.[34] In the church wedding situation, for example, there is a definite sequence of expected events. Scripts are also prominent in settings like job interviews, Christmas gatherings, eating at a restaurant, or going to the supermarket. It is probably the case that as naive psychologists and person perceivers we only really get interested when the impact of situations is ambiguous or problematic—when we are not confident of our estimates of consensual response or when our estimates lead us badly astray. So it is not situational constraint per se that baffles and befuddles us; our troubles begin when there is constraint but we're not sure how much, when there is constraint but we misread or underestimate it. It is then that both the naive and the scientific psychologist need help. Such help is complicated by the many factors I have discussed, including the essential fact that situations are typically created by the combined actions of the perceiver and the target person. They are constructed, defined, and negotiated as part of the social interaction process.

The fact that the topic of situational constraint raises some complex issues does not move me very far from my conviction that the great person–situation trade-off is the most fundamental of attributional priorities. The discounting principle involved is almost always in use, at least when a target person's actions create enough surprise to set the attributional process in motion. But as we shall see in the next chapter, the calibration of trading off is often crude and flawed. Our person perceiver seems to respond to the actor in the situation not by ignoring the person–situation trade-off, but by assigning the wrong values in carrying out his or her attributional arithmetic.

Correspondence Bias

I have a candidate for the most robust and repeatable finding in social psychology: the tendency to see behavior as caused by a stable personal disposition of the actor when it can be just as easily explained as a natural response to more than adequate situational pressures. We have already come upon this tendency in several previous discussions, but in this chapter I shall go into more detail in discussing the evidence of its pervasiveness as an empirical phenomenon, its most likely causes, and its most important consequences. I have been waging a campaign to call this ubiquitous tendency "correspondence bias," a term that seems to capture the idea that we see behavior as corresponding to a disposition more than we should. In other words, we have a greater tendency to make a correspondent inference than correspondent inference theory itself (or any other attribution theory for that matter) would predict. Others will continue to refer to the phenomenon as the "fundamental attribution error," a dramatic depiction introduced by Lee Ross, but I find this needlessly controversial[1] and not helpfully denotative. Nevertheless, Ross and I agree that the biasing tendency is basic and important in ways that will be amply documented in this chapter.

Although the data base for this phenomenon has been developing for only the past couple of decades, the notion that people are generally biased in applying the great person–situation trade-off—in the direction of overattribution to the person—has been with us in various forms for some time. In 1949 Gustav Ichheiser argued that perceivers are prone to exaggerate the consistency of personality over a variety of situations.[2] More specifically, Heider spoke in 1958 of the salience of behavior, such that "it tends to engulf the field rather than be confined to its proper position as a local stimulus whose interpretation requires the additional data of a surrounding field—the situation in social perception."[3] It is but a small step to argue that behavior, in all its salience, will be seen more easily as caused by the person than as elicited by the situation. That step is to assume that the act and the actor form a perceptual unit and that the act belongs more to the actor than to the setting.

Correspondence bias is also strongly implied in the discussion by Nisbett and me of actor–observer differences in attribution.[4] In our essay we argue that observers attribute to personal dispositions many actions that the actors themselves see as caused by the situation. We suggest that both actors and observers are wrong, but we devote more space to document observers' "dispositionalism" tendencies than actors' tendencies to attribute their own choices or preferences to intrinsic features of the objects chosen or preferred.

Watson has reviewed the many studies concerned with the validity of the actor–observer proposition,[5] and in general the proposition fares rather well, at least by a simple count of studies favoring versus studies opposing the proposition. Though the evidence concerning actor attributions is somewhat equivocal, the evidence for correspondence bias among observers has become quite overwhelming. Let us take a quick look at some of the evidence and consider the major alternative accounts that treat the correspondence bias results as artifacts of particular samples or particular experimental arrangements.

The Early Evidence for Correspondence Bias

I have previously described a set of experiments by Harris and me, designed to provide an early test for correspondent inference theory in the domain of attitude attribution.[6] In our experiment subjects were asked to evaluate a male student's attitudes toward Castro after reading an essay he allegedly wrote under free choice or under the constraint of having the essay direction assigned. The results were generally supportive of the theory: Stronger attitudes were attributed under choice conditions, and this was especially true with the pro-Castro essay, an essay in the "undesirable" direction.

However, what most caught our attention was the reduced but nevertheless very significant tendency of subjects to attribute correspondent attitudes to the target person even when the target person had no choice. Even when people knew that the essayist *had* to write the pro-Castro essay, they still were inclined to infer that he *really was* sympathetic to Castro. This "overattribution" tendency was found in many other experimental studies involving different topics and different ways of varying constraint. Topics including attitudes toward desegregation, marijuana legalization, amnesty for draft evaders, and federalized support for medical care have been used within the attitude attribution paradigm.[7] To create situations that should have been viewed as highly constraining, the experimental cover stories included a course examination question, a debate assignment, a highly paid task, and a variety of other instructions that would normally elicit 100 percent compliance to a request by an experimenter. Regardless of the attitude topic or the particular form of manipulated constraint, observers were biased toward correspondent inferences, that is, toward attributing dispositions in line with the behavior observed.

Is Correspondence Bias Merely an Artifact?

There was something about these early demonstrations of correspondence bias that aroused considerable skepticism — not about the findings themselves, but about the particular circumstances under which they were produced. In short, many social psychologists were convinced that the phenomenon could be explained with reference to "local" features of the procedures, that the findings of correspondence bias have limited generality. Let us take a look at some of the artifactual explanations and consider their merit.

THE BEHAVIOR PROVIDES CLUES ABOUT THE TRUE BELIEFS OF THE TARGET PERSON   In the initial demonstration of Harris and me, the essays on Castro and the speeches on desegregation were made up by the experimenters. We attempted to make these offerings quite unexceptional, and it was made clear to subjects that the target persons had access to supporting materials in constructing their arguments. Nevertheless, these first experiments were vulnerable to the contention that the behavior content may have conveyed something about the expertise or the passion of the actor that could only suggest that he or she was more of a true believer than the average person. Sensitive to the thrust of this contention, Melvin Snyder and I conducted several experiments in which the target persons were the same as the perceivers; that is, all subjects wrote assigned essays on one or another side of an opinion issue that were then exchanged, after which subjects evaluated the true attitudes of those authors of the essays they received in the exchange.[8] Correspondence bias was very significant under these conditions. Subjects may have *thought* the essays provided clues suggesting correspondence, but they were wrong in the aggregate. In this and most subsequent studies, furthermore, there was no relationship between the true attitude of the essay writer and the attitude attributed to the writer by the subject reading it.

We have found, in general, that subjects are quite insensitive to variations in extremity of content or enthusiasm of delivery. In fact, Ajzen and his colleagues did an experiment in which correspondence bias occurred in the absence of any relevant content whatsoever.[9] Subjects received some unrevealing personal information about the target person, learned that he had complied with an assignment to write an essay, and then were asked to evaluate his true attitude without ever having seen the essay. It would be wrong to conclude that variations in content are always irrelevant. If negative arguments are mentioned or if there are strong signs of a grudging delivery, correspondence bias can be reduced or eliminated. Within wide limits, however, variations in presentation and content play a surprisingly small role in the attribution of attitudes after the general endorsement of a particular position.

TARGET PERSONS REALLY DO HAVE THE FREEDOM NOT TO ENDORSE UNCONGENIAL OPINIONS: THEREFORE, THEY MUST FIND THE POSITION AT LEAST SOMEWHAT CONGENIAL   It is certainly the case that, in all the correspondence bias experiments, people (who become target persons) in the no-choice condition retain considerable freedom: They may refuse to write the assigned essay or refuse to deliver the assigned speech, presumably incurring only the embarrassment of having turned down the experimenter's request or in some cases the loss of the offered payment for helping out. Subjects may assume that persons who strongly endorsed a position opposite to that assigned to them would exercise the option of ultimate refusal. Therefore, observers may view the target persons as belonging to a self-selected group of actors who are at least not strongly opposed to the position assigned. Although this is a reasonable presumption, it flies in the face of abundant data that suggest that 100 percent of all "constrained subjects," in fact, do comply. Thus, even those firmly opposed to the message they have been asked to deliver quite readily turn to the task, and their messages do not reveal that they were even in conflict about their role. Again, perceivers may *think* the target person has considerable freedom in the high constraint condition, but by the criterion of a unanimous acquiescence they are wrong. This suggests that at least part of the bias toward correspondence involves a misreading of the degree of constraint inherent in the experimental procedures. The results do not support the notion that the constraint in the high-constraint condition is only moderate and accurately perceived as such. To put it in a somewhat different way, the question is not whether subjects perceive the constraint to be maximum in some absolute sense, but whether the constraint is perceived as sufficient to induce compliance in a mildly aversive situation.

PERCEIVERS BECOME PERSUADED, OR AT LEAST THINK TARGET PERSONS HAVE PERSUADED THEMSELVES   Perhaps people who are asked to integrate and present arguments in favor of a position are inclined to end up privately more in favor of the position than they were initially. Furthermore, perceivers are clever enough to realize this, and thus their diagnostic judgments are not biased in the correspondent direction; on the contrary, their inferences are accurately correspondent.[10] A more remote possibility is that the perceivers' own attitudes are influenced by the communication from the target person, after which they project their new attitudes onto the ambiguous stimulus figure who has been forced to act under high constraint.

These suggestions are rather easily dispensed with as a general explanation for the many instances of correspondence bias. First of all, when subjects are asked to estimate the true attitude of the target person *before* the assignment of the essay-writing task, the tendency toward correspondence bias remains. Second, little or no relationship has been found between the perceivers' own attitudes and the attitudes that these perceivers attribute to others. Even if they are somewhat persuaded by the message delivered to them, this does not affect the attributions toward the target person to a significant extent.

CORRESPONDENCE BIAS MAY BE TRUE OF ATTITUDES BUT NOT OF OTHER KINDS OF DISPOSITIONS   Perhaps there is something so fragile or flexible about perceived attitudes that correspondence bias is restricted to the attitude domain. Perhaps it is less likely to occur in those domains where personal dispositions have greater stability and are less responsive to persuasive information. We know already, from the Ross, Amabile, and Steinmetz[11] experiment presented in Chapter 4, that correspondence bias does occur in the attribution of "general knowledge." The contestant who (quite naturally) fails to answer most of the difficult questions contrived by a questioner is seen by observers to be lacking in general knowledge, even though the constraints inherent in the situation should have been obvious to all participants.

Also, in Chapter 3, I reviewed a study showing correspondence bias in the attribution of an anxious personal disposition. Subjects observing target persons presumably responding to anxiety-eliciting questions (presented via a soundless videotape) not only perceived her as anxious in the situation, but proceeded to attribute a disposition to be more anxious than the average person in a variety of other situations as well.[12] This is a particularly strange error since it totally belies the discounting principle: People in an anxiety-arousing situation should be seen as *less* anxious dispositionally than people in a more benign situation since any signs of anxious behavior can be readily attributed to situational provocation.

Finally, Miller, Hinkle, and I were able to show a high degree of correspondence bias in the attribution of personal tendencies toward introversion or extraversion.[13] In our experiment small groups of about six subjects met in a seminar room and were asked to rate themselves on a ten-point scale ranging from extremely introverted to extremely extraverted. After they did that, they were asked to write a brief self-descriptive account designed to persuade whoever might read it that they were truly extraverted or (in the other half of the cases) introverted. These "convincing" self-descriptions were collected and redistributed around the group; then each subject was asked to read an essay by another subject in the group, written under the constraining instructions to which all were exposed. There was no hocus pocus, no hanky panky, and no deception in this experiment. The resulting attributional data showed a strong tendency for those receiving extraverted essays to rate the author as extraverted and those receiving introverted essays to rate the author as introverted. These experimental results not only tell us something about the generality of the correspondence bias effect but also make it more difficult to imagine any explanation that involves perceivers or target persons being persuaded by any arguments presented in the experimental situation. It is difficult to imagine that any subjects were persuaded to become more introverted or extraverted by the essays that they read.

CORRESPONDENCE BIAS IS A REASONABLE RESPONSE OF SUBJECTS TO THE IMPLICIT DEMAND CHARACTERISTICS OF ATTITUDE ATTRIBUTION RESEARCH Some psychologists (e.g., Arthur Miller[14]) have argued that the attitude attribution paradigm — guessing the true attitude of someone acting under highly constraining conditions — establishes an atmosphere in which the perception of individual differences is implicitly stressed. Subjects confronted with the standard task of diagnosing a constrained target person's attitudes must assume that no experimenter would create such a task unless there was some reason to think that the true attitude of the target person could "get through." This biases the subject to look for behavioral evidence while ignoring the degree of situational constraint itself, and since the behavioral evidence favors correspondent inferences, this is what subjects come up with. There are a number of hidden assumptions in this contention that can be challenged, but even if we go along with the assumption that something in the experimenter's manner and the cover story called for individuating diagnostic ratings, why wouldn't subjects be just as likely to show a suspicion bias as show a correspondence bias? In other words, why wouldn't subjects posit an experimental interest in whether dissimulation can be detected? Or put even more strongly, why would experimenters selectively expose subjects to target persons who believed what they were saying under no-choice conditions if they were interested in the perception of subtle behavioral cues? To me, at least, the demand argument could just as easily go in the opposite direction.

In an experiment we have already referred to, on the attribution of introversion and extraversion, half the subjects were specifically alerted to the constraining situational circumstances; the remaining half were urged to concentrate on individual differences as revealed by the introversion/extraversion essays.[15] These instructions had no effect on the outcome, which was correspondence bias in all conditions.

Research in the domain of deliberate deception and its detection takes the argument against an "experimenter demand" interpretation one step further. In their summary of research on the communication of deception, Miron Zuckerman, Bella DePaulo, and Robert Rosenthal describe a general tendency toward a "truthfulness bias" across many experiments.[16] Thus, subjects, even in settings where they are alerted to distinguish between lies and truth telling tend to err in the direction of attributing truthfulness (i.e., making correspondent inferences).

As a final note, in most of the experiments it is explicitly stated that the target person was randomly chosen from many possible target persons; alternatively, subjects are made quite aware that they are receiving a randomly selected communication from another subject in the same room or at least in the same experiment. It is hard to see how any perceived interest on the experimenter's part could override the obvious possibility that a given target person could just as easily be opposed to as in favor of the stand he or she was forced to endorse — or at least that the range of opinions from which the target person's was drawn must be similar to the range in the population from which the subjects themselves were drawn.

Artifactual Explanations: A Summary

I have intended to show in the preceding discussion that correspondence bias cannot easily be explained away with reference to experimental artifacts, i.e., specific procedural features present in contrived experiments but not present in the real world. This is not to say that these artifactual explanations are necessarily implausible or that they could not affect the degree of correspondence inferred. Indeed, each of these artifactual variables could be set in such a way as to enhance or depress the correspondence bias effect. The important conclusion, however, is that one can persistently find examples of correspondence bias in experiments controlling for the effects of particular artifacts, a result suggesting that the presence of the artifact is hardly essential for the effect. In summary, correspondence bias does not seem to depend on experimenter demand, the accurate perception of behavioral cues, the persuasive impact of the message, or the accurate perception that target persons have considerable decision freedom. But if none of these factors is essential to the correspondence effect, why does it occur? I will pursue this in the next section, but to anticipate my conclusion, I believe that correspondence bias is a function of a variety of different factors, any one of which might be sufficient to create the effect.

Fundamental Determinants of Correspondence Bias

"Behavior Engulfs the Field"

Heider introduces us to the likelihood of correspondence bias by suggesting that properties of the surrounding field are not as salient as the behavior itself. Nisbett and I further elaborated on the salience of actions to an observer. Furthermore, observers are handicapped in their attempt to perceive the situation from the actor's point of view. Although people are intellectually aware that situations influence and in some cases determine behavior, there is much more perceptual immediacy to the connection between act and actor. Heider emphasized that the actor and his act are immediately apprehended as a "causal unit," a natural, fundamental Gestalt. As I have said elsewhere, "What is more reasonable, after all, than the brute palpable fact that there can be no action without an actor? The notion that situations can cause action is abstract and derivative, almost metaphoric in its implications. At best, situations capture and direct the energies provided by the organism. Situations are contextual shapers; they vary as more or less potent background conditions but they nevertheless remain part of the background."[17]

Insufficient Adjustment

The salience of behavior and the ready apprehension that act and actor form a primitive causal unit both seem plausible contributors to the correspondence bias effect. But people certainly do use situational information in judging others. They are, as it were, well aware that the strength of the causal connection between the act and the actor is variable. People are not always free to act "authentically" — in faithfully expressive ways. Without some awareness of situational constraint, the world would be a very different place indeed. And even the typical data pattern in an attitude attribution experiment shows large differences in attribution of behavior produced under different levels of constraint. If we are victims of the perception of act and actor as a causal unit, how does this awareness of situational factors fit in? The most reasonable conclusion, it seems to me, is that there is a secondary adjustment to situational influences, an adjustment that is important but insufficient. It is as if perceivers said to themselves, "Well, he did it [or he said it] — but, wait a minute. There was some constraint: He may not have wanted to do it, but he wasn't given much choice." So perceivers back off from a straightforward correspondent judgment; they simply do not back off as much as they should.

Amos Tversky and Daniel Kahneman have alerted us to the fact that such insufficient adjustment is a common error in the perception of information.[18] Initially presented information — or in the attitude attribution case the most salient information — becomes an anchor in the judgment process. Perceivers then adjust in the light of other facts or circumstances, but they are highly conservative in their adjustments, and the adjustments turn out to be insufficient. Tversky and Kahneman have presented a number of compelling examples of this "anchor-and-adjustment heuristic," in which the anchor is a completely arbitrary starting point and yet the consequences for a final judgment are powerful. In one such example, subjects were asked to spin a wheel to obtain a presumably totally arbitrary number and were then asked whether there were more or fewer African countries in the United Nations than the number on the spinner. The numbers were actually controlled to be either definitely under- or overestimations of the actual number of African countries. But subjects starting from an anchor that was too small ended with much smaller estimates than those starting from a larger number. They had presumably anchored on the small or large number (which had been presented only as an arbitrary starting point) and then adjusted the estimate to a more realistic figure. Unfortunately, what seemed to be realistic was strikingly different, given the two starting points.

George Quattrone has specifically extended the notions of anchoring and (insufficient) adjustment to explain correspondence bias.[19] Furthermore, he proposes that the degree of insufficiency — and therefore the degree of bias — can be predicted from information about the most likely position of the target person prior to observing that person's behavior. As part of what I have called a category-based expectancy, people have in mind a range of plausible values of underlying attitudes or beliefs before they read an essay or listen to a speech that takes a stand on an issue. For example, Princeton University students, listening to a speech opposing affirmative action made by a Princeton undergraduate, would approach their observation task with some idea concerning the range of opinions one is likely to find at Princeton. From such an expectancy range, students could roughly assess the likelihood that a particular statement, made under no-choice conditions, should be taken at face value.

If the constrained speech, essay, or other form of opinion statement is the anchor and the statement implies a position outside of the range of plausible expected positions, we can predict that the observer will adjust his or her attitude attribution toward the expected value. But the observer will not adjust as far as the most probable initial expectancy. The observer will, Quattrone argues, adjust until shortly after entering his or her range of plausible values and then stop.

To test this set of ideas, Quattrone and Bonnie Sherman obtained category-based expectancies from Stanford University undergraduates concerning the positions they considered typical at Stanford toward capital punishment and unisex (versus coed) dormitories.[20] These students were also asked to demonstrate the range of attitudes they thought would include 75 percent of the Stanford population. As one would expect, the expected range of attitudes toward capital punishment was much larger than the expected range toward coed dorms. When other Stanford undergraduates participated in an attitude attribution study, reading an essay alledgedly written under no-choice instructions on either capital punishment or unisex dorms, correspondence bias was more pronounced when subjects tried to estimate the essay writer's true attitude toward capital punishment. Thus, the larger the range (the wider the category-based expectancy), the larger the anchoring effect.

The Effects of Cognitive Load

Unfortunately, to explain correspondence bias as a case of anchoring and insufficient adjustment is to substitute one error as an explanation for another. It is true that the anchoring-and-adjustment heuristic fits in with a larger literature on conservatism and judgment, and it does somehow seem more general and more basic. But is there any clear evidence that this is what is happening in the case of correspondence bias? Daniel Gilbert has recently completed a fascinating series of experiments that comes close to providing such evidence.

One implication of the anchoring-and-adjustment heuristic is that anchoring is a more automatic, primitive process than adjustment. This is certainly consistent with Heider's notion that the act and the actor form a natural causal Gestalt, a perceptual unit.[21] If situational adjustments require more complex inferential processing, it should follow that such adjustments would require more conscious attention, more cognitive effort than the anchoring itself. In Gilbert's experiments various ways were found to burden subjects with additional cognitive tasks while they were engaged in watching a videotape of a target person defending an attitudinal position under no-choice conditions.[22] For example, some viewers were led to expect that they would soon have to give a speech; others were asked to be ingratiating toward a person they had reason to dislike.[23] Still others were told *not* to pay attention to words at the bottom of the screen, a task of self-control that proved to be cognitively very demanding.[24] In all such cases the tendency toward correspondence bias was enhanced. That is, cognitively taxed subjects were more convinced than untaxed subjects that the speaker was expressing sincere beliefs. The extra effort required to make the appropriate situational adjustments was apparently undermined by the added cognitive burdens that Gilbert imposed.

Gilbert's research by no means proves that the anchoring-and-adjustment heuristic is at work, but it is certainly consistent with the idea that some kinds of information are more basic and more easily and automatically processed than others. The use of information about situational constraints appears to be a more complex inference than the perception of act and actor as a causal unit. It is therefore more vulnerable to any distracting requirements that make such inferences difficult to perform.

Seeing Is Believing, and Vice Versa

Gilbert offers an even more fundamental proposition that he traces to Spinoza's view of perception and inference, dating from the latter part of the seventeenth century.[25] Spinoza believed that there is a natural human tendency to accept what one sees or hears *before* one engages in any tendency to assess or correct this judgment. Thus, comprehension and assessment go together, in his view, to be followed only later by a process of "certification" or "unacceptance." This is contrasted with the view of Descartes—and perhaps the great majority of modern philosophers, as well as persons—that we first comprehend and then decide whether to accept or reject.

Of course, these views often leave the perceiver in the same place, but the differences in Spinozan and Cartesian positions is nevertheless important. For one thing, the Spinozan position implies a bias toward acceptance. To use one of Gilbert's examples, if someone tells us, "Wombats love pickles," and this does not conflict with any existing knowledge we have, the Spinozan view would have us going along with the statement, whereas the Cartesian view would have us suspending judgment in the absence of a reason either to accept or reject the statement's validity.

The Spinozan view is more consistent with the anchoring-and-adjustment heuristic, though Gilbert's Spinozan formulation would add that the anchor is a combination of immediate comprehension and immediate acceptance, followed by attempts at adjustment that often falls short of what a more "objective" Cartesian system would achieve. I surmise that the results of the cognitive load experiments would have pleased Spinoza, for they clearly suggest that the *unacceptance* of a statement made by a target person requires a certain amount of cognitive effort. Therefore, a person "distracted" while processing a speech or essay is less able to question its validity and to reach the conclusion that a highly constrained target person may or may not believe what he or she says.

Even so, the use of a Spinozan view to explain correspondence bias does require a fair amount of inference. Most specifically it requires that the behavior and the disposition be comprehended as a unit and initially accepted as true and that situational constraint be an inferential afterthought, part of the certification or unacceptance process. Finally, there is no inherent reason why even a Spinozan would adjust *insufficiently* when he or she does adjust. We may conclude, then, that although the Spinozan view accounts nicely for the cognitive load experiments conducted by Gilbert and his colleagues, it does not fully account for the phenomenon of correspondence bias in the first place. That requires some additional assumptions locating perceived behavior in the comprehension/assessment stage and perceived situational constraints in the potential correction stage.

What Is Functional About Correspondence Bias?

If one takes a functional or evolutionary perspective, the task is to consider the possible adaptive purposes served by a tendency of human beings to attribute acts to dispositions rather than to situations. This is a challenging task indeed because correspondence bias certainly implies the potential for frequent mistakes in our judgments of others, and one assumes that incorrect perceptions of the dispositions of others will prove maladaptive more often than not. And indeed it can, as Quattrone has shown.[26] He adapted the previously reviewed experiment in which Questioners were assigned the role of providing difficult questions to Contestants, and Observers concluded that the Contestants were deficient in general knowledge.[27] Quattrone arranged it so that an erroneously "correspondent" judgment of the Questioner's and the Contestant's general knowledge could end up losing the subject money. In the experiment, subjects observed a typical Questioner–Contestant session and were then put in the position of deciding whether to rely upon the Questioner or the Contestant for answers in the subsequent task. They showed a strong preference for relying on the Questioner, even though this was often a mistake that cost them prize money. The point of Quattrone's experiment was to show that correspondence bias is not simply a matter of putting checkmarks on an attributional questionnaire; in a situation with clearcut consequences the tendency proved self-damaging and therefore quite maladaptive.

But perhaps the tendency to make correspondent inferences even when they are not warranted is adaptive most of the time. The tendency may therefore be an understandable example of cognitive inertia, satisfying the cognitive miser model.[28] Although the perceiver is misled occasionally, that expense is worth bearing for the advantage of usable cognitive energy that is then released. If, indeed, it requires cognitive effort to assess or reassess the truth value of everything we hear or see, one can imagine a poor, ineffective, overtaxed organism, too busy wallowing in doubt to get through the day. Furthermore, it is probably fair to say that most of the things we see and hear need little correction. This is clearly true of our perceptions of the natural environment, where our amazing sensory receptors do a remarkable job in accurately reflecting colors, distances, textures, and odors. As for the social world, most societies are probably constructed so that people are rewarded for saying things they believe to be accurate, at least in most circumstances. This is certainly true in our society, even if people do occasionally dissimulate for ulterior purposes. If people generally say what they believe, to perceive them uncritically as believing what they say is generally adaptive, especially since it requires a minimum of cognitive effort and leaves us free to ponder more important things.

In the social sphere there are additional reasons to accept what we see and hear as not worthy of open challenge. In Erving Goffman's scheme of things, society is only possible if people generally refrain from challenging the questionable statements of others.[29] If we stop to think about it, people often make claims or offer self-insights that we recognize as false or as stretching the truth. We may also sense that even the communicator doesn't believe what he or she is telling us. What do we do when this happens? Usually nothing. We let it pass, just as we seem to realize that others will let our *faux pas* pass. There is, in Goffman terms, a lot of mutual face protection going on. And if this is the usual state of affairs in our social world, it seems less surprising that we would take what our experimental target person says as containing at least a kernel of truth or would at least give him or her the benefit of the doubt. The tendency to save another's face, in other words, may spill over to the tendency to try to believe everything that others tell us — at least to believe that *they* believe it.

To take a slightly different approach to the question of adaptation, it is important to realize the imperfection of our social feedback and the infrequency with which we learn that we have made an error in judging another person. Our judgments are likely to be pretty loose and flexible in the first place; we are not all that firmly committed to most of them. Second, as part of the very face-saving tendency mentioned above, our judgments of particular others will seldom be challenged in an authoritative way by those particular others. But most important, in the vast majority of our interactions we do not need to have an accurate reading of the interior dispositions of our interaction partners. The importance of perceptual accuracy in assessing target persons is circumscribed by the purposes of our interactions with them and by the requirements of the settings in which such interactions take place. Furthermore, social interaction inevitably involves the mutual negotiation of identities; neither party to the interaction is a fixed behavioral or even dispositional entity, and each may try to influence the other concerning the person he or she would like to be seen as. One consequence of this is that I am not the same person with different interaction partners, nor are they constant across the settings of social behavior. So all I basically need to know, as Swann suggests, is "How will this target person behave with *me?*" — and not how this target person behaves with everyone else. Swann could easily have added, "How will this individual behave in the settings in which I'm likely to encounter him or her?"[30]

So the relation between accuracy and successful adaptation is a complex issue, and one can begin to see that perceivers can be biased toward correspondent inferences without necessarily paying a very heavy price. The truth is that in most of our interactions it does not make any difference whether or not we have misjudged the "true nature" of the other persons involved. And when it becomes important to make accurate dispositional attributions, as in actual or potential close relationships, we are usually blessed with the richer information that comes with more behavior in more varied settings, the kinds of information patterns that should facilitate accurate dispositional inferences.

One can still raise many questions, however, about the potentially threatening implications of the correspondence bias phenomenon for adaptive social behavior. One is always tempted to find some purpose that underlies a tendency toward cognitive bias and, in the case of correspondence bias, to suggest that this must in someway facilitate effective action or at least give the actor an illusion of cognitive control over his or her environment. But it is not clear how it does such things. Why would it not be more adaptive to have a discerning understanding of the powerful role that situations play in constraining behavior? Clearly, as Quattrone's research has shown, there are social contexts in which the cognitive bias tendency can be personally maladaptive, even if the tendency does not normally interfere with attainments of most of our interaction goals. It is not difficult to generate examples in the political and international sphere to point up the potential dangers of a correspondence bias tendency. If we fail to appreciate fully the constraints on political discourse during a national campaign, the tendency to pick the best candidate may be seriously compromised. Many observers of the political scene have suggested that the qualifications for getting elected have little to do with the qualifications for governing effectively. At the level of attributing dispositions to national governments, it can be of vital importance to grasp how things look from the other nation's perspective; i.e., what is the situation its leaders confront? It is not hard to imagine the damage that can be done to international understanding, and therefore to international relations, when our nation's leaders erroneously draw correspondent inferences from the particular actions of another nation's leaders, inferences not corrected by the realization of constraining forces in their situations. We attribute *their* arms buildup to their hostile disposition, whereas our own buildup is seen as a "natural" response to the threat of their hostile intentions.

A Phenomenon of Western Civilization?

One may concede that correspondence bias is indeed a robust phenomenon among American college students but wonder how widespread the phenomenon is in different cultures. It is tempting to link the bias to the Western, and perhaps especially the North American, emphasis on the individual. Are Americans more systematically socialized than non-Westerners to view the person as a separate, independent, autonomous agent? Does our individualistic emphasis at least contribute to the ubiquitous tendency to view a person's actions as caused more by his or her dispositions than by the surrounding situational context?

Such is the contention of Joan Miller, who compared narrative accounts by middle-class Indians from Mysore with those provided by middle-class Americans from Chicago.[31] Subjects from each country were asked to describe two prosocial and two deviant behaviors from their recent experience and explain why the behavior happened. Not only did the Chicagoans show a stronger tendency than the Indians to attribute the behaviors described to personality dispositions and a weaker tendency to refer to contexts, but the comparative differences became more clear-cut with age. Thus, whereas the children did not differ greatly in their explanatory responses, adult Chicagoans were much more prone than adult Indians to draw correspondent dispositional inferences.

These results are highly suggestive, and the developmental data tend to support the notion that different socialization practices result in the use of different attributional premises in radically different cultural settings. Many more studies of this kind need to be done in order to establish more clearly the degree to which correspondence bias is indeed a Western phenomenon, but these results are plausible, and comparable differences might be expected in comparing Americans with Chinese or members of tribal African communities.

Sources of Correspondence Bias: A Summary

The preceding discussion was forecast by the statement that we are not likely to find a single cause of correspondence bias. Indeed, one can point to many villains, including the relative salience of action versus settings or situations, the residue of social pressures toward mutual face saving, and the high probability that people usually mean what they say. I have devoted the largest part of the preceding discussion, however, to the anchor-and-adjustment heuristic and to the related propositions of Spinoza, emphasizing the tendency to accept or agree initially with whatever we see or comprehend. There seems to be good evidence for such a tendency, and a strong evolutionary explanation can be deduced. Such an explanation is largely based on the assumption that attributions and inferences share processes that were originally developed at the more primitive perceptual level. Organisms must be constructed to respond quickly to the behavioral challenges in their environment, and thus it makes sense most of the time for them to go along with their initial perceptions, which are typically not problematical. The evaluation and critical assessment of our perceptions' validity is cognitively taxing and time consuming. The obsessionally skeptical organism is probably an organism trapped in indecision.

On the other hand, the tendency toward correspondence bias can threaten appropriate adaptive behavior and can have seriously damaging consequences for individuals and for nations. Furthermore, we have already seen — and we shall continue to see in the remainder of the book — that the correspondence bias tendency underlies a variety of important social psychological phenomena. So in addition to being a robust and ubiquitous phenomenon, it is one that has multiple consequences in our social world. One of these is that correspondence bias paves the way for the interpretations of behavioral confirmation that make possible self-fulfilling prophecies in the interaction sequence.[32]

Perceiver-induced Constraint

A central feature of the interaction sequence is the fact that the perceiver is part of the stimulus context to which the target person is responding. In the self-fulfilling prophecy scenario, the perceiver's erroneous expectancy affects his or her behavior, and this in turn modifies the behavior of the target person in the direction of confirming the erroneous expectancy. For this confirmation to have any impact on the perceiver — in other words, for the perceiver to take the target person's reactions as independent confirmation of an expectancy — the perceiver must fail to discount his or her own contribution to the behavior confirmation process. The perceiver must fail to recognize the extent to which he or she has elicited the expectancy-confirming behavior just observed. Thus far, we have seen how poor observers generally are when it comes to recognizing the power of the situation; are they any better when they both observe and are themselves part of the action? The quick answer is no. In fact, if anything they are worse.

Active perceivers, those who play some role in eliciting the behavior they observe, have a difficult attributional task. They not only have the observer's normal challenge of allocating behavioral causation to the situation or the person but must consider their own contribution to the construction of the situation. To do this, an active perceiver must evaluate his or her own impact: How does the perceiver appear to the target person, and what does the target person make of him or her? How much leeway does the perceiver's behavior allow the target person? In other words, how constraining is the perceiver's behavior, and along what dimension does this constraint fall? Presumably, to answer such questions active perceivers must somehow put themselves in the target person's shoes and try to see themselves from the perspective of the other. By comparison with the perceiver who is also an involved actor, the passive observer of a social interaction between two other people is usually in a better position to share the target person's orientation—to assess one actor's constraining elicitations by imagining how the observer him- or herself would be constrained by them.

As if their problems of empathizing with the target person weren't formidable enough, active perceivers must also devote attention to their own actions. If the interaction is at all consequential, the perceiver who is also an actor must consider and prepare for what to do next. Clearly, there is a lot going on even in the most casual interactions, and we can imagine how the process of keeping track of everything can be cognitively taxing. Under the circumstances, what kinds of precision should we expect when we ask the perceiver to tell us what is causing the target person to behave as he or she is behaving?

Our own research on perceiver-induced constraint began with an experiment designed to test the extreme case in which a perceiver fully controls the behavior of a target person. In a highly constrained and very artificial interview situation interviewers were assigned the role of signaling interviewees to answer questions concerning social or political issues. However, it was made clear to the interviewer that the answers he was to hear had been previously prepared for the experiment and that the interviewee was to read them verbatim. On each of several trials, the subject, alone in a room with sending and receiving equipment, asked a question and then pressed a button signaling either for a liberal or for a conservative response. Subjects were given schedules that "by chance" contained either a high proportion of liberal signals or a high proportion of conservative signals.

When the interviewers were later asked to rate the interviewee on a scale anchored at the end points by "Extremely Liberal" and "Extremely Conservative," those faced with a predominately conservative responder tended to rate him on the conservative side, whereas the predominately liberal responder was rated on the liberal side. In other words, there was a very strong tendency for the perceivers who induced the observed behavior to display, nevertheless, a strong degree of correspondence bias. In this same experiment, other subjects served as observers. They, too, saw the interviewer's schedule of signals and heard the verbatim reading by the target person (actually a previously recorded version delivered in a rather bland monotone, always the same in each experimental session). Observers showed roughly the same amount of correspondence bias.

Within that experimental situation[33] the active perceiver does not have much to do that would tax his cognitive resources. The only thing that distinguishes the active perceiver from the passive observer is the former's participation in a fairly undemanding task of reading a schedule and pressing an appropriate button on each trial. In a number of subsequent studies, however, Gilbert and his colleagues have clearly shown that active perceivers show a greater degree of correspondence bias than passive observers when confronted with a target person behaving under highly constrained, no-choice conditions.

Even if active perceivers are indeed more cognitively taxed than passive observers, we have presented a fair amount of information earlier in this chapter suggesting that observers who are distracted or engaged in multiple tasks will show greater correspondence bias than those allowed to give their full attention to the observational and attributional task. The only question remaining is whether one can demonstrate that acting and the anticipation of action are indeed comparable to other kinds of distraction, such as keeping eight-digit numbers in mind.

This last step has been made quite clear in an experiment by Gilbert, Pelham, and Krull.[34] Subjects listened to a pro- or an antiabortion speech prepared and delivered by a male target person operating under the usual no-choice conditions. The degree of constraint was emphasized for all subjects; it was stressed that the diagnostic task would be very difficult because the target person had no choice about which side of the issue he would defend. Half the subjects were given the additional instructions that they would soon be switching places with the target person after he gave his speech, and therefore they would have to give a speech on the same topic. It was assumed that these subjects would be preoccupied with thinking about and preparing for the speech task to come, thus depleting their cognitive resources while dealing with the prior task of attributing attitudes to the other person.

The results clearly support the reasoning that the discounting principle requires more resources than does taking behavior at its face value. When cognitive resources are ample, in the absence of any instructions to anticipate constructing their own speech, there is the usual finding of correspondence bias, even though strong steps were taken to emphasize the situational constraints involved. When subjects were cognitively taxed by instructions that they would later be switching places with the target person, the tendency to show correspondence bias was clearly enhanced. This "cognitive load" manipulation — instructions causing the subject to reflect on his own plans for action — seems at least closely analogous to the pressures of self-distraction with which I have characterized ongoing social interactions and the plight of the active observer.

Gilbert, Pelham, and I pursued another form of distraction that can occur in a group setting, namely the distraction that can come from trying to determine whether you have any constraining power over another member of the group, and if so, how much.[35] Imagine a meeting, for example, in which a variety of topics are discussed, opinions expressed, and votes taken. Most of us would be at least mildly interested in any evidence reflecting our power to influence the outcome of such discussions. But is it possible that in trying to determine how much influence we have over others, we fail to realize that a person not influenced by us may be influenced by someone else and not simply be expressing personal dispositional tendencies?

We designed a pair of experiments to determine whether subjects could keep track of multiple sources of influence if they were at the same time intent on finding how much power they did have in a complex social situation. The behavior in question was, once again, the expression of opinions on a liberal – conservative dimension. As in our very first experiment, in which the subject was in a position to influence a target person to express a particular opinion, the subjects could induce a target person to express a particular opinion either by giving him a direct signal or, in a second experiment, by asking a biased or loaded question. However, it was made clear to the subjects that the signals or the particular biased question might or might not get through to the target person. Furthermore, the subject was also aware that there was another potential influencer in the situation whose signals or questions might determine the opinions expressed by the target person. By experimental arrangement, we could control the degree of covariation between the signals sent by the subject and the target person's response. In other words, we could determine whether the subject had little or a lot of constraining power.

When subjects were ultimately asked to indicate the extent to which the target person privately endorsed the opinions espoused, we found that subjects who could discover trial by trial that they had little power to elicit specific opinions tended to make correspondent attributions. In other words, low-power subjects assumed that the target person believed what he said. This would be plausible, except that they had been told that the target person's responses would (on all but a few "free-response trials") be determined either by themselves or by the other influencing subject, and they could easily see that, although they were not controlling the target person's behavior, the other subject was.

On the other hand, if the subjects were informed beforehand that their influence wouldn't get through very often, this tendency to show correspondence bias did not exist. Thus, we argued, the interest in discovering how much power you have in a group situation can divert or distract you from realizing how much power someone else may have. In any event, the attempt to track one's influence in a social situation involves another kind of cognitively taxing preoccupation that amplifies correspondence bias.

Without the benefit of such research findings, we might have been able to argue that active perceivers ought to be in a particularly good position to appreciate their constraining influence over a target person. After all, their own behavior and its social implications are at stake.[36] We can now see, however, that although perceivers may be quite aware of their own actions, the more they are distracted by the pressures of acting, the more difficult it may be for them to appreciate the social and attributional implications of their own behavior. This is revealed in results from an experiment by Linda Ginzel, William Swann, and myself.[37] In this experiment subjects played the role of opinion-polling interviewers, asking a series of questions that were loaded to elicit either liberal or conservative answers to a series of political questions. The answers, delivered on a standard videotape (presented as "live" closed-circuit TV), were uniformly conservative in tone. According to the discounting principle, subjects in the liberal-loaded question condition should have subsequently rated the target person more conservative than subjects asking questions loaded in the conservative direction. This clearly did happen when subjects themselves (as instructed) chose those questions that fulfilled the criterion that they were biased in a specified (either anti or pro) direction. This selection of the questions by the subjects was designed to "rub their noses" in the possibility that the answers received would be partly determined by their own questioning behavior.

When subjects were simply assigned the questions to ask, they showed no tendency toward discounting conservative responses after conservative questions or toward augmented attributions of conservatism after liberal questions were asked. This was in spite of the fact that they later reported clear awareness that the questions were biased. In addition to showing the power and tenacity of correspondence bias, such results show that it is one thing to be aware of one's potentially constraining actions and another to draw the appropriate attributional conclusions—to observe the logic of the person–situation trade-off.

Some other results from this experiment suggested to us that certain tasks are more likely to "prime" an attributional script than others. Some subjects were merely told that their task was to try to *influence* the target person to respond in a conservative (or a liberal) direction. These subjects were quite aware that they were asking very loaded questions, but they showed little tendency to discount. The task seemed to focus them on the behavior of the other person, without having to raise the question of what the person truly believed. Other subjects were specifically given the task at the outset of the experiment of *diagnosing* the true beliefs of the target person after going through the same procedures of attempting to influence his response by choosing a set of extremely biased questions. These subjects showed a stronger discounting effect, seeing the conservatively responding target person as more conservative when he was answering questions designed by the perceiver to elicit liberal responses. Our interpretation of these results is that the preliminary instructions to "diagnose" the target person's true beliefs triggered off the attributional script, with a resulting adherence to the person–situation trade-off. The script is obviously there in our minds, but it is not inevitably or routinely applied without appropriate priming.

Correspondence Bias and the Interaction Sequence

In the present chapter I have tried to convince you that the tendency to attribute even highly constrained acts to dispositions is indeed a pervasive one. Correspondence bias is the most robust and ubiquitous finding in the domain of interpersonal perception. We do not know precisely why people succumb to bias, but a variety of determinants probably conspire to produce the biasing effect. If a particular interaction episode or a particular experimental design removes one factor, the bias may be sustained by a combination of those determinants that still remain. The various determinants may include:

1. Action is more dynamic, figural, or salient than the situational context in which it occurs. Because of this, it is perceived quite automatically as part of a causal unit linking the act to the actor.

2. While we have a rich vocabulary to describe personal dispositions or traits, our vocabulary for describing situations is quite impoverished. Because of this differential availability of constructs, we may be more naturally drawn to dispositional thinking. This may be especially true in Western cultures, with our emphasis on autonomy and individual responsibility. Our vocabularies may reflect this culture-derived attributional preference.

3. The fact that situations control the behavior of most people much of the time is perhaps so obvious that we lose interest in highlighting situational factors. They become taken for granted as either present or absent, even though there are many subtle gradations of influence that are nevertheless highly relevant for explaining an actor's behavior.

4. People are socialized to accept the acts of others at face value, and even if they are wrong, their errors are rarely maladaptive. This tendency to save the face of others may become so ingrained that it makes it difficult to suspect others of dissimulation or deception.

5. Most social interactions can proceed without a hitch in the absence of accurate dispositional attributions. Seldom will inaccurate inferences about others' traits be unequivocally challenged as we interact with them or in other ways impede or disrupt the interaction process. Therefore, if there is any initial tendency for correspondence bias, it is unlikely to be corrected by social feedback. Since we usually suffer no negative consequences for this persistent tendency to accept behavior at face value, it is probably easy to convince ourselves that we are correct. By the kinds of experimental procedures we have highlighted in this chapter, however, it can be demonstrated that this assumption is often incorrect.

No doubt there are other plausible determinants contributing to the omnipresence of correspondence bias, but I hope that this list is sufficient to strengthen the argument that the tendency is multiply determined. Beyond making that point, I have stressed the particular relevance of the anchor-and-adjustment heuristic, bolstered by the findings that increased cognitive load is accompanied by more striking biases in the direction of correspondence. The phenomenon of anchoring an act to an actor and thus perceiving the act as part of a causal unit is apparently very primitive and very automatic, requiring few cognitive resources. This view of act and actor as a causal unit goes back to Fritz Heider's early (1944) paper on phenomenal causality, where he stresses the perceptual bases of dispositional attributions.

But Heider stressed that attributions could also involve complex inferential processes. The adjustments one must make to provide a fuller account of behavioral causation involve more effortful cognitive work. Thus, accounting for situational factors as causal determinants of behavior is a matter of "secondary inference," of somehow correcting the simple perception of an exclusive act–actor unit. The idea that we anchor and then adjust — and that adjusting involves greater cognitive demands than anchoring — is certainly supported by Gilbert's cognitive load findings. What remains unexplained, however, is precisely why the adjustment — the situational correction, if you will — remains *insufficient* even when the perceiver has ample time and, one can infer, ample cognitive resources.

In any event, the cognitive bias tendency is robust and appears to be at least as persistent when situations are produced by the perceivers themselves. The findings showing bias under conditions of perceiver-induced constraint are especially relevant for understanding the percolation of expectancy effects in social interaction sequences. Because perceivers fail to discount, to adjust for their own influence over the actions of others, they erroneously treat these actions as dispositionally determined. Correspondence bias is thus an essential part of the behavior confirmation phenomenon, and without this tendency, self-fulfilling prophecies would presumably be nipped in the bud. Perceivers' belief that their expectancies are confirmed by the actions they observe is reasonable only if those actions are indeed independent of their own or only after they have made appropriate discounting calculations to take account of their self-fulfilling influence.

Interaction Goals and

Strategic

Self-Presentation

As I write this, in the early days of George Bush's presidency, there is considerable public debate concerning "the real George Bush." Is George Bush the deferent "wimp" who served Ronald Reagan as vice-president? Is he the mean-spirited, unfair campaigner who orchestrated the destruction of Michael Dukakis? Is he the genial conciliator who took over the presidency arguing for a kinder, gentler nation? Or is he the decisive, aggressive commander-in-chief of the Panama invasion? Such questions throw into sharp relief the central concerns of this chapter. To begin to answer the "Who is Bush?" question, the concept of interaction goals becomes crucial. Being a vice-president, being an election candidate, and being president obviously involve goals that require different personal characteristics for their successful fulfillment. It is not surprising, therefore, that each of these different roles elicited the projection of different personal qualities in George Bush's "presentation of self." We may be tempted to believe that there is a "real George Bush" who will eventually surface, but it may be more useful to view George Bush as a coherent pattern of responses to the different interaction goals that expose him to public scrutiny.

In a less dramatic way, perhaps, the sides of ourselves that we reveal to others are obviously shaped by the objectives or goals we seek to promote through our social (and nonsocial) actions. The fact that person perceivers must take interaction goals of the target person into account should hardly come as a surprise to readers of the preceding chapters. Presumably, interaction goals are heavily influenced by the situations in which actors find themselves, and we have repeatedly emphasized the errors associated with failing to take situational context into account. Thus, it is often the case that recognizing a target person's interaction goals is part and parcel of recognizing the situation from the target person's point of view. But now I want to get more specific about the particular impact of a persons' interaction goals on the persons' presentation of self.

It is important to recognize at the outset that most interaction goals are concerned with or are mediated by the actor's attempts to manage the general impression others form of him or her as a person. There are, to be sure, interaction goals that do not seem to entail impression management. Perhaps the behavior episode initiated by "Please pass the salt" would qualify as an example of an interaction goal devoid of self-presentational features. With the exception of such ritual exchanges, however, the vast majority of interactions have implications for each actor's impressions of the other. Indeed, it is often the case that the achievement of our interaction goals is fundamentally dependent on how our pursuit of these goals informs others about our characteristics.

There are several ways to approach the problem of self-presentation. Perhaps I can tie some of these together with a bit of personal history. Given my own early exposure to an approach to social perception that emphasized the effects of motives and expectancies, it is no surprise that I argued early in my career (in a paper with John Thibaut,[1] as noted in Chapter 2) that our perceptions of others are affected by our goals in interacting with them. Thus, we will be selectively attuned to different behavioral features and process behavioral information differently as a function of our interaction goals — what we want out of an interaction. If our goal is to test or confirm our values, we will be especially attentive to those features of another person's behavior that are relevant to our value positions. If our most important value is honesty, we will pay special attention to all those cues relating to honesty and integrity. If our most important concern is with getting ahead in the world, we will be especially alert to symbols of power and status in our social environment. We may become very adept at discerning who is most likely to help us reach the top — or after whom we should model ourselves. Thibaut and I would include these examples under the heading of "value maintenance." If our primary goal is to understand another person, what makes the person tick, what her motives are, this orientation will lead us to look for different things than if we are in a "value maintenance set." Such a concern with antecedent determinants theoretically puts the perceiver in a "causal genetic set." Thibaut and I also identified a third set of interaction goals, "situation matching set"; this refers to the perceiver's role when looking at another person's behavior to determine whether it fits some norm, rule, or standard. Presumably, most of us are generally oriented toward value maintenance most of the time. Clinical psychologists, psychiatrists, and psychoanalysts in particular are often in a causal-genetic set. Examples of someone likely to be primarily in a situation-matching set are a judge, a member of a jury, and a college admissions director. Parents in relating to their children can find themselves shifting from one set to another as situations throw them into the different roles of companion, adviser, or disciplinarian.

I still believe in the crucial impact of the perceiver's interaction goals on what he or she perceives and infers about another person, but as I have continued to conduct experiments on person perception, the other side of this coin has struck me as equally important. For Peter to understand Tony, he must take Tony's interaction goals into account. He can surmise what these goals are by taking note of what might be instrumental actions in the service of goal attainment; he can also try to understand the situation that Tony faces. For example, Peter may decide that Tony wants something from him both because Tony has lately been lavish with his compliments and because the situation is clearly one in which he has something that Tony wants. Peter is thus putting his attributional understanding to work in the service of understanding Tony; Tony, on the other hand, is putting his attributional understanding to work in his attempt to influence Peter's impression of him. To put it as simply as possible, the study of impression management and self-presentation is an integral part of the study of interpersonal perception. We cannot understand how people perceive each other without at the same time understanding the dynamics of self-presentation. The self that we present is, after all, the focal stimulus that must be evaluated through the attributional process. And the same attributional reasoning is available whether an actor contemplates how to create an impression or when a perceiver forms an impression based on an actor's self-presentations. And so, some thirty years ago, I began to theorize and conduct experiments on the conditions affecting the nature and recognition of self-presentation.[2]

Returning to Chapter 1 and the schematized interaction sequence presented there, this means that students of interpersonal perception must realize that both perceivers and target persons have interaction agendas, and each will typically have a stake in the impressions of self created for the other's appreciation. In some cases the interplay of interaction goals is obvious. A favorite example of those of us who study self-presentations is the job interview. Here, the interviewer wants to pick the best person and the candidate wants to present him- or herself as the best person for the job. Furthermore, each is basically aware of the other's interaction goals and will undoubtedly take these into account in forming his or her impression. Though it is useful to keep this setting in mind as a clear prototype, the attempts to relate actions to interaction goals are important in all social interactions, even though the actors' agendas may be not as transparent as they are in the job interview.

Because of the subtle and complex way that goals and motives insert themselves into social interactions, one of the major premises of social psychology involves the *diagnostic ambiguity of behavior*. Behavior is often an unreliable and misleading indicator of internal states, thoughts, and feelings. We have already seen that there are many areas of phenomenal unawareness: We can be affected by stimulus conditions that we fail to identify, and we can be moved by motives that are not accessible to our own insight. But beyond such considerations, we are also deceptive — often benignly and for good reason, but deceptive nevertheless — in concealing or misrepresenting feelings or inaccurately referring to purposes underlying actions that are actually in the service of different, unreported goals. How different our lives would be if people always said everything on their minds! And what a radical difference this would make for the field of social psychology!

Power Maintenance: A Fundamental Interaction Goal

As my own theorizing about self-presentation has evolved, I have been led to distinguish between strategic forms of self-presentation and what Roy Baumeister has called "constructive self-presentation."[3] Constructive self-presentations are those in which we try out selves — perhaps actualizing different potential selves with different audiences — to decide, with or without the help of social feedback, whether a presented self should be incorporated into a more stable identity.

Until very recently, most of the research on self-presentation has been concerned with *strategic* self-presentations. These I would define as actions designed to maintain or augment an actor's power by the management of an impression. This linkage of self-presentation to power requires some discussion of the concept of power and the strategies most likely to promote it.

The word *power* conjures some unpleasant associations for many of us. One thinks of ruthless autocracies, of the strong exploiting the weak, or at least of various forms of dominance and submission in which the person who submits cannot be as happy as the person who dominates. But we should try hard to strip away these negative connotations because the concept of power must be a crucial feature in any serious scientific analysis of interpersonal relations.

As used by our premier students of social interdependence, Thibaut and Kelley,[4] power is simply a way of talking about the distribution of potential outcomes in a relationship. You have power over me, or I am dependent on you, to the extent that your actions can reward or punish me — to the extent that you can move me through a wide range of outcomes by the way in which you behave toward me. My dependence on you, however, is limited by my counterpower over you. In most peer relationships, each partner can reward or punish the other to roughly the same extent; the outcome ranges of peers tend to be equivalent. But there are many relationships in which power may not be equally distributed. Employers can typically move employees through a wider outcome range than employees can move employers. Similarly, power asymmetries typically characterize relations between teachers and students, parents and children, judges and defendants, and doctors and patients.[5]

The more dependent one person is on another for favorable versus unfavorable outcomes, the more motivated the dependent person will be to increase the likelihood that those favorable outcomes will be forthcoming. Such motives become connected to interaction goals that generate strategic presentations of the self, presentations designed to tilt social outcomes in a favorable direction, i.e., to maintain or augment one's power.[6] We will shortly consider the particular strategies that people use to achieve the basic interaction goal of power maintenance and augmentation, but first, a brief historical digression will help to set the stage.

Historical Antecedents:
The Dramaturgical Approach

To the shame of psychology, whose scholars took too long to recognize the importance of impression management concerns, the historical roots of self-presentation theorizing lie in the subfields of sociology known as symbolic interactionism and role theory. Symbolic interactionism is a reference to the image of society as interaction, "the reciprocal influence of persons who as they act take into account one another's characteristics."[7] The most relevant aspect of such interactions is the exchange of symbolic meanings, and these exchanges involve both the expression and the construction of the "self." Though symbolic interactionism has diverse origins in social philosophy, George Herbert Mead[8] is often cited as the single most important influence shaping symbolic interactionism. Mead emphasized the emergence of "self" from social interaction, a precursor of the more contemporary idea that our identities are negotiated as we interact with others.[9] The self thus becomes in part a reflection of the reactions of others to us. It is but a small step to realize that these reactions of others can be partially controlled by instrumental actions of the self.

The attention of sociologists to the concept of social roles was also crucial to later theorizing about self-presentation. Role theories have basically been concerned with analyses of social structure and the linkage of such analyses to social behavior. Since the concept of role is taken from theatrical discourse, it fits into what has been referred to as the *dramaturgical approach*. Erving Goffman became the preeminent spokesman for such an approach as he blended elements of symbolic interactionism and role theory to characterize interaction "encounters." In his classic book, *The Presentation of Self in Everyday Life* (1959), he speaks not only of participant roles, but also of audiences, performances, and stage settings, including on-stage and off-stage doings. For Goffman each encounter is like a play in which the participants project definitions of the situation of which a concept of their selves is a part. One of the most crucial rules governing social interaction is that each participant must try valiantly to support the other's definition. Successful interactions thus require appropriate "dramaturgical discipline." Since a participant's projected self is part of his or her definition of the situation, this crucial rule often involves "face work," mutual efforts of each participant to protect the face, the claimed self, of the other participant. If players do not have proper dramaturgical discipline, there will be gaffes, disruptions, or embarrassing "scenes." The view that Goffman projects is that interactions are not fun and are often dangerous — hazardous to our emotional health and threatening to our identities. It is therefore best to get in and out of them as gracefully and self-protectively as possible. His main conception of social interaction emphasized the maintenance of a delicate social fabric.

Thus, for Goffman, the presentation of self is not strategic in the sense that I mentioned above but is rather embedded in a larger set of structural considerations reflecting the motive of each participant to conduct interactions smoothly and without incident. Although occasionally touching on the problem of impression management, Goffman did not emphasize or focus on the personal motives that are satisfied by creating particular kinds of impressions in others. This latter emphasis has been more characteristic of the approach psychologists have taken to the topic.

Prominent Self-Presentational Strategies: A Tentative Taxonomy

Pittman and I define strategic self-presentation as "those features of behavior affected by power augmentation motives designed to elicit or shape others' attributions of the actor's dispositions."[10] We go on to note that features comprise all aspects of behavior, including gestural and other nonverbal nuances, style of expression, and the actual verbal content communicated by the actor to the target person. The reference to features is also meant to convey that a given communication cannot be defined as either self-presentational or not.[11] Responses are not intrinsically self-presentational; self-presentational features are intertwined with social responses that also have other purposes. Though it is undoubtedly true that certain kinds of behavior are likely to have instrumental components, whereas other actions are typically expressive or "authentic," almost any action can have self-presentational significance, depending on the context and on the expectations of the audience. It is important to keep in mind that self-presentational features typically involve selective disclosures and omissions, or matters of emphasis and timing, rather than blatant deceit or dissimulation.

This latter consideration is important for those of us who study self-presentation, for it is a common experience to run across people who find the discussion of impression management or self-presentation unpleasant and disturbing, precisely because the terms conjure up images of crass manipulation and exploitation through communications that are consciously planned to deceive. Such images are reinforced by at least the titles, if not the content, of the kinds of self-promotional books that are prominently displayed in airport bookshops. Titles like *Winning Through Intimidation*[12] or *Power: How to Get It, How to Use it*[13] — to say nothing of the granddaddy of self-salesmanship, *How to Win Friends and Influence People*, written by Dale Carnegie more than half a century ago[14] — suggest a genre offensive to those who treasure candor, authenticity, and the gaining of respect through performance rather than claims of personal influence. I recall a conversation with a very famous social psychologist who did not even want to consider the problems associated with impression management because he found the whole topic offensive. He did not deny the existence of such phenomena, he had merely made a personal decision not to concern himself with them.

My own approach has been, on the contrary, inspired by a fascination with the extent to which our social behavior is influenced by considerations of impression management. I cannot escape the conviction that self-presentational strategies must be identified and analyzed for any comprehensive understanding of interpersonal perception. Like anyone else, I can be offended by particular instances of deceitful audience manipulation, but I try neither to condone nor to condemn the generic fact that *all* of us are concerned about what others think of us and our actions are in part designed to affect these impressions in the direction of self-protection or self-enhancement (or more technically, in the direction of power maintenance or augmentation). If we stand back a step or two, what could be more naturally human than the wish to be liked, listened to, or respected, and even on occasion to be feared? Alternatively, what could be more human than learning various behavioral strategies that improve the likelihood of getting more social rewards and fewer social punishments from the important people around us?

There is a tendency for each of us to acknowledge that whereas others are engaged in such strategies, I personally am not. Because this tendency is so widespread, there is a daunting methodological limitation that confronts us: We are not likely to gain much insight into the determinants and forms of self-presentation by asking people about their interaction goals and the strategies they have devised to implement their achievements. Here above all places, the experimental method is invaluable. We identify strategic self-presentation by creating experimental settings that should theoretically arouse impression management motives and then by observing those features that distinguish the resulting responses from behavior that is relatively devoid of such deliberately implanted motivation. This is the method of approach followed by psychologists concerned with impression management, and though it is not an easy approach to follow in many cases, we surely have more insight into self-presentational processes than we did when Erving Goffman wrote his classic book over thirty years ago.

The experimental approach is valuable not only because people don't want to talk about their private strategies of impression management (since "personal PR" is not highly regarded in our culture); this happens also to be an area of behavior determination that is particularly inaccessible to actors themselves. Why might this be so? It helps to begin with the realization that our social environments are from birth the preeminent sources of variations in our welfare. Parents, siblings, teachers, and peers become sources of those outcomes that we most treasure and fear as we grow into adulthood. Out of the thousands of repeated experiences of social interaction, experiences in which we are often dependent on the good auspices of others, it is reasonable to expect the learning (indeed the overlearning) of a comprehensive and differentiated social repertory. This response repertory eventually grows to serve as a largely automatic set of action patterns that are triggered by dependency settings. Shaped by such multiple experiences, we respond naturally and without reflection to those ubiquitous conditions where our social power is at stake. We may be aware that we are shading our opinions in order to gain the respect of our supervisor, for example, or that we have made a special effort to get on the good side of the boss's female secretary by commenting on her stunning hairstyle. But then again, we may do these same things without any awareness of their ultimate strategic significance. With or without such awareness, the features of self-presentation are of central importance in any attempt to provide a comprehensive account of interpersonal relations in general and interpersonal perception in particular. Though the discussion that follows may at times read like a manual of tactical advice for manipulators, I hope this will be treated more as a rhetorical failing of the author than as an invitation to dismiss the topic as one that concerns only a selected sample of salespersons and politicians.

Ingratiation as a
Self-Presentational Strategy

The wish to be liked by others is undoubtedly a pervasive human desire. In my attempt some years ago to present a theory of strategies for being liked, I defined ingratiation as "a class of strategic behaviors illicitly designed to influence a particular other person concerning the attractiveness of one's personal qualities."[15] The word "illicitly" needs clarification. I wanted to restrict the term to acts and overtures that go beyond routine politeness or mere obedience to the social norms that govern civil discourse. I wanted to point to a subversive quality that is not captured by the explicit formulations of social exchange; ingratiators do not openly say, "You do y for me and I'll do x for you." Ingratiation exploits the logic of social exchange while subverting it. The goal of being liked merely because one has made an effort to be liked can best be attained only if it is concealed. It is not, in other words, contained in the implicit contract underlying social interaction.

It is this set of considerations that sometimes leads people to refer to the ingratiator as having "ulterior motives," motives to secure and or augment our power by the indirect means of making others like us. In cost–benefit terms, ingratiation is a potential means of gaining more than we have paid for. If we can get another person to like us, that person's power over us will be diminished as those of our actions that may be under his or her control become more predictably positive. So ingratiation is illicit because it bypasses the open channels of social exchange, but, as I have argued above, the strategic character of the ingratiator's behavior does not typically involve conscious awareness or deliberate planning. It is strategic, it is illicit, but it remains cognitively inaccessible.

There is a rich amount of culturally shared knowledge concerning the particular tactics that are successful in enhancing an actor's likability. In my initial presentation, I singled out opinion agreement, compliments, favors, and presenting or making salient one's most favorable characteristics as promising ways of managing a likable impression. There is little secret or surprise in the contention that we like people who agree with us, who say nice things about us, who seem to possess such positive attributes as warmth, understanding, and compassion, and who would "go out of their way" to do things for us. In fact, I no longer have to appeal to the homespun plausibility of these prescriptions for being liked. In an experiment to be summarized more fully below, Debra Godfrey, Charles Lord, and I asked subjects to list freely those strategies they would consider if it were terribly important to get a particular other person to like them.[16] The degree of agreement among these undergraduates was remarkable: The best strategy for being liked almost invariably included showing interest in the other person and drawing the person out, displaying such "approach" gestures as smiles and eye contact, indicating agreement with stated beliefs and opinions, and (to a somewhat smaller extent) the use of flattery or compliments.

Since these social facts are part of shared cultural wisdom, one wonders why such obvious tactics as agreement and flattery are employed and why they work in such an illicit domain. I think the answer points to a kind of "autistic conspiracy." As Pittman and I note, "the very success of ingratiation usually depends on the actor's concealment of ulterior motivation or the importance of his stake in being judged attractive. The illicit nature of ingratiation may also lead ingratiators to deceive themselves concerning either the importance of being judged attractive or the relationship between this desired goal and the strategic features invading their action decisions. A tantalizing conspiracy of cognitive avoidance is common to the actor and his target. The actor does not wish to see himself as ingratiating; the target wants also to believe that the ingratiator is sincere in following the implicit social contract."[17]

Thus, the autistic conspiracy involves a combination of ingratiator self-deception and target person vanity. After many years of research attempting to analyze the dynamics of ingratiation, I tend to agree with Lord Chesterfield that "Vanity . . . is . . . the most universal principle of human action."[18] In an earlier passage in his famous "Letters" the good lord said, "If a man has a mind to be thought wiser, and a woman handsomer than they really are, their error is a comfortable one to themselves, and an innocent one with regard to other people; and I would rather make them my friends, by indulging them, than my enemies, by endeavoring (in that to no purpose) to undeceive them."[19]

The best evidence that vanity plays an important role in episodes of ingratiation comes from experiments comparing the reaction of those who are the targets of ingratiation attempts with that of those who are bystanders or observers. In several early experiments such comparisons invariably showed that the targets of flattery and agreement are more likely to consider such tactical comments authentic or justified than are those bystanders for whom the particular ingratiating overtures are not intended.[20]

The theory of ingratiation, as more elaborately spelled out in my 1964 book, involves three independent variables: incentive value, subjective probability of success, and perceived legitimacy. Incentive value refers to the importance of getting a particular person to like you, a factor that is usually equivalent to the degree of your dependence on him or her. The greater the asymmetry of power in a relationship, the higher the value of a "likable" attribution for the person who is lower in power. The subjective probability of success simply refers to the likelihood that any strategic overture will be effective in securing the "likable" attribution. This part of ingratiation theory is, then, but a variant of many motivational models emphasizing that goal-directed behavior is a joint function of the value of a goal on the subjective probability of success in achieving it.[21]

A third determinant in the theory of ingratiation involves a question of the value placed by the potential ingratiator on candor and authenticity, on the one hand, and interpersonal skill and manipulative success, on the other. In *Ingratiation* I applied the label "perceived legitimacy" to this value domain, attempting to capture the notion that some people in some contexts will consider illicit strategic behavior to be more legitimate, more excusable than will others. There are, thus, considerations beyond the matter of "Will it work?" that affect behavioral decisions to cultivate positive impressions, especially if these can only occur at the expense of dissimulation or deceptive agreements and compliments. Originally, I suggested that perceived legitimacy factors probably serve as a stop-and-go signal, but now I see no reason why the same considerations could not strongly influence the actor to modify his or her strategic behavior in the direction of greater authenticity, rather than completely eliminating its strategic significance.

There is a fascinating dilemma embedded in the first two components of ingratiation theory. Generally speaking, the more important it is to be liked, the more sensitized the target person will be to any cues suggesting deceit or inauthenticity. Thus, the greater the incentive value, the lower the subjective (and probably the objective) probability of success. How the potential impression manager handles this ingratiator's dilemma adds some intriguing complexity to the realm of self-presentation.

Handling the Ingratiator's Dilemma

One consequence of the ingratiator's dilemma is that strategic overtures can be more open, more straightforward, when they are delivered by a higher- to a lower-status person than when they move in the opposite direction. Compliments from a boss to an employee need not be very subtle to be effective. Why? Because the incentive value, being presumably rather low, coexists with a high value for the subjective probability of success. The boss may not need to cultivate the employee's loyalty, but it does no harm and involves little risk. Furthermore, it is very often the case that the boss is more dependent on the employee than the employee realizes; thus, each has a somewhat different view of the other's dependence.

The low-status person, however, faces the dilemma more sharply. I have noted above that the autistic conspiracy helps a little in paving the way, but there are some strategic consequences of the ingratiator's dilemma that can be identified. First of all, our early research on conformity as an ingratiation strategy suggested that people in low-power (or high-dependence) situations tend to complicate their strategic agreements.[22] They find ways to establish their credibility by, for example, disagreeing on trivial issues and agreeing on the important ones, or showing low confidence when one disagrees and high confidence with agreement. Another way to reap the benefits of seeming to be in agreement while avoiding the risks of perceived hypocrisy is for the ingratiator to speak first on those issues where he or she can reasonably infer, but has not yet openly learned, the target person's opinions.

When performances and one's ability are at issue, another cluster of strategies involves modesty, self-deprecation, or humorous forms of self-mockery. Boastfulness and exaggerated claims are unattractive, so a person can at least avoid that road to social disaster by bending over backwards in acknowledging inadequacies, flaws, and weaknesses. A recent study by Linda Ginzel shows how available the modesty strategy is for those who are exclusively concerned with making themselves liked.[23]

When self-deprecation becomes blatant, however, the tactic can undermine related dimensions of competence and social adjustment by indicating that the individual is crippled by low self-esteem and insecurity. Modesty can even boomerang as a means of being liked when it becomes an excessive burden in the interaction process; persistent self-deprecating comments seem to invite reluctant expressions of reassurance, the constant need to provide which can become increasingly aversive. The trick for the successful ingratiator is to let modesty reflect the secure acceptance of a few weaknesses that are obviously trivial in the context of one's strengths.

That is not always easy to do, but it might be easier if one could somehow be modest "by association," modest in a way that did not undercut one's projected competence. A remarkable study by Cialdini and deNicholas shows that people will seize upon such an opportunity if it presents itself.[24] Subjects who did well or poorly on an initial task were subsequently asked to participate in a presumably unrelated second experiment by judging a person named Donald from a vignette describing some of his characteristics and accomplishments. Donald was presented either in a very positive or in a rather negative, unfavorable light. By a seeming coincidence actually arranged by the experimenter, it so happened that Donald had the same birthdate as the subject. In the process of conveying their impressions of Donald, the crucial question was whether the subject called attention to the birthdate coincidence. The relevant result for our present purposes was that subjects who did well in the prior task tended to mention the birthdate coincidence only when Donald was described in negative terms. Subjects who did poorly tended to mention the coincidence only when Donald was positively described. The tendency of the successful subjects to associate themselves with the negative Donald can best be seen as a subtle form of modesty. The subjects seemed to be magnanimously aligning themselves with an inferior other, but the alignment is really meaningless, and anyone would agree that it should not in any way demean each subject's own accomplishments. After all, coincidental birthdates should have no attributional significance. Perhaps, then, these successful subjects unwittingly drew attention to the coincidence as a way of having their modest cake without suffering the unpleasant negative consequences of overindulgence.

A major strategy to cope with the ingratiator's dilemma is for the actor to conceal the extent of his or her dependence or to reduce its salience. The former is more difficult than the latter. Lloyd Stires and I were able to show that the subjects who are assured that a target person is unaware of his or her power to reward and punish them tend to use more blatant ingratiation tactics, such as self-enhancement.[25] When the awareness of dependence is shared by the subject and the more powerful target person, on the other hand, there is a stronger tendency for the subject to be modest. Such contrived knowledge asymmetries are probably rare in the real world, so these results may offer little help for the would-be ingratiator. As noted above, however, it is probably the case that low-power actors consistently underestimate the degree to which those who have power over them also are dependent on them.

Though it is probably the case that both parties to a social interaction are usually aware of each actor's power to hurt or help the other, salience of one's dependence is another matter. Clearly, this can be manipulated by clever or well-trained ingratiators. The salience of an employee's dependence is presumably higher when in the plant or office and on the job than when socializing with the boss at a company picnic or when the employee bumps into the boss at the theater or a vacation resort. Whenever the obviousness of differential power is reduced, the subjective probability of an ingratiator's success should be increased. Timing may be crucial: Employees should perhaps refrain from laughing too hard at the boss's stale jokes just before Christmas bonus time.

The question of timing makes it appropriate to introduce the notion of a power bank. The ingratiator should strive to build up a bank account or reservoir of good will and can do so most safely by distributing ingratiation over those occasions when his or her dependence is not salient. The power banker can subsequently be counted on when crucial decisions are made that can affect the ingratiator's outcomes. Salience may be reduced not only by judicious timing, but also by the use of compliment mediators. Sally, who is woefully dependent on her supervisor, Nancy, may want to contribute to the power bank that Nancy controls. She might do this by telling Nancy's secretary how much she admires her supervisor's fairness and good judgment. If this is said in casual context and in sincere tones, there is a good chance that the secretary will eventually transmit some version of this compliment to Nancy herself. In this way Sally can gain some of the advantages of ingratiation while running few of the risks — risks that include being labeled an obsequious flatterer.

In the (I hope, facetious) manner of a self-presenter's manual for successful manipulation, Table 7-1 summarizes these recommended tactics and injunctions.

TABLE 7-1   How to Handle the Ingratiator's Dilemma
(*In the Manner of a "Manipulator's Manual"*)

---

1. Complicate your opinion conformity

    a. Disagree on trivial issues; agree on the important ones.

    b. Express low confidence when you disagree, certainty when you agree.

2. Be (selectively) modest

    a. Be humorously (and securely) self-mocking.

    b. Deprecate your own abilities in areas tangential to success.

3. Reduce the salience of your dependence

    a. Don't be "tactical" when your dependence is obvious.

    b. Corollary: Create a "power bank" for those rainy days.

    c. Use "secondary sources"—get others to ingratiate for you.

4. Connect yourself to symbolically appropriate others

    a. Note coincidental relations with stars (self-enhancement), or . . .

    b. With losers (modesty)—but only when the relation has no genuine attributional significance.

Ingratiation, the Ubiquitous Leaven

Being liked is obviously not the only impression management goal in social interaction, nor is it the only way for an actor to maintain or augment his or her power. I shall shortly discuss the alternative power strategies of self-promotion, intimidation, exemplification, and supplication.[26] Though these alternatives help us to appreciate the variety and riches of self-presentation features, I strongly believe that ingratiation is the most ubiquitous—and perhaps the most fundamental—of the strategies. There are so many different reasons why it is nice to be liked and so many interactions where such a goal is relevant!

But ingratiation is important not only because it is common; it is important as a leavening ingredient in most of the other strategic variants. For many decades psychologists have been aware of the human tendency to augment the consistency of one's evaluations of another person, the tendency known in the rating literature as the halo effect. To like someone is to give him or her the benefit of doubts in many different domains. It seems to be extremely difficult for people to judge target persons objectively as possessing both positive and negative characteristics. At least there always seem to be pressures toward consistency of evaluative judgment. Thus, being liked might be expected to influence the target person's judgments on traits ranging from competence to character strength and moral purity. For this reason, I am suggesting that a pinch or two of ingratiation helps to leaven the other self-presentation strategies as well. One can strive to be competent, but if one succeeds in being liked as well, the rewards of a competence impression will be more firmly secured. The chances are also excellent, because of a halo effect, that a likable competent person will be seen as more competent than a less likable person of equal competence.

Self-Promotion

In the early stages of our work on ingratiation my students and I did not draw a careful distinction between the interaction goal of being liked and the goal of being seen as competent. For example, subjects in one experiment were instructed to play the role of a student being evaluated for a very attractive fellowship and told to "say the things calculated to make the interviewer think highly of you."[27] They were also told to "try to figure out what kind of person the interviewer probably likes and then try to act like such a person." In this early study, then, subjects were in effect urged to be both ingratiating and self-promoting, though the study was presented as being concerned with ingratiation.

As Thane Pittman and I tried to consider alternative self-presentation strategies, those linked to a variety of desired attributions, it became apparent to us that ingratiation and self-promotion involve quite different behavioral decisions. Subsequent research has clearly borne this out. The two strategies are not only distinctive in the behaviors they suggest, but in certain contexts they may be in conflict. I have already noted some of the potential negative consequences of the tactics of modesty — tactics that may increase liking but undermine others' impressions of competence. It seems even more apparent that certain kinds of self-promoting claims can make the claimant less likable.

Indeed, this conclusion is consistent with the results of an experiment comparing strategies of ingratiation and self-promotion.[28] In this study same-sex undergraduates met for two get-acquainted conversations approximately a week apart. After the first conversation each of the subjects rated the other on the two dimensions, likable–unlikable and competent–incompetent. Prior to the second conversation one of the subjects (randomly selected) was taken aside and assigned a particular interaction goal to pursue during the upcoming conversation. These preinformed subjects were given either the goal of successful promotion or that of successful ingratiation. That is, either they were told to focus in the second interview on convincing their partner that they were highly competent persons, or they were instructed to do everything possible to get the partner to like them more than the partner did after the first interview session. These strategic self-presenters were not told how they had initially been rated, but the self-promotion subjects were led to believe that there was room for improvement in their competence ratings, and those in the ingratiation condition were led to believe that they could improve on their likability ratings.

The actual changes in ratings showed that the ingratiators did indeed become more likable in response to the instructions in their condition. However, not only did self-promoters fail to convince their partners that they were more competent than the partner originally assumed, their efforts to do so also caused their partners to rate them as less likable the second time around.

How did these interaction goal instructions actually affect the behavior of the preinstructed subject — and that of the naive conversation partner? A main difference, as predicted, is that ingratiators spoke less and self-promoters spoke more during the second session than they had during the first. (A control group with no specific instructions did not show any change in conversational volume.) When the contents of the conversation were analyzed in various ways, there were few striking differences in the frequency of specific tactics. We were unable to show that ingratiators smiled more, nodded their heads more, or claimed fewer accomplishments than self-promoters. About the only easily detectable difference in content was that ingratiators increased their tendency to agree with their conversational partners from week 1 to week 2, and self-promoters showed a decrease in such "confirmations."

However, judges who were shown videotapes of the end of the first conversation and the beginning of the second conversation had little difficulty identifying which subjects were trying to ingratiate and which were in the self-promotion condition. Even though single measures of specific tactics were not very discriminating, as suggested above, obvious differences in the patterns of verbal and nonverbal behavior clearly distinguished the two assigned strategies. Representative comments of the raters, summarized in Table 7-2, help us grasp the nature of this pattern for both successful and unsuccessful strategists. Several things are apparent from these comments. The differences between successful and unsuccessful ingratiators seem to hinge on the successful subjects' appropriate, "natural" use of the same strategies that the unsuccessful subjects apparently used to excess. This goes along with my earlier contention that we all agree on many of the tactics involved in ingratiation. In this case, however, excessive eye contact, flattery, and agreement led to strategic failure through "overkill."

The picture for successful and unsuccessful self-promoters is slightly different. Here the subjects who were unsuccessful in securing increased competence ratings tended to be seen as awkward and inept, converting their concern with promoting competence into gestures of disinterest and aloofness. Successful self-promoters were able to get their own

TABLE 7-2 Representative Comments of Raters by Condition and Success

Ingratiation	Self-promotion
Successful	
Pair 1	*Pair 1*
Asks questions. Relaxed, bright, sensitive. Less promoting; less opinionated.	Awkward, dull. Self-conscious. Controlling conversation. More assertive. Talked about computers. Friendly, interested.
Pair 2	*Pair 2*
Successfully friendly. Open to other, less focused on own life. Searched for common ground.	Talked about coordinating job and school. Haircut and tie. Did all of talking. Emphasized successful job. Self-aggrandizing.
Pair 3	*Pair 3*
More animated, leaned forward. Listened well. Self-deprecating. Made other person laugh.	Knows professors, rattles off course numbers. Less animated. Seemed depressed. Made sure partner knows taking 5 courses. Shy, awkward.
Pair 4	*Pair 4*
Friendlier. Seemed very interested in other. Did not dwell on self. Smiles, nods. Drew other out, leaned.	More person-oriented. Agreement, support. Asks lots of questions. Drew other guy out. Does not seem to self-promote, but I think this is natural state for him.

	Unsuccessful
Pair 1 Less animated, smiles less. More self-promoting. Listened more. Tons of questions. Incredible eye contact. Generally dislikable.	*Pair 1* Less animated. Other person dominates conversation. Thinks can do well in fifth course. Trying to appear competent at expense of friendliness.
Pair 2 More awkward. Less animated. Much more tense. Trying to appear interested. Leaned forward, smiled, made positive comments.	*Pair 2* Puts self forward as character: abstracted, mature. Mentions not getting work done. Looks at table quite a bit. Socially inept.
Pair 3 Laughed before other guy finished story. Obvious space cadet. Weird laugh. Says "you are awesome!" Conformity.	*Pair 3* So quiet. Very business-like. Tries to make self better by putting someone else down. Took control but didn't seem interested.
Pair 4 More self-conscious. Questions. Compliments. Flattery. Drew other guy out. Tells other he is "dressed nice."	*Pair 4* Seemed not interested in what target person was saying. Emphasized successes. Dull. Other guy dominates. Sort of a lump.

Source: (From Godfrey, Jones, and Lord, 1986).

Note: Comments made by different raters are separated by periods.

achievements across and at least some of them seemed "natural" and "friendly" while doing so.

Self-Promotion and Performances

Although the preceding study provides some insight into the distinctive features of self-promotion and ingratiation, it is important not to generalize these results too glibly to other settings. Self-promoting subjects were generally unsuccessful, but this may have been largely due to the constraining context in which they had to operate. Get-acquainted conversations between peers are perhaps not the best settings to impress others with one's competence. A study by Linda Ginzel suggests that would-be self-promoters can more readily succeed in settings where performance itself is an issue.[29] Her subjects were instructed to put together a brief speech describing the applicability of a Shakespearean drama for contemporary business decisions. After their speeches they were asked to evaluate their own performance in answer to a series of questions posed by another subject, one who had monitored their speech. Speechmakers preinstructed to answer the questions in a self-promoting manner were generally successful in conveying an image of competence. In fact, in contrast to our earlier results, self-promotion subjects were more successful in achieving their goals than were speechmakers who were given ingratiation instructions.

The relation between various self-promotion tactics and actual performances is one of the constraining features that makes self-promotion so distinctive. It seems self-evident that claims of competence unrelated to performance will eventually fall of their own weight. Not only will the claimant be unsuccessful, there is even a "self-promoter's paradox."[30] Since it is known that certain kinds of people exaggerate their abilities, the listener quite naturally wants to link claims with concrete evidence of actual performance. The paradox arises in that outstanding performers do not need to make claims; the performance can usually "speak for itself." This is why outspoken self-promoters run such a risk: Claims cannot be a substitute for performances that unequivocally reflect competence. The corollary is that truly competent people should have a reduced need to claim competence. Perhaps this is true in part because those who are insecure about their competence are more likely to put forth competence claims as a means of gaining reassurance from those around them. After all, perhaps if they can convince others, they can convince themselves. In addition, however, to the extent that competence-relevant performances are known, verbal claims of competence become unnecessary.

There is typically an asymmetry involved in attributions of competence.[31] Successful achievements are more likely to signal competence than are unsuccessful achievements necessarily to reflect incompetence. One can do poorly for a great variety of reasons, whereas good performances typically can only be achieved by competent people. Failures are thus attributionally ambiguous: The task may have been extremely difficult, the performer may not have tried very hard, people are sometimes sick and under the weather, they have bad days, etc. I have argued elsewhere that not only do we want to be seen as competent in our culture, but we are especially interested in having our achievements attributed to native or natural ability.[32] Most of us would prefer to be seen as lazy rather than stupid; as naturally gifted rather than dependent on laborious training; as brilliant, musical and athletic, rather than doggedly persevering.

This desire to have our successful performances reflect our natural abilities — and our failures not detract from such attributions — has a variety of interesting consequences for the tasks that we choose, the effort that we exert, and the way in which we "handle" success and failure. In the present context, however, the main point of relevance is that a major class of self-promotional strategies are those that go beyond claims of competence to the particular manner in which our performances are arranged, displayed, and perhaps commented on. Thus, the framing of our performances is a crucial part of the more general framing of competence. The adept self-promoter will figure out ways to have his or her responses seen in the most impressive way and will devise strategies to link his or her successes to native talent, to natural abilities that contain the potential for even greater performances in the future.

Such performance-framing strategies are illustrated in an experiment that George Quattrone and I did several years ago.[33] We wanted to show in this experiment that people are capable of using their understanding of attributional logic so as to frame the implications of a performance in the direction of native ability. Subjects in one experimental scenario were asked to imagine that they were trying out for the role of Scrooge in a Broadway production of A Christmas Carol and were given an opportunity to convey selected information about themselves to the play's director. Half the subjects were to imagine that they had been through an audition for the part, after which there was enthusiastic applause from an audience that included the director. No audition was mentioned in the hypothetical scenario given to the remaining subjects. When subjects were confident of meeting the specific self-presentational objective of winning the Scrooge role—in other words, when they were led to believe that the audition had been a successful one—they went out of their way to emphasize inhibitory factors that made their performance difficult or unlikely and therefore all the more diagnostic of a more general (or "natural?") underlying competence. Specifically, the "successful audition" subjects were eager to disclose they had previously received excellent notices for their performance in another play as a generous, lovable sucker—just the opposite of the Scrooge role. Subjects without the opportunity of a Scrooge audition indicated that they would avoid the disclosure of this information, presumably because it would have been damaging to their effort to convince the director that they could be a plausible Scrooge. Thus, the successful audition subjects seemed to be saying, "My ability to play the Scrooge role is part of a broader and more basic versatility." Results for an entirely different scenario with the same conceptual features were almost identical.

To sum up, a major difference between ingratiation and self-promotion is that the latter can at some point usually be tied to measurable performances. I suppose one could say that in theory, at least, ingratiators can voluntarily become the likable persons they present themselves as; attributes like friendliness and congeniality are more under a person's control than are the capacities reflected in consequential performances.

Attribution and Self-Presentation: Two Sides of the Same Coin

Before concluding with further discussion of alternative goals and strategies that may influence the interaction process, let me break in to restate the major thesis of this chapter. If we want to understand interpersonal perception as a dynamic process embedded in ongoing social interaction sequences, we must recognize the crucial roles of perceived and enacted interaction goals. Perceivers are also actors, and target persons are also perceivers. Both are motivated to attain certain goals through the process of social interaction. At a minimum, each actor may want to "get through" the interaction and to escape without endangering his or her social identity. Interactions can, at this extreme, be ritual interchanges of scripted pleasantries, homilies, and so on. The vast majority of interactions are more interesting. They involve intersecting agendas that require creative improvisation in the actions designed to pursue them. Almost all of our interactions involve opportunities for social rewards and punishments. Sometimes these outcomes are immediately delivered and sometimes they are remote and probabilistic. Because outcomes and potential outcomes are interwoven throughout the interaction process, each actor's power and social identity is involved. Furthermore, our relevant outcomes are in part contingent on the impressions we create. We therefore have an investment in how we are seen and how our actions are attributed. Insofar as such considerations enter into our behavioral choices and our actions are shaped or influenced by the effects we desire to have on others, we obviously make use of our knowledge of attributional processes. Different acts are attributed to different dispositions; the same act can mean different things in different settings. These are elementary ingredients of our social wisdom, of our "naive" attributional theories. The trouble is that such ingredients of attributional understanding are available to us both as actors and as perceivers. My interest in managing an impression must contend with your stake in sorting out what I am really like from how I would like to be seen. Since I don't want to be seen as merely managing a desirable impression, because that could have just the opposite effect, I must exploit the attributional process while not appearing to do so. (This is the illicit, though generally not conscious, aspect of ingratiation.) But if actors make use of the attributional process in planning their behavior, perceivers must also be aware of the actors' stake in creating a positive impression.

These considerations prompt us to reexamine the potential for situational attribution throughout the interaction sequence. A perceiver can infer a target person's interaction goals if the perceiver has a target-based expectancy based on prior knowledge of the target person's motives. But such goals, and certainly their specific modes of implementation, are more typically a function of the situation. Thus, the boss who recognizes the employee's dependence does so because of the situation that ties them together. The context often alerts us to the likelihood that certain goals will be implemented, and this can create hazards for impression management strategies. Thus, I have spoken of the ingratiator's dilemma and the self-promoter's paradox. I have also suggested that the target person's vanity, the desire to believe the best about oneself, often comes to the rescue of the self-presenting actor. We should also note that when interaction goals are tied to situational contexts, correspondence bias can come to the self-presenter's rescue as well. The chances are good that the self-presenter's situation, the one that gave rise to his or her goals, will be given insufficient causal weight by the perceiver.

Additional Self-Presentational Strategies

Power oriented strategies in social interaction also include exemplification, intimidation, and supplication. Exemplifiers attempt to elicit attributions of *moral worthiness*, intimidators want to be seen as *dangerous* (not to be "messed with"), and supplicants hope that others will see them as *dependent* and needing help or support. These distinctions can be buttressed by anecdotes and perhaps by theoretical reasoning, but there have been few systematic research efforts to establish the conditions under which they occur. Nevertheless, it may be appropriate to recapitulate briefly some of the distinctive characteristics of these strategies.

Exemplification

Exemplification has much in common with self-promotion and invites many of the same dangers. One who persistently dons the mantle of saintliness, of superior virtue, obviously runs the risk of being seen as sanctimonious and hypocritical.[34] Truly virtuous people do not claim virtue; those of high moral standing presumably are known for their selfless acts, their generous contributions to the commonweal, especially at the expense of self-aggrandizement. Exemplifiers often come across as lost in a cause, absorbed by devotion to ideological or political commitment. Most of us consistently try to project honesty and integrity, whether this is part of convincing an audience or convincing ourselves. Those who want special credit for moral virtue or strength of character must therefore seek out special circumstances before such exemplary traits can be demonstrated in action. These can be created with some ingenuity in most organizational settings. They can certainly be found in politics, in ideological movements, in dangerous occupations like the police or the military, and generally in arenas where self-sacrifice and self-discipline can be made apparent.[35] Without such challenging showcases, exemplifiers can perhaps succeed in the long run by establishing a history of consistency, self-discipline, and/or invariable honesty across a variety of occasions. This is presumably the goal of many parents who wish to serve as exemplary models for their children, and the volume and range of interactions within the family can make up for the absence of more focused instances where one's courage or self-sacrifice is put to a dramatic test.

Intimidation

Intimidation has a built-in potential for generating aversion and dislike. Intimidators may get their way by projecting a capacity and the inclination to provide negative outcomes, but they rarely become endearing in the process. For this reason, intimidation is most commonly found in relationships that are nonvoluntary rather than in freely formed relationships among peers. If someone is always threatening to make my life difficult, I shall be highly motivated to avoid interacting with that person. But there obviously are many organizational and familial contexts that preclude such avoidance. Employers cannot easily leave employees and wives cannot easily leave husbands, to note a pair of semibinding relationship contexts.

Intimidators have a certain irreducible power over their target person derived from such barriers to social mobility. The dangers they can pose can, of course, be material — loss of salary, denial of tenure, the withholding of sexual favors, and so on. In many of the more interesting and subtle cases, however, intimidators induce compliance in target persons who merely want to avoid the negative consequences of disagreement or the disruption and emotional disturbance that noncompliance can generate in certain relationships with certain kinds of people. I may be intimidated by a boss who is reputed to be unpredictable and, at least occasionally, irascible. Parents, husbands, and wives often exert control by a capacity to project incipient anger. A gathering frown can prompt a change in activity or a new turn in a conversation, changes designed to bring the relationship back to "safer ground."

Supplication

Supplication is the last resort, the preferred strategy for low-power persons who have little else going for them. Supplicators can parade their weaknesses, hoping to engage the norm of social responsibility or, in some cases, the obligations that superiors are supposed to feel toward inferiors (*noblesse oblige*). Supplicators can be effective to the extent that some exchange of benefits is involved. If I am paraplegic or a fragile, elderly woman, it makes sense for me to induce a friend or a spouse to carry my heavy luggage or to move an easychair. Though social responsibility norms may cover such nurturant help in the short run, the supplicator will obviously be more assured of desired benefits if he or she has something to offer in return. Most marriages and other dyadic relationships involve this kind of division of labor, whether "rational" or traditional, and very stable relationships can be formed on the basis of such compensatory exchanges. In one fairly common exchange, at least in my generation, wives prepare meals and husbands do the dishes and take out the garbage. The supplicator who does not engineer such compensatory benefits runs the risk of driving potential benefactors as far away as their rationalizations will permit.

Are There Still Other Strategies?

The answer to the question posed by this heading must be "Undoubtedly." Pittman and I tried to cover the most important power-relevant attributions that one might try to elicit as an impression management goal, but there is no reason to assume that our list is exhaustive. Table 7-3 summarizes the strategies and indicates the related attributions sought and the dangers involved. Indeed, when one thinks of the various routes to social power, the list of relevant strategies could be quite extensive. How extensive might depend on how many variations we can squeeze under the rubrics of ingratiation and self-promotion, the two major strategic categories about which we know the most.

It is also important to recognize the limitations of our current understanding of self-presentational phenomena. I was once asked by the editor of a popular magazine to do a self-presentational analysis of the presidential campaign between Ronald Reagan and Jimmy Carter. I demurred, largely because I felt that our methods of analysis are not yet ready to contribute much to such comparisons and our conceptual net is too broadly gauged for responsible treatment of such an event as a presidential campaign. Nevertheless, it is tempting to speculate on the reasons why certain political leaders succeed where others fail. The "Reagan phenomenon," for example, will intrigue political analysts for years and certainly poses a challenge for students of self-presentation. What were the

TABLE 7-3 A Taxonomy of Self-presentational Strategies Classified Primarily by Attribution Sought

	Attributions Sought	Emotion to Be Aroused	Negative Attributions Risked	Prototypical Actions
1. Ingratiation	Likable	Affection	Sycophant Conformist Obsequious	Self-characterization Opinion conformity Other enhancement Favors
2. Intimidation	Dangerous (ruthless, volatile)	Fear	Blusterer Wishy-washy Ineffectual	Threats (Incipient) anger (Incipient) breakdown
3. Self-promotion	Competent (effective, "a winner")	Respect (awe, deference)	Fraudulent Conceited Defensive	Performance claims Performance accounts Performances
4. Exemplification	Worthy (suffers, dedicated)	Guilt (shame, emulation)	Hypocrite Sanctimonious Exploitative	Self-denial Helping Militancy for a cause
5. Supplication	Helpless (handicapped, unfortunate)	Nurturance (obligation)	Stigmatized Lazy Demanding	Self-deprecation Entreaties for help

characteristics that made him the "Teflon President"?[36] Jimmy Carter could surely have used some of these ingredients. His presidency was seriously wounded by the Iranian hostage crisis, a crisis that was eventually resolved without any fatalities among the hostages, and yet President Reagan sailed through relatively unscathed when our ill-conceived show of token American force in Beirut ended in the death of more than 250 U.S. Marines. Furthermore, it is hard to imagine another president regaining the affection and respect of the people as quickly as Reagan did after the illegalities of "Irangate" were revealed and highly publicized in televised congressional hearings.

The Reagan phenomenon reminds us that we really don't have much to say as yet about the self-presentation Gestalt known as charisma. A similar gap: What are the components that blend so effectively when we say that someone has "style"? At this point we can only speculate that these qualities have something to do with mixtures of self-confidence and self-mockery, comfort with one's achievements but humility in citing them, the ability to communicate in ways that touch and arouse constituents, and selected aspects of physical appearance and bearing that are difficult to locate in our psychological theories. We "know" these things as lay observers, perhaps, but they are difficult to grasp conceptually and not easy to realize as experimental variables.

Concluding Remarks

But we should not be too despairing. As I hope this chapter conveys, we have learned much about some of the broad outlines of strategic self-presentations. We can proceed from the truism that people care about the impressions they create to specify the particular attributions that are relevant for attaining many of our interpersonal goals. Power, I have argued, is the key consideration in securing these attainments. By considering the different ways that people can gain power, use the power they have, and blunt the destructive potential of the power of others, a number of common strategies can be identified: ingratiation, self-promotion, exemplification, intimidation, and supplication. Of these, ingratiation is the most ubiquitous, though self-promotion does not lag far behind. I have suggested that it never hurts to be liked and that ingratiation is often the leavening factor that makes the other strategies effective.

My analysis emphasizes the relation between attribution and self-presentation. The processes of one cannot be understood without grasping the processes of the other. In emphasizing the impressions or identities that actors are motivated to construct in social interactions, I have omitted consideration of the relationship between self-presentation and self-knowledge. How do we know ourselves and what evidence do we rely upon for this knowledge? This question, basically a question of self-attribution, is the one to which we now turn in the next chapter.

Getting

to Know Ourselves

Interpersonal perception involves getting to know others, of course, but it also involves getting to know ourselves. This is true in numerous respects. First of all, self-knowledge can be a direct consequence of perceptions of others in our presence. From discussions in the preceding chapter, it is obvious that we can learn about ourselves by learning how others respond to us in the interaction sequence. What do their actions tell us about their impressions of us? Do they seem to be patronizing? Deferent? Inattentive? What clues can we read that contribute to an updated self-definition?

Second, in the course of social interaction our behavior is both a confirming reflection of our self and an indicator of

those respects in which the self-concept may need to be modified or adjusted. The following account focuses especially on
those features of the phenomenal self that are most affected by
the information conveyed during ongoing social interaction
processes. (It also emphasizes those theories and findings that
I personally found nonobvious when I first heard about them.)

Relevant Self-Knowledge

The Self as Others See It

Learning about ourselves is an endless process, and much of
this process incorporates the perceived reactions of others.
This is what symbolic interactionists mean when they refer to
the negotiation of identities during the interaction process.
From the point of view of those in this tradition, actors negotiate with each other in subtle ways to establish some implicit
agreement concerning the role of each in the interaction and
the "face" that each projects to, and accepts for, the other.
These notions of what Charles Horton Cooley once called the
"looking glass self"[1] were incorporated in variations of social
comparison theory emphasizing "reflected appraisal."[2] The
basic phenomenon referred to in these and related concepts is
that we learn who we are by observing how we are reflected in
the "mirror" others provide by their actions toward us.

The Self as Norm or Standard

The self-attributions emerging from past negotiations can in
turn have a direct influence on interpersonal perceptions.
Think about how often we use our own implicit decision processes as an anchor in evaluating the behavioral decisions of
others. "What would I have done in that situation?" is a ques-

tion we silently pose as we observe the problematic actions of others around us. The answer to such a question becomes a pivotal starting point for many of our attributional efforts. We thus not only treat ourselves commonly as an element of consensus but go well beyond this to assume that our own reactions are ordinarily the consensual ones. Lee Ross and his colleagues have documented this "false consensus bias."[3] If others behave as we do, or as we think we would have, we typically attribute their behavior to the situation. But we also attribute distinctive personal dispositions to those whose behavioral decisions tend to differ from our own.

The Self as Rational Decision Maker

These attributional patterns, suggested by Ross and his colleagues, are consistent with the actor–observer divergence proposition discussed more fully in Chapters 3 and 5. We, as actors, tend to view our own actions as rational responses to the world as it really is (i.e., as other reasonable people would judge it to be). If, as observers, we notice some one acting in a different manner, we account for those out-of-consensus actions by making dispositional attributions. However, this outcome depends on our identification with consensus, and there are some important occasions in which we can be led to feel that our behavior or our inner states are idiosyncratic. When inner states are involved, we may have what is commonly referred to as a case of pluralistic ignorance. We may feel anxious or fearful in a setting in which others appear to be calm, not realizing that the others are just as successful as we are at covering up their emotional state.[4]

The Distinctive and
Internally Consistent Self

We may also reach the conclusion that our overt behavior is somewhat idiosyncratic, a condition that will lead us to attribute distinctive dispositional attributions to ourselves. As pointed out in Chapter 3, it was Harold Kelley who first raised this kind of question and, in the process, expanded attribution theory to include attributions about the self.[5] Kelley tried to provide an attributional explanation of attitude change observed in subjects induced to express opinions going against their private attitudes. In the early 1960s a rapidly growing body of research stimulated by cognitive dissonance theory[6] was showing that subjects induced to engage in actions whose implications ran counter to their own beliefs ended up changing those beliefs so as to make them more congruent with their induced behavior. In dissonance theory terms, subjects reduce the cognitive dissonance associated with counterattitudinal behavior by bringing their attitudes more into congruence with their actions. Thus, a political conservative induced to endorse a liberal position in a recorded speech or a written essay would subsequently rate himself as more liberal than his previous self-ratings would have suggested.

But a crucial condition for this to happen was the illusion of freedom. If subjects were required or handsomely rewarded for endorsing a particular position against one of their own private attitudes, there was no observed opinion change. Attitude change only occurred if subjects were tricked or cajoled into thinking they could have chosen to write on the other side of the issue. Experimenters in the condition supposedly producing cognitive dissonance might create an illusion of freedom by saying something like "Because we already have a lot of essays on the opposite side, I wonder if you would mind writing an essay favoring capital punishment? I would appreciate it, but of course the choice is completely up to you." In experiments involving such subtle inducements to comply, all subjects do tend to go along with the experimenter's induction. And when they do so, they are left with the realization that, after all, they freely chose to endorse the counterattitudinal position. Kelley proposed that they were therefore led to shift their self-understanding in the direction of the "freely chosen" opinion, even though it ran counter to their firmly held initial beliefs. In line with the familiar attributional trade-off, if their counterattitudinal behavior could not be attributed to the situation, then it had to reflect a personal disposition—i.e., the behavior must not have been so counterattitudinal after all.

The Self as Observer of Self

In this same essay Kelley noted that Daryl Bem was vigorously proposing a very similar notion to account for the results of induced compliance. In an earlier paper on self-persuasion Bem had proposed that actors are no more privileged than observers when asked to report their inner convictions, but instead must decide what they believe by observing their own behavior and its situational context.[7] Bem adopted the radical position, in other words, that people are very poor judges of their own internal states and are forced to rely on observations of their own reactions in order to define and clarify these internal dispositions.

The Self-Perception/Dissonance Controversy

Two years later, in the same year as Kelley's own essay, Bem published an extensive critique of dissonance theory embodying these radical assumptions.[8] In this critique he proposed that the effects of induced compliance on attitude change, effects whose reality he did not challenge, could be explained without positing an aversive arousal state (i.e., a state of dissonance). They could be explained by principles of self-perception very much like those involved in the situation–person trade-off featured in attribution theory. To reinforce his argument, Bem conducted a series of simulations in which subjects were told about other alleged subjects in high-choice influence conditions who complied to the subtle cajoling of the experimenter. The real subjects were asked to estimate the true opinions of the hypothetical subjects. They attributed attitudes to the hypothetical subjects very much in line with what dissonance theorists would predict. Therefore, Bem argued, in this situation observers are like actors themselves, and it follows, actors are like observers.

Those in the cognitive dissonance camp understandably objected to what they perceived as Bem's cavalier reinterpretation of dozens of cognitive dissonance experiments, some of which involved very subtle conditions leading to complex statistical interactions actually predicted by the theory. They contended that Bem's simulation studies of induced compliance did not include the crucial information that all subjects complied in the original experiments or that subjects were randomly assigned to choice and no-choice conditions. Thus, Bem's observer subjects in the simulation experiments could have simply assumed that the target persons whose attitudes they were attempting to estimate were already in favor of that opinion and *therefore* willingly complied to the experimenter's permissive request. Bem's response to these contentions was a kind of perverse agreement with the opposition: "Exactly," he said, "subjects behave, look at their own behavior, realize that they didn't have to behave that way, and conclude that they must have always agreed to some extent with the position they expressed." In other words, subjects do not realize that they have changed their attitudes; they infer that they must have held that attitude all along, just as Bem's simulation judges assumed.

Dozens of experiments and thousands of words failed to end the controversy over dissonance versus self-perception accounts of attitude change after induced compliance. At one point, even Leon Festinger, the father of cognitive dissonance theory, confessed that he saw no reason to prefer one explanation over the other; the two explanations were, in his opinion, interchangable.[9]

As Bem continued to think and write about how people perceive their internal states and dispositions, two things happened. First of all, he became less radical (more sensible?) in realizing that actors do have some privileged information about their internal states. Thus, in his most formal statement of self-perception theory he begins with the proposition that "individuals come to 'know' their own attitudes, emotions, and other internal states partially by inferring them from observations of their own overt behavior and/or the circumstances in which the behavior occurs. Thus, *to the extent that internal cues are weak, ambiguous, or uninterpretable*, the individual is functionally in the same position as an outside observer, an observer who must necessarily rely upon those same external cues to infer the individual's inner states."[10] The italicized portion of this proposition represents an important concession that was absent in Bem's earlier statements.

A second feature that became clear in Bem's summary of self-perception theory is his general acceptance of an attributional framework for expressing his ideas. Thus, one can trace the evolution of his theory from a starting point in Skinnerian conditioning, ultimately to discussions of self-attribution. (As he himself put it, the "Skinnerian parentage of the theory has been increasingly muted in successive translations."[11]) In this final statement of his theory, Bem explicitly acknowledged the clear influence of Kelley and saw his contribution as part of a more general trend toward the explanation of a great variety of psychological phenomena in cognitive terms.

Whether or not one wants to call this trend a paradigm shift, it surely is the case that social psychologists have always generally preferred cognitive to motivational explanations when both were applicable. Bem's research and his persuasive prose fit nicely into this preference and accelerated the decline of interest in dissonance theory and other consistency theories having motivational implications. It is interesting that Bem, at least in his final statement, was quite the gracious scientific statesman. He did not assert that his theory was completely superior to dissonance or other motivational theories; he basically argued that it seemed to be just as useful in accounting for relevant empirical phenomena and required fewer complex assumptions about motivation to reduce aversive states like dissonance. In short, he and Festinger seemed to share the position that, because there was no obvious way to distinguish between self-perception and dissonance theories, no crucial experiment could be designed to prove that one theory was superior to the other.

The Perception of One's Own Emotions

In the meantime, another important development was feeding into the mainstream of self-understanding. Whereas Bem focused primarily on such inner experiences as preferences and attitudes, Stanley Schachter, with very different theoretical origins, emphasized the role of cognitions—i.e., attributions—in our emotional experience. In fact, his major theoretical contribution[12] preceded Daryl Bem's self-perception theory, but Kelley recognized the attributional implications of Schachter's research and incorporated both Schachter's and Bem's positions in his synthesizing essay. Schachter's basic argument was that emotional experience is the product of an interaction between physiological arousal and cognitive labeling. He boldly proposed that our physiological states have no definitive informational value, that they essentially pose a question that is then answered by cognitive readings of surrounding circumstances. With his student Jerome Singer he conducted what may in retrospect be called the first misattribution experiment. Subjects received injections of epinephrine, a drug that normally causes symptoms of increased heart rate and the general bodily vigilance associated with sympathetic arousal. Some subjects were given an accurate description of the typical side effects; others were given a misleading list, including itching and headaches; still others were told nothing about side effects and were given either epinephrine or a placebo. All subjects were subsequently exposed to elaborately contrived social experiences designed to arouse anger or euphoria. In line with Schachter's claim that arousal is an important but informationally neutral ingredient of emotional experience, the misinformed and uninformed subjects showed more extreme anger *or* euphoria (depending on the experimental condition to which they were assigned) than did subjects who were not given epinephrine or those who were given the drug along with an accurate description of its side effects.

This was Schachter's most famous experiment on emotional experience, but several other demonstrations of his theory also provided at least partial support for his emphasis on cognitive labeling as the major determinant of the particular content and direction of emotional experience.

More than a quarter of a century later, most researchers in the emotion area view Schachter's bold cognitive labeling proposal with considerable skepticism.[13] Just as Bem initially wrote as though our inner experience had to be constructed and inferred from external circumstances and our own behavior in response to them, Schachter had treated physiological arousal as nothing but a pattern of ambiguous stimulation begging to be explained. Bem later made concessions about the role of such inner experiences as memories and stored beliefs, whereas Schachter went on to other concerns. But subsequent research makes it clear that not all patterns of physiological arousal are equally ambiguous, and the more intense emotional states are not likely to be misattributed; thus, Schachter's theory was, to say the least, an oversimplification. Nevertheless, I like to cite it as the kind of theoretical statement that is so simple it cannot possibly be true (as I am sure Schachter realized[14]), but also so robust and provocative that it led us in a number of fruitful directions.

What concerns me here is the contribution of Schachter's emphasis on cognitive labeling to the growing literature on self-attribution, and particularly to the possibilities of misattribution. His classic epinephrine experiment should show how subjects could be tricked into labeling the same quantum of physiological arousal in terms of very different labels cued by the experimental context. If the sources of our inner experience can be so easily manipulated, so easily misidentified, the way is paved for research illuminating the role of psychological factors in the perception of pain, anxiety, and other physical symptoms — at least those ambiguous enough to be flexibly interpreted. And, indeed, the past twenty years have witnessed waves of research at the attributional forefront of behavioral medicine. Such research has ranged from attempts to understand placebo effects[15] to penetrating analyses of the role of external incentives in the self-perception of motivation.[16] But perhaps the most direct extension of Schachter's approach is represented by Dolph Zillmann's research on *excitation transfer*.

Zillmann's major contribution was to consolidate Schachter's contention that people can be led to attribute arousal from one source to a second source that is in fact totally unrelated to the original arousing circumstances. Whereas Schachter created arousal by the administration of epinephrine, Zillmann produced similar arousal symptoms by a variety of interventions, most prominently including physical exercise. When people ride a stationary bicycle, their body produces a standard physiological reaction of excitation, measurable by increased pulse rate, skin responses, and other indicators of an aroused organism. In a series of experiments Zillmann was able to show how subjects could be led to transfer their arousal to other potential sources of excitation made reasonable by unrelated experimental experiences. For example, Zillmann's subjects in one experiment were asked to perform the role of teacher by administering electric shocks as corrective feedback to a learner who had previously (by prearrangement) shocked the subject.[17] Subjects had either engaged in vigorous exercise immediately prior to this "opportunity," or the exercise had been followed by six minutes of rest prior to the teaching experience. The results showed that those who had been given six minutes to recover partially from the arousal administered shocks of greater intensity than did those who had been aroused in the immediate past. The reasoning here is very Schachterian: Those who entered the teaching task immediately after physical arousal could readily attribute their experienced arousal to physical exercise. Therefore, the arousal could be conveniently segregated from any other emotion engendered by the task of teaching. However, subjects in the delay condition, though still actually aroused, did not as readily attribute their arousal to the previous exercise. Zillmann's results show, among other things, that subjects are very imprecise in monitoring the decay of arousal symptoms. After six minutes, in this case, excitatory residues persisted in the absence of cues of prior arousal.

In other experiments, Zillmann and his colleagues were able to show that subjects exposed to provocative reading material or exciting movies, such as a Beatles montage, subsequently showed the effects of such arousal in responding to unrelated tasks of judging cartoons or evaluating a good or bad guest lecturer.[18] The conclusion of this line of research sponsored by Schachter and extended by Zillmann is this: *If people for any reason misperceive the circumstances of physiological arousal, their emotions will fit their misperceptions rather than the true state of affairs.*

Dissonance Really Does Motivate

Bem's thoughtful essay was no doubt designed to end the running debate between dissonance theorists and those who favored the more purely cognitive self-perception view. He himself expressed the hope, "The demise of the precious controversy between dissonance theory and self-perception theory is a consummation devoutly to be wished. It is resolved that, henceforth, nothing more on this subject shall be heard from this quarter."[19] Bem remained true to his word, but the controversy continued as a series of "crucial experiments" were never quite decisive in ruling out one or the other theoretical alternative.

Mark Zanna and Joel Cooper then published an experiment strongly suggesting that (1) standard induced compliance procedures do produce an aversive state that (2) subjects are motivated to reduce or eliminate, and (3) if this aversive state can be misattributed to some irrelevant feature of the experiment, attitude change will not result.[20] If this could be shown to be the case, the inference would be inescapable that some kind of internal state of arousal was linked to the attitude change process in those conditions in which a person has been led to assume some responsibility for a counterattitudinal statement.

In the Zanna and Cooper experiments subjects were recruited for a study allegedly concerned with the effects of a particular drug on memory. In preparation for this memory test, they ingested a placebo pill whose side effects were described either as making them feel tense or as making them feel relaxed; alternatively, no effects were mentioned. While presumably waiting for the drug to take effect, these same subjects were asked to help in a second experiment, which turned out to be a typical choice versus no-choice, induced compliance experiment, ending with all subjects writing a counterattitudinal essay favoring the restriction of speakers having controversial views.

When subjects' attitudes were subsequently measured, it turned out that those in the high-choice "no side effects" condition showed the usual attitude change toward the counterattitudinal position they had been cajoled to espouse. No-choice subjects, on the other hand, showed no such attitude change. In those conditions in which high-choice subjects had been forewarned that the pill they ingested would have definite side effects, dramatic differences were predicted and observed as a function of the particular side effects cited. Those who expected to be more tense did not show attitude change, even in the high-choice condition. Those who expected the pill to relax them, on the other hand, showed the greatest attitude change of all.

These findings (summarized in Table 8-1) confirmed the dissonance theory expectation that counterattitudinal statements under free-choice conditions produce an aversive arousal state. Reasoning backward from the results, if the aversive state can be misattributed to the innocent placebo, the subject has an explanation for his or her aversive state and therefore there is no "need" for attitude change. The aversive state will presumably go away by itself, eliminating any basis for a motive to change one's attitude in order to achieve greater consistency between behavior and belief. Subjects who expected to feel relaxed, on the other hand, must have felt especially motivated to reduce such an inconsistency. Their discomfort could hardly be explained by attributing it to a pill that was supposed to make them feel less tense!

These results were replicated and extended by an even more dramatic experimental demonstration in which subjects were actually given small doses of an arousing drug (dextroamphetamine), a tranquilizer (phenobarbital), or a placebo (milk powder).[21] All subjects were led to believe that they were in "the placebo condition." In an immediately following induced compliance experiment, subjects who were actually aroused (by the amphetamine) showed the greatest attitude

TABLE 8-1   **Subjects' Opinions Toward Banning Speakers on Campus (Mean Scores)**

	Potential Side Effect of the Drug		
Decision Freedom	*Arousal*	*None*	*Relaxation*
High	3.40	9.10	13.40
Low	3.50	4.50	4.70

Source: (From Zanna and Cooper, 1974.)

Note: Cell $n = 10$. The larger the mean, the more agreement with the attitude-discrepant essay (Control group $\overline{X} = 2.30$).

TABLE 8-2 **Attitudes Toward the Pardoning of Richard Nixon (Mean Scores)**

Decision Freedom	Drug Condition		
	Tranquilizer	Placebo	Amphetamine
High choice	8.6	14.7	20.2
Low choice	8.0	8.3	13.9

Source: (From Cooper et al., 1978.)

Note: n = 10 subjects per cell. Higher means on the 31-point scale indicate greater agreement with the attitude-discrepant essay.

change, whereas those who were actually tranquilized showed the least (see Table 8-2).

The great irony of the Cooper and Zanna experiments is that the investigators used the misattribution principles of self-perception theory to show that self-perception theory is inadequate. Bem had argued that the positing of an aversive motivational state to reduce inconsistency was not necessary. He would have great difficulty maintaining such a position in the face of the results of these demonstrations of misattributed arousal.

Cooper, Zanna, and their colleagues conducted several additional studies to confirm their argument. The most interesting of the subsequent studies for my purposes was a study by Fazio, Zanna, and Cooper, attempting to integrate or reconcile dissonance and self-perception theory.[22] These investigators may have been from the "dissonance camp," but they were not inclined to ignore completely the reasonableness of Bem's main contention: A person's recent actions are generally salient because of their recency. Therefore, when the person is asked to describe him- or herself, it would not be surprising if these actions were in some way represented in the person's self-description. In short, except when we are forced to do something we normally would not do, we are what we do. Fazio and his colleagues proposed that little or no dissonance is involved when we are asked to tell a white lie — for example, to espouse an attitude that may not be exactly what we endorsed but is close enough to our favorite position to be congenial to us. In considering a continuum of statements differing from this favorite position, these investigators were reminded of a distinction drawn earlier by Muzafer Sherif and Carl Hovland between opinions one finds generally acceptable (falling within one's "latitude of acceptance") and those that one would definitely not endorse (falling within one's "latitude of rejection").[23] Seizing upon this distinction, Fazio, Zanna, and Cooper proposed that subjects induced to espouse "freely" an opinion discrepant from their preferred stand but still within the latitude of acceptance would show subsequent attitude change, but there would be no dissonance experienced. The attitude change would presumably come about because of "biased scanning." The subjects, when asked about their attitudes, would scan their most recent behavior, behavior that most prominently included the endorsement of a slightly discrepant position, and conclude that their new position indeed represented their true attitudes.

When a person "chooses" to make a counterattitudinal statement in his or her latitude of rejection, on the other hand, there is cognitive dissonance, which can be reduced, presumably by changing one's attitude to bring it closer to that implied by the statement. But since there should be attitude change within both the latitude of acceptance and the latitude of rejection, how can we distinguish between what are presumed to be different underlying processes? Again, Fazio and his colleagues attempted to do so by exploiting the logic of misattribution. If subjects who have been induced to espouse an opinion in their latitude of rejection experience the aversive state of dissonance, attitude change will not be necessary if they are cued or primed to misattribute the aversive state to some extraneous circumstance. This, in fact, is what these investigators found. Some subjects were asked a number of questions about the confining isolation booths within which they had to work during the experiment, thus raising the likelihood that these subjects would begin thinking about—and be aroused by—their cramped surroundings. Subjects who had thus been primed did not show any effects of cognitive dissonance, even in the high-choice conditions. In the absence of any mention of the confining booths, subjects "choosing" to espouse a position in the latitude of rejection showed the typical attitude change effect expected by dissonance theory. The misattribution manipulation (i.e., whether the confining nature of the booths was made salient) had no such effects when the subjects "chose" to espouse an attitude in their latitude of acceptance. If one is not feeling tense or uncomfortable, as in the alternative case where one espouses a strongly counterattitudinal position, there is no reason for mention of the confining booths to have any effect.

The predicted and observed pattern of results led Fazio and his colleagues to conclude that dissonance is only aroused when one's actions decisively depart from one's existing attitudes; more modest discrepancies can be handled nicely by self-perception theory. In the latter case, we need not posit any aversive state of arousal.

■

The controversy between dissonance and self-perception theories was a constructive, fruitful interchange. As the debate oscillated, dissonance theorists were forced to adopt a more sophisticated view of the self and the externally arranged conditions of attitude change. This view continued to emphasize arousal and motivation, but linked them to properties of the self-concept rather than to the aversiveness of inconsistency per se. One revised version of dissonance theory notes that what is aversive is acting in ways that suggest that one is not a decent human being—that one is willing to mislead others without sufficient justification.[24] Cooper and Fazio's more recent "new look at dissonance theory" also emphasizes the aversiveness of having to accept responsibility for producing negative consequences, a responsibility that is incompatible with a positive self-concept.[25] Much of the evidence growing out of the dissonance/self-perception controversy centers around potential changes in attitude. What fascinates me about the dissonance story is the more general point that we can be socially induced to behave in a way that is inconsistent with our self-image, which may subsequently change to accommodate the implications of this induced behavior. It is this more general point that I next pursue in considering how we learn about ourselves as we interact with others. Specifically, when do we internalize the roles that we have been induced to perform?

When Presentations Become the Self

In the preceding chapter I dealt with attempts to manage a particular impression in the social interaction process. Now that we are specifically concerned with self-perception and self-understanding, it is natural to focus attention on the implications of self-presentations for the presenter's self-concept. Such a discussion can begin with a return to the notion of an autistic conspiracy between ingratiators and target persons. Unless I am a completely shameless strategist, when I tell a lady that she is brilliant, witty, or beautiful, I will want to convince myself that she at least falls within the general range of those to whom such encomia would be applicable. If I express enthusiastic agreement with her feminist opinions, I should face some internal pressures toward privately embracing feminist positions. In short, the autistic conspiracy predicts shifts in the self-presenter's private beliefs that make them more consistent with his or her public statements.

Armed with the above discussion of self-perception and cognitive dissonance theories, we are now prepared to take a closer look at the conditions under which such accommodations will take place. If the processes of self-concept change follow the same principles as changes in attitude toward political or social issues, then we should expect to find that self-referring statements we would normally wish to avoid, i.e., those in our latitude of rejection, should affect the self-concept when conditions are otherwise favorable for dissonance arousal and reduction. On the other hand, self-referring statements falling into the latitude of acceptance should nudge the self-concept toward greater consistency with behavior under the conditions of self-salience appropriate for self-perception theory.

Fred Rhodewalt and I conducted an experiment to explore these implications using self-esteem as our dependent variable.[26] We induced male undergraduate subjects to say self-enhancing or self-deprecating things in an interview and then measured the effects of these self-presentations on self-esteem in a different, supposedly unrelated context. We reasoned that self-deprecating statements would, for most college students, fall within their latitude of rejection. In fact, subjects typically felt uncomfortable when randomly assigned to the self-deprecating interview condition, finding it very difficult to construct and deliver such self-critical answers to the interviewer's questions. For those subjects instructed to present themselves in a favorable light, on the other hand, the task was considerably more pleasant. Presumably, we are more practiced in calling up self-enhancing statements under a variety of different conditions. Though people are not always, or even typically, as consistently self-enhancing as our instructions urged subjects to be, such statements would presumably fall within most persons' latitude of acceptance. Since, at least, people would like to believe that such statements in fact could be true of themselves, the statements cannot be expected to generate an aversive state of cognitive dissonance.

According to Fazio and his colleagues, for dissonance to be aroused the behavior must implicate beliefs in the latitude of rejection under conditions of free choice. That is, the individual must feel responsible for acting in a manner that is uncharacteristic and that implicates a self view that he or she finds objectionable. To test these hypotheses, half the subjects were explicitly reminded after being assigned their specific interview task that they, "of course," were free to withdraw from the experiment at any time. For self-deprecating subjects, all of whom in fact proceeded with the interview, this should be theoretically a condition of high dissonance — dissonance that should be reduced by a lowering of self-esteem. When self-esteem was anonymously measured in a different setting and compared to a measure of self-esteem taken weeks before the experiment, this is precisely what happened: Subjects who "chose" to self-deprecate showed lower self-esteem; those who were not explicitly given the option of avoiding the interview task showed little or no change in self-esteem. This variable of whether or not choice was made salient did not affect subjects who were given the task of describing themselves favorably, confirming our expectations that there would be no dissonance in the self-enhancement condition.

But according to self-perception theory, self-enhancing behavior should result in elevated self-esteem under conditions in which the behavior is clearly self-referring, but not otherwise.[27] Half the subjects (cross-cutting the choice manipulation) were left to construct their own interview responses to fulfill the self-deprecating or the self-enhancing instructions. Each of the remaining subjects was randomly "yoked" to a particular subject in the "self-referring" half of the experiment — he was given a script indicating how to respond, a script faithfully reproducing the remarks of the yoked partner. Self-perception theory would not predict changes in self-concept following the recitation of scripted remarks having no necessary reference to one's own mode of self-enhancement. On the other hand, those making their own decisions about how best to present themselves favorably should, at least momentarily, show an upward shift in self-esteem. When the final self-esteem measure was administered (again, in a different situation and under conditions of anonymity), only those self-referring subjects in the self-enhancing condition showed such upward self-esteem changes. Those yoked to them did not, and this variable of self-reference did not affect self-deprecating subjects.

We interpreted these finding as offering strong support for the proposal by Fazio and colleagues that dissonance and self-perception theories are each applicable within conditions differing in the acceptability of the attitude-discrepant behavior displayed. Subjects explicitly choosing to present themselves in ways that they would normally reject apparently experienced dissonance; those who improvised their own self-referring responses within the latitude of acceptance showed accommodating shifts toward elevated self-esteem.

Though the results are consistent with such interpretations, they provide no direct evidence that the subjects in the self-deprecating condition were operating in their latitude of rejection or that self-enhancing statements necessarily fell into each subject's latitude of acceptance. A subsequent study by Rhodewalt and Agustdottir helps to pin down this pair of assumptions and, in the process, offers further support for the application of the proposal by Fazio and colleagues to the internalization of self-presentation.[28] Following precisely the same procedures of induced self-enhancing and self-deprecating interview instructions, Rhodewalt and Agustdottir replicated the original results with a sample of undergraduate subjects comparable to those used in the initial experiment.

Rhodewalt and Agustdottir also ran a group of undergraduates whose scores had placed them toward the depressed end of a widely used scale[29] to measure depression. The clinical evidence regarding depression, in addition to our common experience, suggest that depressed people reject reassurances about their positive features, and are quite willing to accept many negative statements about themselves. To the extent that such tendencies characterize the depressed subjects in Rhodewalt and Agustdottir's sample, the results of the original study should be reversed. This in fact was the case. Depressed subjects in the self-enhancement conditions responded as if they were experiencing dissonance when their freedom to choose was made salient (compared to the no-choice condition); depressed subjects in the self-deprecating condition, on

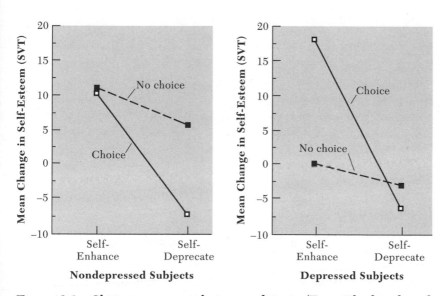

FIGURE 8-1   Choice versus no-choice conditions. (From Rhodewalt and Agustdottir, 1986.)

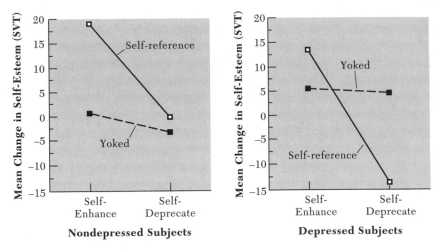

FIGURE 8-2 Self-reference versus yoked conditions. (From Rhodewalt and Agustdottir, 1986.)

the other hand, were not affected by choice but were affected by being in the self-reference versus yoked condition. These results are summarized in Figures 8-1 and 8-2. The suggested rationale or underlying assumptions are portrayed in Figure 8-3.

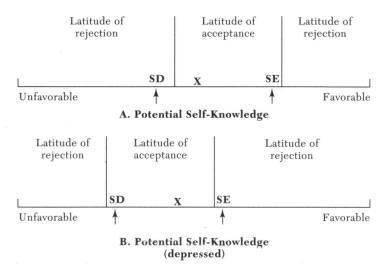

FIGURE 8-3 Latitudes of acceptance and rejection of the phenomenal self (X). SE = self-enhancement; SD = self-deprecation. (From Rhodewalt and Agustdottir, 1986.)

General Conditions of Self-Concept Change: An Interim Summary

The evidence and argument presented thus far seem to suggest that the self-concept is highly malleable. Our self-concept can be changed under the same conditions that induce us to change an attitude toward a social issue or modify our beliefs about other aspects of the world. The studies just discussed imply that induced changes in self-presentation lead to induced changes in the self-concept. If I can be tricked into acting in uncharacteristic ways while believing that I had the choice not to, I am likely to internalize some aspects of what I have done and end up judging my uncharacteristic behavior as not so uncharacteristic after all of the real me.

But how important and how lasting are these changes in the daily evolution of self-understanding? How often can we be induced to behave in uncharacteristic ways under precisely the conditions necessary for self-concept change? These are important questions, especially because so much of the history of psychology has emphasized the stability of the self and the difficulties of bringing about constructive educational or therapeutic changes.

In attempting to answer questions about the stability of the self, it is important to sort out several definitional and methodological issues. Perhaps the most stable self-feature is our identity. I am the same person when I wake up in the morning that I was the night before. Oh, yes, I am a little older, I might have been shaken by a bad dream, or a virus might have stolen upon me, but I am not likely to conclude that a stranger inhabits my body. My identity has obviously a considerable degree of continuity over time. I am confronted with a persistent challenge of assimilating new experiences and integrating them with my self-relevant expectancies to achieve new syntheses. The syntheses are new, but they still represent "me." My self-knowledge reflects my experiences — my successes, failures, insights — and represents an accumulated accretion and storage of self-relevant information. My identity evolves slowly, but the changes do not destroy my sense of who I was and whom I seem to be becoming. It is especially important that my identity is anchored in what I do and in my continuing social relationships. I am a professor, a social psychologist, a father, a husband, a grandfather, a colleague, and so on. Each of these roles adds ballast to my identity and provides boundaries that are not readily breached.

Dramatists and ordinary human beings take for granted the continuity of personal identities. It is therefore a matter of special interest and potential high drama when we run across such rare cases of multiple personality as the fictional Dr. Jekyl and Mr. Hyde or the actual case of Eve and her "three faces."

In addition to my identity, anchored in my professional role and social network, I have a *phenomenal self*. Gerard and I defined this as "a person's awareness, arising out of interactions with his environment, of his own beliefs, values, attitudes, the links between them, and their implications for his behavior."[30] In the present context I would emphasize the mixture of stability and change within this phenomenal self. Part of the phenomenal self is our identity, perhaps represented in the original definition by the integrity and coherence of our belief system and our self-definition. But not every aspect of the self is simultaneously available to us. The phenomenal self involves a stable background of identity anchorage, perhaps, but it also involves the differential salience of self-features reflecting the priming of recent and striking events. Our phenomenal self is "tethered" to our identity, but it is also free to move within the tethered boundaries in response to recent experiences and preoccupations. If we attempt to measure the self-concept at a point in time, typically by asking subjects whether or not they endorse adjectives or statements as self-descriptive, we undoubtedly end up with a mixture of the stable and the transient. That's what the phenomenal self is.

Two related questions now become relevant in assessing the evidence I have reported on attitude- and self-esteem change. The first concerns the degree of resistance to self-concept change in general. Are people motivated to protect a particular self-concept so that they take every opportunity to assert and verify the self? And second, if there is evidence of motivated self-verification, how can we reconcile this evidence with the data just presented indicating self-concept change under fairly benign laboratory conditions? Before turning directly to these concerns, however, it is important to deal at least briefly with the issue of egocentric biases in self-perception.

The Egocentric Bias Issue

As the attributional approach evolved and gathered momentum in the 1970s, a major feature was the identification of numerous departures from strict rationality. The most prominent early candidate was egocentric bias, the tendency to color our attributions in ways affected by self-concern or self-interest. I have already noted the important shift from using attribution theory as a source of empirical predictions to using it as a "rational baseline model," effective in isolating errors in judgment and biases in inference. Though correspondence bias is the most prominent example featured in the preceding chapters, the phenomena that one might collect under the label of egocentric bias are so much a part of everyone's naive psychology that they have not received the same attention as a nonobvious violation of rationality.

Before concentrating on some of the variant theories of egocentric bias, some attention should be drawn to additional biases that have been identified and demonstrated. As I have noted previously, we are cognitive misers in the sense that there are pressures to conserve intellectual resources for those moments when they are most needed. These pressures lead to the allocation of routine decisional processes to automatic processing whenever possible, thus permitting conversations while one drives a car, enjoyment of a television show while one knits, and other combinations of mindless and mindful mentation.

This tendency toward automatic processing is vital to normal human functioning, even though it can lead us astray. In a similar fashion, our tendency to develop problem-solving shortcuts and rules of thumb can also get us in trouble. Tversky and Kahneman have identified several heuristics, or strategic decision-making shortcuts, that are widely used.[31] Though it can be assumed that these heuristics are normally helpful in providing useful approximations to the correct solutions for the problems of everyday life, it is easy to trap people into misapplying them. We use the "availability heuristic" when we operate on the assumption that what is most accessible in memory is accessible because of frequency, although there are often other reasons for its accessibility. Thus, we assume that words beginning with *r* are much more frequent than words having *r* as the third letter, when the opposite is the case. We make this mistake because words beginning with *r* are much more accessible, presumably because of the way we read and use dictionaries. Or we apply the "representativeness heuristic," the tendency to assign automatically those instances that seem to typify or represent a social category to that category, ignoring the frequency with which such prototypic instances are likely to fit in other larger or more numerous categories. We may jump to the conclusion that the swarthy Hispanic with long sideburns and narrow eyes is the drug dealer in a police lineup because he fits our image of the prototypical Colombian drug dealer. When we do this, we are very likely to be in error since the vast majority of Hispanics with long sideburns and narrow eyes are not Colombian drug dealers. Furthermore, many other kinds of drug dealers are much more prominent in American cities. The representativeness heuristic involves insufficient sensitivity to population base rates.

These heuristics are among the many unfortunate by-products of the requirements of cognitive economy. Rules of thumb are useful but far from foolproof. We presumably develop heuristics and other simplifying strategies because they usually do not betray us; they free us for more important cognitive work.

The subset of biases referred to as egocentric not only represent a more ancient theme than the heuristic biases, they reflect the supposedly adaptive human tendency for all of us to be concerned, above all else, with our own welfare. Egocentric biases spring from two motives related to the maintenance of self-esteem: (1) a motivated self-reference bias, a sensitivity to events that are relevant to our personal welfare, and (2) a self-serving bias, wishful thinking about ourselves. Let us take up each of these in turn.[32]

Self-Reference Bias

There are undoubtedly important individual differences in the extent to which people think that everything out there is directed toward or concerned with themselves. Otherwise, psychotherapists would not have identified and described those paranoid personalities who wallow in self-reference ideation (e.g., "They are whispering about me," "They are waiting to surprise me"). Granted there is a range from relative detachment to extreme paranoid egocentricism; each of us is probably aware of a special sensitivity to those things in the environment that concern us and seem relevant to our welfare. Out of the gaggle of voices at a cocktail party, we are likely to be sensitive to the mention of our own name in an otherwise unintelligible stream of conversation. Heider clearly recognized this tendency toward egocentric cognition, citing the frequency with which we see ourselves as the focus of other people's actions. "Let us say that change A implies changes B, C, and D. If B is most important to me by virtue of the fact that it has personal effects upon me, then I have a tendency to assume that A was produced in order to bring B about even though C may actually have been the intention."[33]

Keith Davis and I tried to develop this notion further by introducing the concepts of "hedonic relevance" and "personalism."[34] The effects of another's behavior are hedonically relevant when, for whatever reason, they make us feel better or worse about ourselves. If I overhear someone expressing an opinion similar to my own, this support for my views may be hedonically relevant even though the speaker was not aware that I was listening. Personalism refers to the perception that an effect of someone else's actions were definitely intended to help or hurt us. In our discussion of correspondent inference theory, Keith Davis and I proposed that the effects of other actions that affect us positively or negatively would be perceptually fused or joined together as a single effect feeding into the attributional process. There would be a strong tendency to see hedonically relevant effects as intentional, for hedonic relevance to be readily converted into personalism.[35] Though this still makes good intuitive sense to me, no one has been completely successful in demonstrating the precise cognitive consequences of either personalism or hedonic relevance.

My early experiment with Richard deCharms did show that I will perceive someone who lets me down as less dependable than someone who behaves identically but without personal consequences for myself.[36] That finding, however, can be handled without any specific reference to correspondent inference theory.[37] A study by Michael Enzle, Michael Harvey, and Edward Wright comes a little closer in support of our theoretical notions.[38] Subjects observed an interview and learned that the interviewer had given the interviewee a negative rating. Then they were told that the interviewer had rated four previous interviewees rather positively. As would be predicted by Kelley's model,[39] these subjects took the distinctiveness of the event into account and decided that the negative rating revealed something about the particular interviewee rather than the interviewer's personal disposition. Other subjects saw and heard exactly the same information except that *they* were the interviewees. These subjects disregarded the distinctiveness information and decided that the negative rating said quite a bit about the interviewer's rather nasty disposition.

This tendency for hedonic relevance to be easily converted into personalism may be part of a more general tendency to see our relationships in a self-centered way. Michael Ross and Flore Sicoly present several findings indicating that people tend to allocate more responsibility for a group product to themselves than others would allocate to them.[40] This is not necessarily self-serving, since team players not only think that their teamwork contributes more to team victories, but also take more personal blame for team defeats. The tendency extends to such homely enterprises as taking out the garbage. Husbands and wives each claim more responsibility for such household chores than their spouses attribute to them. Each spouse even claims more responsibility for starting arguments with the other!

Although the conformity and social comparison literatures emphasize pressures to uniformity in social life, toward seeing ourselves as similar to others, self-reference bias is consistent with a countertendency toward seeing ourselves as distinctive or unique. C. R. Snyder and Howard Fromkin have tried to capture the "human pursuit of difference," i.e., the desire to be unique, as an individual difference dimension,[41] but none of us probably wishes to think of him- or herself as just a face in the crowd. Melvin Snyder and Robert Wicklund have tried to relate this to a broader concern with control and with freedom of action.[42] We often want to avoid being pinned down by a particular attributional label. In the interest of emphasizing our freedom to be different and to defy the constraints of easy understanding, Snyder and Wicklund suggest that we at times deliberately act in inconsistent ways. This conveys to ourselves as well as to others the message that we are free to engage in a wide range of action, that we are not slaves to particular traits or propensities. In this spirit Snyder and Wicklund explore the circumstances most likely to arouse a motive to act in ways that will prove to be attributionally ambiguous.

Self-Serving Bias

Except in cases where our assumptions of responsibility extend to negative events, it is not easy to distinguish the general self-reference bias from wishful thinking about our abilities and personal characteristics. Nevertheless, the two are conceptually distinct. It is one thing to be self-preoccupied and hypersensitive to the relevance of other's actions to our own welfare; it is another thing to structure our attributions so that they always give us the benefit of the doubt in making us look good. Few would question the general tendency to take more credit for successes than failures, to tailor our attributions, at least when the circumstances are even slightly ambiguous, in ways that will bolster our self-esteem. And there is ample empirical evidence of such tendencies in the psychological literature.[43] There have been attempts to explain self-serving biases in purely cognitive or experiential terms. We intend and expect to succeed, and usually do, if only because we usually don't tackle tasks that offer little chance of success. Therefore, it is not surprising that we attribute success to our efforts and ability and failure to task difficulty or bad luck.[44] I accept this as plausible alternative in some cases, but I see no reason to question the ubiquitous role of the motive to maintain self-esteem. If our readings of naive psychology tell us anything, they tell us that it is human nature to be blame avoidant, to embrace our successes and to externalize our failures — not always, but whenever we can plausibly do so.

A more difficult question is whether we make self-serving attributions for private as well as for public consumption. Do subjects in self-attribution experiments provide self-serving attributions as a way of justifying their experimental actions to others, or do subjects really believe what they are conveying to their experimenters? As Philip Tetlock and Tony Manstead have convincingly argued, it is virtually impossible to distinguish empirically between private and public attributions.[45] The very act of trying to measure attributions means that those attributions are being conveyed to an audience — even if the measures are supposedly anonymous and transmitted only to an experimenter. A recently expressed conclusion seems sensible: "At times we are concerned with explanation, at times with justification; at other times we are concerned with both, and still other times with neither."[46]

But I would still argue that we can go beyond such a conclusion to say something about the conditions favoring explanation over justification, or what we tell ourselves and what we tell others about our responsibility for good and bad events. Depending on particular circumstances, self-presentation motives can move our public self-attributions either in the direction of defensive self-enhancement or in the direction of modesty. I have already discussed some of these pressures in the preceding chapter. I believe it is reasonable to assume that we have learned from bitter experience the importance of realism in our private self-attributions.

When are we likely to be realistic and when are we likely to be self-serving in our private self-attributions? The key lies in what Harold Gerard and I have called "the basic antinomy."[47] We were trying to understand why people are sometimes defensive, distorting their perceptions and inferences in self-enhancing ways, and sometimes vigilant, acutely focused on objective reality. We argued that people tend to be vigilant prior to decisions and defensive after the fact, when there are commitments or outcomes that cannot be changed. The concept of the basic antinomy was formed to emphasize the decision point as a watershed separating these two basic tendencies toward realism and wishful thinking. I'm confident that this distinction is relevant in considering the manner and likelihood of self-serving attributions.

It seems obvious to me that our desire to see ourselves as paragons of talent, wisdom, and virtue has to be tempered by reality. We would court disaster if we constantly involved ourselves in tasks requiring talents that we lack or if we thought our most dedicated competitors were out to help us. Like a politician deciding whether to run for office, one must be realistic about one's chances. Before all of life's important decisions, it is obviously adaptive to be realistic in our self-evaluations. Once the decision has been made, after we have committed ourselves and must proceed with actions that follow through on the commitment, it is understandable that we try to make the best of it. There seems little harm in the self-serving bias that characterizes postdecisional phases, as long as we can effectively segregate decisions and avoid the consequence of self-inflating attributions contaminating subsequent predecisional phases, where vigilance and realism again become important.

Such reasoning does suggest that self-serving attributions may be more immediate and impulsive than are realistic self-assessments. I confess that I have caught myself making self-serving attributions on the tennis court (e.g., my points are deserved; my opponent's are lucky), whereas I can later look back with a more balanced perspective in assessing the relative contributions to victory or defeat of my own abilities, effort, line calls, crosswinds, self-destructive attitude, and so on.

This discussion only scratches the surface of a large and fascinating domain that includes the study of excuses,[48] accounts,[49] self-handicapping,[50] and learned helplessness.[51] Before moving on, however, it is important to note that realistic self-assessments need not be ruthless self-assessments. In fact, some fairly clear evidence has emerged that, in the interests of good mental health, they should, if anything, be shaded in an optimistic direction. Yes, it can be a disaster to take on tasks that we are bound to botch, but it may be worse to entertain such a negative self-view that we never risk failure. Shelly Taylor and Jonathan Brown present impressive evidence concerning the role of illusions about one's positive attributes in contributing to mental health.[52] Optimistic self-evaluations lead to increased motivation, task persistence, and generally more effective performance. Insofar as we are successful in convincing ourselves that we have certain kinds of talents, a range of potential activities may beckon and challenge us. We may quickly learn, of course, that we cannot follow through on the competences we have attributed to ourselves, but we may also succeed in validating attributions about the self that were hitherto based on very ambiguous evidence. Our beliefs in our own competence may lead us to fail, but without them, we would not even attempt to succeed.

Resisting or Accepting Self-Concept Change

In earlier sections of the chapter I focused on various conditions of self-concept change, implicating the role of uncharacteristic behavior in producing shifts in self-esteem. The immediately preceding discussion implies that there are important boundary conditions that normally contain such shifts. To the extent that people engage in self-serving attributions, reconstructing events in their favor, self-esteem seems to be driving other cognitive processes rather than driven by them. Is it possible to reconcile views of self-esteem maintenance and self-protection with experiments that show how self-esteem changes can be induced?

A logical consequence of self-serving attribution bias is that favorable self-concept changes ought to be easier to induce than negative self-concept changes. If negative experiences are effectively rationalized and externally attributed, whereas positive experiences are internally attributed, the results should be a steady escalation of self-esteem. At least this should be the case if positive and negative experiences are comparable in frequency, and we have already suggested that successes are likely to be more common than failures for a variety of reasons. Though one can make this logical case for ever-expanding optimism, there are obvious reality constraints that intervene. In addition, Carolyn Showers has called attention to "defensive pessimism," a widely used strategy that involves expecting the worst so that one can only be pleasantly surprised.[53] As in many of our attempts to conceptualize features of human nature, it seems that whenever there's a yin, there's a yang. In any event we must acknowledge that our self-concepts are at least loosely constrained by memories of past achievements and failures, as well as by the competing pressures of optimism and pessimism.

The very fact that we talk about self-esteem clearly implies that we are not, and can never be, completely neutral about the self. But to what extent are we invested in our current self-concept and to what extent are we therefore resistant to self-concept change? One might suppose that the extent depends on how "satisfied" we are with our current identities, but William Swann puts forth a more radical proposal that is reminiscent of earlier self-consistency theories. He assumes that we develop a strong investment in our identity and will seek opportunities to defend and verify it.

In a series of striking studies, Swann and his students have shown that subjects with strongly held concepts about the self in certain domains will adopt numerous strategies to verify these self-concepts.[54] They will perceive and interpret ambiguous feedback as confirmatory, and when confronting those who have a discrepant impression of their self-concept features, they will act in ways that exaggerate the challenged components of the self-concept. This is not surprising when these components are positively valued, but Swann contends that people will even find ways to verify negative self-conceptions. In one study Swann and Pelham showed that college students with negative self-concepts preferred to room with those who also viewed them unfavorably rather than with those who held a more discrepant — and more positive —

impression of them.[55] More generally, Swann argues, people tend to seek out social situations and opportunity structures where they can be themselves. They will seek out or "gravitate toward social relationships in which they are apt to receive self-confirmatory feedback."[56]

This certainly sounds reasonable to me in the vast majority of cases when we want to verify hard-won self-concept features that we value positively, either because they suggest ability or virtue or because they enhance our sense of distinctiveness. What does not make quite as much intuitive sense is that we would want to verify negative self-conceptions — and especially that we would seek out and prefer to interact with those who have negative opinions about us. Many years ago Steven Jones reviewed the evidence supporting self-esteem theory versus self-consistency theory and concluded that self-esteem theory received more support.[57] Abraham Tesser has impressive support for his "evaluation self-maintenance theory," which proposes a number of strategies by which people maintain a comfortably positive self-evaluation.[58] Claude Steele holds a similar position, emphasizing self-enhancement motives in his "self-affirmation theory."[59] Since self-verification is essentially a self-consistency theory, how can Swann's research and his contentions be reconciled with the vast bulk of research suggesting strong self-enhancement motives?

Swann makes a number of points in an effort to reconcile his findings with the earlier literature:

1. Most people have positive self-conceptions in most domains, and therefore self-verification often masquerades as self-enhancement. It is important to note that Swann picks his negative self-concept subjects from the extreme low end of a large distribution of self-esteem scores made by Texas undergraduates.

2. People feel good in the short run when they have negative self-concepts and receive positive feedback, but they prefer more sustained relations with those who agree with them about their negative qualities. Thus, Swann endorses the idea that those with a negative self-view can affectively enjoy positive feedback while cognitively appreciating those who

are realistic and perceptive in sharing their pessimistic self-view.

3. People don't self-verify a global positive or negative impression; they are concerned with specific positive and negative features of the self-concept, with concrete dimensions or domains.

These reconciling considerations are crucial, and Swann has more recently sought to clarify when people self-enhance and when they self-verify, recognizing that there are basic human tendencies toward both.[60] Clearly, as he puts it, people want to be praised and loved, but they also want their worlds to be stable and predictable. So people are self-enhancing to nourish their self-worth. They are gratified and relieved when they receive favorable feedback about themselves. But people also strive to maintain their self-conceptions and therefore appreciate valid, self-verifying information. A recent study by Swann and associates nicely shows both processes at work.[61] People with either low or high self-esteem indicated a preference for personality feedback concerning positive versus negative self-attributes. However, among those positive and negative self-attributes that they acknowledged, they preferred favorable information about their self-attributed personality assets and negative information about their acknowledged shortcomings.

Though the interplay between self-enhancement and self-verification processes is undoubtedly complex and will remain controversial, I certainly agree that people develop their self-concepts within a network of social relations and find comfort and solace in interacting with those responsible for shaping and defining the self-concept. Our confirmatory opportunity structures do appear to maintain the stability of our self-concept in the real world. Certainly, basic values and ability conceptions are not easily changed, and resistances to therapeutic pressures or political propaganda can be easily documented.[62]

Swann suggests that this confirmatory real world is likely to trivialize any minor self-esteem or self-concept changes that one can bring about in a brief laboratory experiment. Since I have been involved in a number of such laboratory experiments resulting in measures of self-concept change, I can be expected to have some reservations about this conclusion. I do. Laboratory-induced self-concept changes may be transient, but they are not trivial: "If we reliably can produce changes in the laboratory, we gain insight into how such changes can occur in everyday life. One hardly needs to argue any more the general case that induced behavior can affect attitudes. To this general case can be added the many specific cases in which behavior constrained by the situation leads to differences in self-perception that lead to further actions that are committing or reinforced and therefore become part of a process of cumulative and an ultimately very important self-concept change."[63]

The major point I would emphasize is that, both within the laboratory situation and in everyday life, overt behavior and the reactions it elicits from others are crucial. As I hope this chapter has abundantly documented, it is relatively easy to induce either uncharacteristic behavior or new behavior under circumstances such that the power of the induction is unrecognized or underestimated. Such occasions, I would submit, are very common in everyday life. The important questions are how often they occur, how consistent is their implication for identity, and how do others respond to such uncharacteristic or novel actions? Hochschild's work with flight attendants[64] illustrates how role demands in a chosen career eventually become internalized when they are consistent and unrelenting. Even when faced with such recurrent conditions as crowded planes, delayed flights, risky landings, and offensively demanding passengers, flight attendants must remain calm, reassuring, "genuinely" warm, and endlessly cheerful. Interviewed attendants make clear their realization that the role requires sensitivity to inappropriate feelings and vigorous efforts at "feeling work" to bring their emotions into proper alignment with role expectations.[65]

Each of us is aware of occasions when we wonder quite what "made us" say what we did, why we made a particular purchase, or why we declined a particular invitation. These kinds of "uncharacteristic" actions become a little more characteristic when they occur in the absence of obvious external justification. The principles of change demonstrated in the laboratory are hardly irrelevant in the world of everyday social transactions.

Summary and Concluding Remarks

There can be no obvious conclusion, given this glancing blow to the topic of self-knowledge, but I will nevertheless venture a few remarks in the spirit of taking stock. Festinger, Bem, and Schachter have given us provocative new ways to look at the relationships between thought, feeling, and behavior. It is a major part of their legacy that we now take for granted that people can be induced to act in uncharacteristic ways and, under some circumstances, will accommodate perceptions of their new behavior by adjustments in their self-concept. It is easy to forget that this message was strange and controversial not so long ago — and still remains so in some benighted quarters!

This chapter has not emphasized the obvious, more traditional assumptions about self-knowledge. These assumptions are nevertheless important, even though they are not controversial. Each of us is a product of our experiences interacting with genetic endowment. Our self-knowledge is infused with memories of these experiences, how they happened to us and how we reacted to them, whether we came to them or they came to us. Bem's radical proposal aside, we can easily access many of these memories, which then provide a sense of continuous identity, a continuity nevertheless featuring some growth and evolutionary change. We know who we are because, more and more clearly, we know where we've been and what we've done. We have had to make many decisions, and in so doing we have had to develop and draw on our beliefs and values. We've had to decide what is important to us and, chances are, been forced on occasion to analyze why.

I have included this chapter on self-knowledge because no treatment of perceiving others could possibly be complete without some consideration of how we perceive ourselves. Given a framework of person perception as embedded in processes of social interaction, self-perception can be seen as vitally involved in both the initiation and the continuation of any sequence of interaction. We enter interactions with purposes linked to our preferences and values, typically open to any social information that is relevant to self-understanding and typically concerned with the implications of the interaction for our own welfare and self-esteem. As the interaction proceeds, there may or may not be self-concept change. If there is, the change may or may not represent the confirmation or fulfillment of our partner's expectancies. In the final chapter I shall try to flesh out the bare bones of the interaction process presented in Chapter 1 and in doing so shall keep in mind the continuous impact of self-perception on cognitive decisions regarding the intentions and dispositions of the interaction partner.

The

Fate of Expectancies

in Social

Interaction

A distinctive rationale for the present inquiry is the attempt to study the perception of persons as a cognitive activity embedded in the social interaction process. Simply put, I have tried to emphasize a unique characteristic of interpersonal perception: We act while we see, and what we see is in part affected by our own actions. In the introductory chapter I outlined the steps of a typical interaction sequence, a sequence that starts with expectancies of the perceiver, features their alteration or confirmation, and ultimately ends in changes in the target person's self-concept. In this final chapter I should like to consolidate the preceding discussions by focusing on the issues involved in what is known as behavioral confirmation, the circumstances under which one person's false expectancies about another become confirmed by the behavior of that other person. This is sometimes referred to under the older label of the self-fulfilling prophecy — the expectancy is the prophecy, and when it results in confirming behavior, the prophecy fulfills itself.

The concept of self-fulfilling prophecies can be traced to a provocative paper by Robert Merton in 1948. According to Merton, "The self-fulfilling prophecy is, in the beginning, a *false* definition of the situation evoking a new behavior which makes the originally false conception come *true*. The specious validity of the self-fulfilling prophecy perpetuates a reign of error. For the prophet will cite the actual course of events as proof that he was right from the very beginning."[1] Self-fulfilling prophecies have been discussed in a variety of social science contexts, ranging from the effects on stock prices of authoritative forecasts to escalating cycles of mutual arms buildup in international relations.[2] In cases like these one person's (or one nation's) prophecies or expectations result in actions that trigger off confirmatory reactions. Thus, when country A expects country B to be hostile and threatening, A may divert more of its gross national product to "defensive" armaments. Country B interprets this buildup as a threat to its survival, thus diverting more of *its* capital to arms. This buildup is then interpreted by A as an independent confirmation of its initial expectancy.[3]

The self-fulfilling prophecy paradigm cries out for the application of experimental design logic. Some perceivers must be randomly given false expectancies while others are not. The ultimate interest is in whether the behavior of randomly designated target persons is affected by the presence of the expectancy in such a way as to confirm it. Without such experimental comparisons it is difficult to ensure that the confirming action would not have occurred in the absence of the false expectancy. In the arms race example there is no way of showing what country B would have done if country A did not escalate its own armaments.

Robert Rosenthal and Lenore Jacobson were the first to apply this experimental logic in the study manipulating teacher expectations of their students' performance.[4] The teachers in their study were led to believe that some of their students were late bloomers, likely to show spurts of high performance in the future. Although the students so designated were actually randomly chosen, they in fact did better subsequently than did students who were not designated late bloomers. This study became quite controversial and was attacked on several methodological grounds. Follow-up studies did not always confirm the Rosenthal and Jacobson results, but there seems little question that performance effects can vary with teacher expectations. In a review of fifteen years of research on such effects, Rosenthal and Rubin concluded that some sort of teacher expectancy effect occurred in approximately two-thirds of the 345 studies they reviewed.[5]

It is hard to see why there should be any controversy about the possibility that teacher reactions could affect the level of student performances. Although the Rosenthal and Jacobson study and other early investigations did not focus on mediating processes, one can well imagine that the teachers paid more attention to the late bloomers, gave them more challenging work, reinforced them more strongly when they succeeded, encouraged them more when they failed, and so on.

More pertinent to our present purposes, and also capturing the mediating behavior to some extent, is a well-known study by Mark Snyder and his colleagues.[6] These investigators showed how a fairly benign set of stereotypes based on physical attractiveness can function to influence social interactions in such a way as to produce behavioral confirmation of the stereotype. Male undergraduates carried out a get-acquainted telephone conversation with female undergraduates. There was one deceptive intervention: Males were given pictures of their female partners that were actually pictures of another female who was either very attractive physically or rather unattractive. The pictures, designed to establish a particular kind of expectancy, were dealt to the males by random assignment. Raters who later listened to tapes of the interaction judged males who thought they were interacting with an attractive female to be more friendly, open, and sociable than were those who thought they were interacting with an unattractive female. Furthermore, these different interaction patterns were generally reciprocated by the females, who were unaware that any pictures were involved in the reaction of the male at the other end of the telephone line. Thus, they were judged by another set of raters to be more gregarious, poised, sociable, and self-confident. Loosely interpreted, at least, these differences in female behavior must have had the effect of confirming the males' stereotype that attractive females are poised and friendly whereas unattractive females are rather awkward and aloof.

To what extent are the underlying processes of behavioral confirmation at work in interpersonal perception? When and why do a perceiver's expectancies ultimately bring about confirming actions in a target person, actions that would not have occurred in the absence of the expectancy that predicted them? Conceptually, a two-step sequence is obviously involved as a minimal condition of the self-fulfilling prophecy. The crucial thing about this sequence is that it jumps the gap between perceiver A and target person B:

1. A's expectancy about B affects A's behavior toward B.

2. A's behavior toward B affects B's behavior in such a way that it confirms A's expectancy.

Let us now examine what conditions are necessary for such a particular sequence of events to occur.

The Perceiver

Effects of Perceivers' Expectancies on Their Behavior

In Chapter 4 I presented a discussion of expectancy effects, focusing on the ways in which people cope with information that does not completely fit with preexisting expectations. The distinction between category-based and target-based expectancies was introduced, along with considerable evidence to support the proposition that perceivers will perceive or interpret ambiguous information in a biased manner, assimilating the information in such a way as to make it more compatible with the expectancy. This is especially true, it was argued, when target-based expectancies are involved. Thus, there is general support for one important effect of prior expectancies: Once an expectancy is established, it is likely to be maintained because there is a bias toward perceptual confirmation.

Actually, confirmation bias may involve a mixture of cognitive assimilation and biased data gathering. Perceptual or cognitive assimilation is a well-established phenomenon,[7] one that is built into Trope's dual-process theory of attribution and contained in many other theories of schemas, categories, and stereotypes. I include under the heading of cognitive assimilation those instances in which anomalous or ambiguous data are explained in ways that render them more consistent with expectations. Biased data gathering is not as well documented, but Mark Snyder and his colleagues have provided several examples of its occurrence. The study most often cited is an experiment showing that when subjects are asked to discover whether a particular target person is extraverted, they chose to ask questions that one would inevitably answer in an extraverted manner. Thus, when introverts were confronted with questions like "What would you do if you wanted to liven things up at a party?" even they sounded extraverted in trying to come up with an answer. Other subjects were asked to choose interview questions that would give them the best chance of discovering whether the other student was an introvert. They chose questions like "What factors make it hard for you to really open up to people?" Again, even extraverts can probably come up with an answer to this question that will make them look introverted.[8]

Trope and Bassok contested the generality of this finding of biased (confirmatory) data gathering.[9] They were able to show that people will prefer truly diagnostic information if the alternatives are clearly presented and subjects are not constrained by the kinds of questions available. More recently, Swann and Guiliano have found support for the initial Snyder and Swann position, showing that subjects will spontaneously generate hypothesis-confirming questions as well as retain hypothesis-confirming information better than disconfirming information.[10] Although the issue and the determining conditions have not been decisively determined, it appears that unless specific diagnostic questions are provided, expectancies can affect one's information-gathering behavior, as well as one's perceptions and interpretations of the information that is available.

But how do expectancies affect the bearer's behavior when the bearer is not specifically instructed to gather diagnostic information? A number of interesting possibilities emerge that affect what, whether, or when self-fulfilling prophecies will occur. Here, I believe, expectancy content may be crucial. Most of the experiments dealing with potential behavior confirmation effects have been specifically designed to demonstrate the existence of such effects in a variety of interesting domains, such as teacher–student interactions, telephone conversations between prospective dates, settings of bargaining and negotiation, and so on. Perhaps quite unwittingly, the investigators in these studies chose domains and specific procedures that would most likely yield self-fulfilling prophecies rather than other alternatives (including, indeed, self-defeating prophecies). These studies, in other words, speak more to the question of whether self-fulfilling prophecies *can* happen than to any questions concerning their frequency, prominence, or importance in everyday life.

To appreciate the role of expectancy content, it may help to consider the null case: What kinds of expectancies would *not* be likely to affect the actions of the expectancy holder? If one were to pursue this question, it would obviously make an important difference whether or not a lasting interaction was anticipated. If we assume that such prospects are at least unclear, we can make some initial headway by specifying expectancy types falling on a dimension ranging from strongly determinative to weakly determinative effects on perceiver behavior.

At the strongly determinative end, I would include those expectancies directly linked to affect and its expression. If I expect you to be a very anxious and unpredictable person, this expectancy may lead me to be quite skittish or anxious in return. If I am told that you are a very warm and friendly person, it is likely that I'll behave in a warm and friendly manner. At the other, weakly determinative end, there is undoubtedly a wide range of expectancies that have no effect on the expectancy holder's actions, especially in the case of casual

short-run interactions, those not expected to result in persist-
ing relationships. Consider the following illustrative expectancies:

He may be gay

She is probably not dependable in a pinch

She appears to be deeply religious

I am told he cheats at games

In each case, those who hold these expectancies would not act
differently toward the expectancy targets than would those
who do not hold them—assuming, of course, that the hypothetical characteristics are not rendered particularly relevant
by the interaction context itself. Thus, my expectancy that
John is inclined to cheat may definitely have an effect on my
actions toward him when we play a game of tennis or bridge.
Unless the context is specifically relevant to the disposition,
however, the expectancies involved are not of the sort that
elicit specific behavioral reactions, regardless of one's private
feelings. If experimenters had chosen to implant these or similar expectancies in their initial study of self-fulfilling prophecy
effects, my hunch is that they would have been discouraged
and that our present view of such effects would contain considerably more skepticism.

The Behavioral Consequences
of Behavior

The next step is to consider how the target person's behavior is
affected by the perceiver's behavior. It is important to remember that the actions of target persons are affected by more
than the preceding actions of the perceivers with whom they
are interacting. In Chapter 7 I considered the crucial role of
interaction goals as behavioral determinants. Obviously, such
roles provide an important context for interpreting and react-
ing to actions of the perceiver. Thus, even if an employer
behaves toward Susan in a hostile manner, she may for strate-

gic reasons respond with a docile, friendly overture. Under other circumstances and with other interaction goals, she might be much more likely to respond in an equally hostile manner.

• **Three Interaction Scripts** In spite of this caveat, it seems useful to distinguish three "scripts" that are likely to guide a target person's reactions to the expectancy-linked actions of a perceiver. *Reciprocation scripts* are perhaps the most common features of social interaction since they call for a kind of tit for tat. If you smile at me, I am very likely to smile at you. Frowns elicit frowns. The use of hostile maneuvers in a competitive game is likely to elicit hostile maneuvers in the recipient.[11] Reciprocation scripts seem to be activated by considerations of approach and avoidance or considerations of challenge and threat versus comfort and security. Behavioral confirmation is presumably very common when such considerations are prominent. They almost guarantee that a reputation for friendliness or hostility, deserved or not, will generate behaviors eliciting confirmatory reactions.

Complementarity scripts, on the other hand, call for reactions that are different from — indeed, in a sense the opposite of — the actions that preceded them. In most interaction contexts, assertive actions produce submissive responses, whereas submissive and tentative actions often elicit take-charge behavior in others. If a perceiver is led to believe that her teammate is a submissive type, she may try to complement the partner's submissiveness by her own assertive action. The obverse might be true if the perceiver expects a teammate to be very domineering. In fact, Keith Davis was able to demonstrate the playing out of complementarity in an experiment in which cooperative pairs were given (randomly assigned) clues about the assertiveness or submissiveness of their partners. Related attribute polarities, such as nurturance and succorance, presumably lend themselves in the same way to behavior confirmation.[12]

Expectancies that normally lend themselves to complementarity scripts may be more sensitive to contextual factors than expectancies eliciting reciprocation scripts. Indeed, another condition in Davis's experiment involved the subjects in a competitive interaction. Under these competitive conditions, where each subject was to be judged on his own ability to come up with the best reasons to support a jointly shared position, subjects who believed that they were confronting an assertive competitor became more assertive themselves, and those with a submissive expectancy were noticeably laid back and polite.

Finally there are what I will call *accommodation scripts*, which arise when I try to adjust my behavior to your apparent needs. If I am told you are stupid, I will speak more slowly and use shorter words. If I am told you are hard of hearing, I will speak more loudly. If I think you are an extremely sensitive person, I will shy away from topics known to upset squeamish people. Berna Skrypnek and Mark Snyder provide an experimental example showing the role of stereotypes in triggering off an accommodation script.[13] Male subjects were required to negotiate a division of tasks with an unseen experimental partner. The tasks were either stereotypical masculine or feminine tasks. When the subjects were led to believe that their partner was female, they managed to induce the target to choose a greater number of "feminine" tasks than when they thought the partner was a male, or when no gender label was applied. In this case, then, the subjects thought they were accommodating to the gender of their partners, but in the process they could easily end up more convinced than ever that this person was a truly feminine female or a truly masculine male.

In general, however, the consequence of accommodative reactions for behavioral confirmation is not consistent. In many cases, the target person's accommodative behavior says little about him- or herself and more about a responsiveness to social norms. Such reactions confirm the *perceiver's* self-view without providing any useful information about the target person.

The preceding discussion gives us some idea of the role of expectancy content as a determinant of behavioral confirmation. The main message I am trying to deliver is that behavioral confirmation of a perceiver's expectancy can occur only if the expectancy affects behavior and that behavior in turn affects the target person's behavior in a confirming direction. These are two of the necessary conditions, but they may not be sufficient. Sufficiency depends on the attributions of the perceiver, how he or she interprets the expectancy-confirming behavior of the target person. First, I shall invite you to reconsider various relevant aspects of the attribution process. Then I shall move on to consider the target person's role and his or her control over behavioral decision processes.

Interpreting Confirmatory Behavior

The essence of the self-fulfilling prophecy is that behavioral evidence consistent with a perceiver's expectancy is treated by the perceiver as independently confirming. The pathology implied is that a false hypothesis generates a sequence of behavioral events that provide hypothesis-confirming evidence and the hypothesis holder does not realize or sufficiently appreciate the causal role of the hypothesis. I have already considered abundant indications of correspondence bias when there is perceiver-induced constraint. My ringing conclusion was that perceivers are notoriously poor at discounting their own behavioral impact on the confirmatory reactions of others. Indeed, if perceivers-while-acting were acutely aware of their eliciting role and drew the appropriate attributional conclusions, there would be no self-fulfilling prophecies—at least in the eyes of the engaged perceiver or in the eyes of passive observers insufficiently aware of the perceiver's constraining behavior. Unfortunately, as we have seen, even when perceivers are aware of their constraining influence, they do not take this sufficiently into account when they are asked about a target person's dispositions.

A study by Roy Baumeister and his associates forcefully reinforces this point.[14] Protagonist subjects induced to present themselves either favorably or modestly to an interaction partner succeeded in establishing a norm for the pattern of partner responses. In other words, their partners responded with similar levels of self-enhancing or self-deprecating behavior. However, although the role-playing protagonists were quite aware of altering their own behavior to fulfill the assigned experimental task, they failed to take this into account when evaluating their partners. Instead, the role-playing protagonists inferred their partner's true self-esteem levels directly from their responsive (i.e., strongly induced) behavior in the interaction.

Nevertheless, one might reasonably expect variations in the degree of correspondence as a function of attributional context and expectancy content. Attributional ambiguity should vary with the presence or absence of all forms of situational constraint, not just those featured in the situation created by the perceiver. Target persons may be acting in response to strong normative pressures, and perceivers must attempt to sort these out in applying the logic of the great trade-off between persons and situations. In spite of their relative insensitivity to such normative pressures, perceivers are not likely to ignore them completely. A warm and friendly person in a competitive situation is likely to be judged as more warm and friendly than the same person behaving in the same fashion in a cooperative setting, regardless of the perceiver's own behavioral input.

This example obliquely suggests the role of expectancy content again, specifically the degree of control that a target person has over particular response patterns. In general, persons have considerable control over the expression of attitudes, preferences, levels of personal enthusiasm, aspects of mood, and social orientation (for example, whether to be warm and friendly). People have considerably less control over performances that are closely linked to ability. It is difficult for a truly stupid person to appear brilliant, one who is tone deaf can hardly be expected to carry a Gershwin tune, and it is hard to imagine a poorly coordinated person performing the complex maneuvers required for the pole vault or the balance beam. On the other hand, it is not too difficult to appear cheerful when one is depressed, or to shade one's opinions toward perceived consensus. Perceivers should presumably be more cautious in drawing confident attributional inferences from behavior under the control of a target person than when confronting performances associated with the less ambiguous attributes of personal ability.

A similar issue concerns the relationship between expectancy content and the target person's *opportunity* for disconfirmation. There are many classes of expectancies that, once established, are very difficult to disconfirm, because they do not lend themselves to frequent tests or the tests themselves are not reliable. If someone has suggested to you that I am a coward, I would have a difficult time disabusing you of this slander in the normal course of events. It is not every day that I will have an opportunity to rescue a child from a burning building or confront a 250-pound bully. Similarly, though for somewhat different reasons, if you think I am dishonest, I will have great difficulty convincing you otherwise. Most people are honest most of the time, especially when under surveillance, and behavioral manifestations of my unrelieved honesty are normally under my own control.

Certain expectancies, such as warmth, friendliness, and persistence, gain their strength from behavioral averaging. Others like courage, dishonesty, and high ability can be established by a single instance. Glenn Reeder and Marilyn Brewer have made the interesting observation that some attribute – behavior linkages are quite asymmetrical; ability-linked attributions are generally of this type.[15] Thus, if you entertain the hypothesis that I am very smart, I can do and say a lot of stupid things before you will relinquish the hypothesis. But if you think I am stupid, as I have noted above, one undeniably brilliant performance might change your mind.

The Perceiver's Interaction Goals

It is important to remember that perceivers are not always and inevitably concerned above all else with valid diagnostic information processing. Most perceivers don't think of themselves as perceivers; they are merely actors swept up in questions of what was just said and what the response should be. Perceivers clearly have many things on their minds, and they have many purposes for engaging in social interaction.

The potential role of interaction goals is nicely demonstrated in a study by John Darley and his colleagues.[16] Subjects anticipated a game modeled after the "$25,000 Pyramid," a television game show in which a sender transmits clues to a receiver who then must give the correct answer. Experimental subjects were told that they would hold brief conversations with several potential partners. They were led to believe that the first of these conversational partners was not likely to perform well under pressure (according to a particular psychological test). The ensuing (simulated) conversation, one that involved audiotaped answers to questions that had been preselected by the subject, revealed the target person to be either a frantic or a composed person. The investigator's crucial interest was in whether the subjects would, in pursuit of their interaction goal of choosing a suitable partner, ask the kinds of questions that would reveal whether the potential partner was likely to perform appropriately under pressure — in other words, whether their initial frantic expectancy would be disconfirmed by the answers of the "composed" target person.

Control subjects went through the same procedures thinking that the experimenter was interested in vocal patterns during casual conversations. Thus, they did not have any particular interaction goals motivating them to assess the validity of their expectancies.

The results showed that the subjects with the interaction goals of choosing the best partner did ask more expectancy-relevant questions designed to get at performance under pressure. When these questions elicited the "composed" target person answers, furthermore, the subjects clearly discarded their initial impression, which had been introduced by the expectancy manipulation. These results are summarized by Figure 9-1.

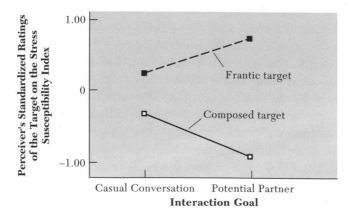

FIGURE 9-1   Perceivers' ratings of the target on the stress susceptibility index. (From Darley, Fleming, Hilton, and Swann, 1988.)

This is one of those studies that might be dismissed as a clever feat of experimental engineering. Subjects are given a negative expectancy ("not good under pressure") and an opportunity to check on its validity. When they are motivated to do so, with an interaction goal of picking a suitable partner, they seize the opportunity. Subsequently, as a function of the programmed characteristics of the target person, they learn whether the expectation is confirmed or disconfirmed. This is all very understandable once the operations are spelled out, but the study is important in demonstrating that perceivers may or may not break through the normal constraints of interaction to elicit those kinds of information that are directly relevant to a negative expectancy. The results are interesting because subjects in the control condition behave the way most of us do most of the time, confirming the important general proposition that negative expectancies will often be maintained unless perceivers are specifically motivated to assess their validity.

The Target Person

Obviously, as I have been at pains to emphasize in several of the preceding chapters, target persons are not inevitably the passive victims of erroneous expectancies. They have their own interaction goals and (typically) an overarching concern with the impression they are creating. We already know, from Swann's research on self-verification, that people do not like to be misconstrued. In fact, they will respond to obvious misconstruals by fighting back, by doing whatever it takes to disconfirm the erroneous expectancy. For example, in one study this took the form of exaggerating one's "true characteristics" in order to undermine the false expectancy.[17]

The study by Darley and his colleagues does not concern the interaction goals of a target person, but there is no reason why the strategic objectives of target persons would not affect their responses to probes and queries by a perceiver. A study by Linda Ginzel demonstrates this possibility in an experiment involving complex patterns of role-playing instructions conveyed separately to two naive subjects.[18] Target persons prepared and delivered a brief speech suggesting some of the business implications of a Shakespearean play. For example, they were encouraged to expand on the suggestion that *King Lear* might be used to consider those factors that could cause a leader to delegate authority to someone other than the "right person" for the job. After delivering their speeches, target persons were asked by perceiver subjects to evaluate their own performances; the perceiver subjects were given questions to ask that were clearly biased either to elicit positive or negative information from the performer. Unbeknownst to the perceiver subjects, the performers were instructed to respond to the perceiver's questions in such a way as to come across as highly likable in one condition and highly competent in another. The resulting answer patterns were distinctly different. Ingratiating subjects came across as modest and self-deprecating. They challenged those questions asking for positive information and went along with questions asking for self-criticism. Self-promoters, on the other hand, challenged the premise of questions biased in the negative direction and gave enthusiastic responses to questions asking for "what went right."

Similar challenges to perceiver questions were observed in a study by Nancy Schoenberger.[19] Here, the interaction goal of the target person was not implanted by experimental instructions; it was implicit in the subject's own level of self-esteem. High-self-esteem and low-self-esteem undergraduates were interviewed concerning a number of mundane college experiences. At a critical point during the interview, the interviewer introduced a series of personal questions that were loaded either to elicit positive or negative self-evaluative information. Subjects responded very differently to these questions as a function of their level of self-esteem. In line with Swann's self-verification theme, high-self-esteem subjects showed a definite tendency to transform the negative questions into positive ones. Low-self-esteem subjects showed just the opposite tendency; they readily answered the negative questions but tended to challenge the premises of the positively oriented questions before attempting to answer them.

Neither of the preceding sets of results was embedded in a full-fledged self-fulfilling prophecy study, since neither was preceded by the introduction of a false expectancy. I have introduced them because they document the potential activity of target persons in following through on certain agendas, even when this involves challenges or transformations of the constraints imposed by a perceiver's eliciting behavior—in this case loaded questions. So target persons can be motivated to confront and disagree with those who seem intent on constraining them to respond in uncharacteristic ways. This is all that is necessary to make the important point that many prophecies will not lead to their own self-fulfillment.

A crucial variable affecting the degree of self-fulfillment is whether a perceiver's constraining behavior is clearly seen as linked to an expectancy that the target person is motivated to refute. Usually, one assumes, expectancies are not announced; they are implied in subtle ways in the complex process of negotiating an identity. I have already considered the variable relationship between perceiver expectancies and perceiver behavior, and it is obvious that a target person cannot go out of his or her way to refute a misconstrual if the target person does not realize that there has been one.

The importance of expectancy knowledge is documented in a study by James Hilton and John Darley.[20] Some perceivers were led to believe that their future interaction partners had a cold personality, while others held no such expectancy. Crosscutting this variation, some target persons were told that their (perceiver) partners expected them to be cold, while other target persons were not given expectancy information. The results, summarized in Figure 9-2, showed that target persons who were told that the perceiver had a negative or invidious expectancy about them were able to overcome this expectancy in the interaction process. When target persons were not informed about the expectancies held by the perceiver, however, they were unable to pick up any implicit clues, and expectancy confirmation was the general result.

This study reminds us of a very important consideration, one with which I shall conclude this section. An important characteristic of most social interactions is that they are governed by certain rules or norms of disclosure and by some powerful constraints on challenges and confrontation. In Chapter 7 I reviewed Goffman's rather pessimistic treatment

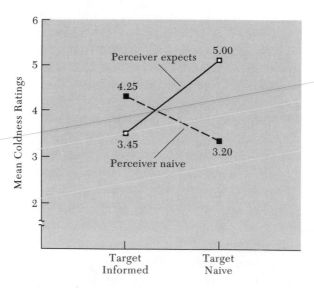

FIGURE 9-2   Perceivers' rating of targets on the warm/cold scale when they expect a cold partner or when they are naive. (From Hilton and Darley, 1985).

of social interactions as settings of danger. Both parties to the interaction normally have an interest in preventing disruption and hope to push the interaction forward without gaffes or embarrassment. There is a strong tendency toward mutual face saving, and an important implication of this is that target persons will often refrain from challenging or correcting perceivers, even when they feel that they are being misunderstood. This is especially the case when the misunderstanding is not so far fetched or insulting as to be intrinsically disruptive, and when the relationship is a casual and transient one. If we do not anticipate an enduring relationship with someone, it hardly seems worthwhile to argue about the impression he or she has of us, especially since the nature of the impression is seldom disclosed, and when it is disclosed, it is typically disclosed only in misleading and disguised ways. As I have said elsewhere: "If the perceiver says, 'I bet you're a Leo,' it's easy to correct him and say, 'no I'm a Taurus,' but many impressions are not that easily identified and corrected. Challenging a false impression normally requires at least a slight disruption of the conversational flow ('what did you mean?'), an attempt to characterize the error ('you must think I'm . . . '), and marshalling of evidence to dispute it ('I'll have you know I was voted the most likely to . . .'). . . . Unless serious negative consequences follow from the erroneous impression, it is the line of least resistance to proceed as if the error had not been surmised."[21] All of which makes me think of the many times I have not corrected a tradesperson or a casual acquaintance who referred to me as Smith or Brown instead of Jones.

The preceding leads us back to a consideration of how common self-fulfilling prophecies are in everyday life. I have already expressed my suspicion that the literature may be badly biased in their favor, simply because the first generation of behavioral confirmation studies were in fact designed to demonstrate the reality of the phenomenon rather than document its extent or analyze the circumstances that favor it. Darley and his associates share my suspicion on this score, but they also provide some basis for expecting prophecies to be confirmed more often than they are disconfirmed.[22] They imagine a six-cell table, composed of two interaction goals (to reach a valid diagnosis as opposed to getting in and out of an interaction without embarrassment) and three cross-cutting sets of target characteristics: expectancy–consistent, expectancy–violating, and ambiguous:

	Diagnose	*Get in and out*
1. Expectancy–consistent	SFP	SFP
2. Ambiguous	SFP	SFP
3. Expectancy–violating	*No SFP*	SFP

Assuming that ambiguous information is normally assimilated to the expectancy, self-fulfilling prophecies will occur in five of the six cells. Only when the perceiver is motivated to find out the target person's relevant characteristics, and only when the target person's characteristics clearly disconfirm the expectancy, will the prophecy not fulfill itself. (Alas, there is no easy way to determine the relative frequency of instances in each of these six cells in everyday interactions.)

Self-Concept Changes

In the preceding chapter I considered the conditions of self-concept change (as well as resistance to change!) at some length. Here, I return to the same phenomena within the self-fulfilling prophecy context. An expectancy or prophecy can confirm itself without any ultimate change in the target person's self-concept. That is, you can get me to behave in line with your false expectancy, perhaps, but it does not necessarily follow that I will change my view of myself to accommodate this uncharacteristic behavior. We know from the theory and experiments of cognitive dissonance that behaviors that are highly constrained do not create the conditions for attitude, or self-concept, change. Cooper and Fazio tell us that dissonance will only occur when there is some feeling of personal responsibility for actions that implicate the self in an aversive way[23] —or, in the present context, actions that fall in the target person's latitude of rejection.

In the preceding chapter I also considered a slightly different alternative to dissonance theory involving self-perception: Without imputing any motive to reduce the unpleasant state of cognitive dissonance, people do make decisions about their dispositional attributes by observing and reflecting on their own recent behavior. Self-perception and dissonance theories both contain important references to situational constraint. Not only do highly constraining situations not produce dissonance, they remove any logical requirement for self-attribution in order to accommodate one's behavior. Bem is very clear in his insistence that "manded" behaviors (i.e., those required because of the situation) do not implicate dispositional characteristics of the actor.[24] Thus, the two related theories of uncharacteristic action share an obvious consistency with the great trade-off principle of attribution theory; that is, what is attributed to situational constraints need not be attributed to the person, in this case, the self.

As we zoom in on episodes of social interaction when behavior confirmation does occur, the issue of self-concept change hinges on whether the target person's expectancy-confirming actions can be readily attributed to situational pressures or whether they reflect an important degree of personal responsibility on his part. How does the target person decide that he has been forced to act in an uncharacteristic way? According to the earlier discussions of situational constraint (especially in Chapter 5), one important key would seem to be the degree of perceived consensus. This perception could involve either explicit or implicit social comparisons; the target person may or may not have the benefit of observing whether others have responded in the same fashion in the same circumstances. Even when deprived of such explicit social comparison information, the target person can use indirect clues to infer what the consensus would be and how others would respond in the same situation. On such extrapolations may hang the fate of potential self-concept change.

Research on this issue is sparse, but a study by Dianne Tice illustrates how actors can use such indirect information to attribute their own constrained actions to self or situation.[25] Tice arranged an experimental situation in which the subject was induced to act in a particular way and clues were then provided concerning the reactions of similar and dissimilar others in the same setting. Tice reasoned that if similar persons behaved like the subject, the subject would make a dispositional self-attribution. If dissimilar people behaved the same way, on the other hand, subjects would be drawn to a situational attribution.

Borrowing an experimental situation previously shown to inhibit sociable conversation,[26] Tice arranged for subjects to wait in the hall prior to the experiment. They were soon joined by an experimental confederate, presented to them as another subject, who discouraged conversation by turning away from the subject and reading a book. In all but a few cases the subjects waited quietly and did not speak, a perfectly appropriate response in this contrived situation. After three minutes of silence, the experimenter summoned the subject and immediately acknowledged that the person in the hall was a confederate; the experimenter went on to say that she was interested in whether the subject initiated any conversation with the confederate. Since no conversations had taken place, the subjects were usually led to recognize that they had not been sociable or gregarious. The main experimental question was whether they attributed their behavior to an introverted disposition or to the situation.

By a convincing series of ruses,[27] subjects were led to believe that their own withdrawn behavior was characteristic of prior subjects who were similar to them or dissimilar to them on a variety of personality dimensions. By comparing various combinations of similar and dissimilar predecessor reactions in the same experimental situation, it became clear that subjects' attributions (to their own introversion or to the situation) were more affected by the observed reactions of dissimilar than by those of similar others. Thus subjects who saw *dissimilar* predecessors speak to the confederate rated themselves as more introverted in general than did those who saw dissimilar predecessors remain silent (as they themselves had been silent). Actions of *similar* others had an obverse— but much less powerful—impact on self-evaluations. Only when similar predecessors were silent and dissimilar ones were talkative did subjects clearly see themselves as introverted.

The muted impact of similar others seems reasonable when we realize that a similar other behaving like us is attributionally ambiguous; perhaps this is because of our shared dispositions, but it might be a function of the situation, unless there is additional evidence that dissimilar people are inclined to behave differently. A final feature of Tice's results was that subjects induced by the dissimilarity manipulation to rate themselves relatively introverted or relatively extraverted also tended to *behave* in line with these manipulated self-concepts. Thus, the experimentally created introverts sat further away from the interviewer and spoke less than those induced to see themselves as more extraverted.

Russell Fazio and his colleagues obtained a comparable set of findings.[28] Subjects in the course of an interview were asked questions systematically biased to elicit introverted responses (e.g., "What things do you dislike about loud parties?") or extraverted responses (e.g., "What would you do if you wanted to liven things up at a party?"). Subjects' subsequent self-descriptions showed the intended effects of this interview manipulation, with the former subjects rating themselves as more introverted. More intriguing were some subsequent behavioral data. After the interview, subjects were led to a waiting room where a confederate recorded whether the subject initiated a conversation and noted how far from her the subject placed her chair. Combined measures of waiting-room sociability confirmed the experimentally engineered self-ratings. Those who were induced to answered biased interview questions in an extraverted direction later tended to sit closer to, and converse more volubly with, the confederate.

One does not have to stretch too far beyond the results of the Tice and Fazio experiments to see a final piece in the self-fulfilling prophecy puzzle. If we imagine these induced changes in overt behavior as part of an ongoing sequence of interaction, it seems clear that induced behavior can not only confirm a perceiver's expectancy but also be internalized by the target person, who will then continue to confirm these expectancies, even in the absence of continuing constraint. This suggests one way in which the self-fulfilling prophecy can be sustained. New behaviors are induced and tentatively internalized, followed by additional new behaviors consistent with the induction. These new behaviors not only confirm the perceiver's initial expectancy, they may be reinforced by the perceiver through further expectancy-enhanced assumptions and labeling processes. The tentative extravert may thus end up finding that it is socially disruptive to be anything else.

Concluding Remarks

In conclusion, I have tried in this and the preceding chapters to convince the reader that it is relevant and realistic to look at how we perceive and understand others in the context of ongoing social interactions with them. Such an "embedded" view of person perception is not only relevant and realistic but useful in pointing to numerous areas of tractable research potential. At each stage of the acquaintance process there are fascinating questions whose answers we are just beginning to divine. Our perceiver comes to the interaction with various "priors" or preconceptions about the interaction partner. These inevitably confront and must be brought to terms with the behavior of the other partner, but this behavior is not independent of the perceiver's eliciting actions. The partner also has preconceptions. Both parties to the interaction have goals that each hopes will be reached—or at least not disturbed—by the interaction. Perhaps they will proceed to interact and then disengage without any lasting consequences. But perhaps one or the other or both will be affected to see themselves differently as an ultimate consequence of being seen incorrectly by others. This is but one of many possible outcomes, but it is one that especially dramatizes the significance that many of our interactions have for personal assessments resulting either in change or in renewed affirmation of the self-concept.

I have not directly addressed questions about the personal value of learning how better to read the dispositional implications of others' behavior. It is always tempting to argue that improving everyone's "diagnostic accuracy" would be good for society and a healthy thing for personal relationships. Certainly there are many kinds of interpersonal misunderstandings that contribute to conflict and tension—and therefore to common themes in fiction and drama. Such misunderstandings, many writers and dramatists want us to understand, can hardly serve as the healthy foundation for a long-term or intimate relationship.

And yet there are undoubtedly times and instances when misunderstandings—or at least failures of complete understanding—can facilitate cohesiveness, cooperation, and eventually interpersonal happiness. It is not always wise to be preoccupied with the values and motives and traits of others. Not only can this get in the way of effective action, but the preceding chapters have identified some of the specific occasions favoring attributional ambiguity.

In a very general sense, however, I believe that our social lives are more comfortably and firmly grounded by a more sophisticated understanding of how interpersonal surfaces reflect personal depths. In addition, our social lives are thereby enriched. What can be more fascinating than the games of insight into others and ourselves? I hope that I am not alone in becoming more intrigued by the mysteries of interpersonal perception, the more I think I have discovered about the processes involved.

Notes

Chapter 1

1. A primary assumption of my approach is that interpersonal perception is grounded in attributions of the causes of behavior. This book is intended to spell out what the "attributional approach" (Heider, 1958; Jones and Davis, 1965; Kelley, 1967; Jones, Kanonse, Kelley, et al., 1971–1972) has to tell us about how people perceive each other.

2. The concept of interaction goals was introduced by Jones and Thibaut (1958).

3. Swann (1984).

4. An argument advanced by Wright and Dawson (1988).

5. This follows similar attempts by others and myself: R. A. Jones (1977); Darley and Fazio (1980); E. E. Jones (1986).

6. Resemblances between this fictitious example and the one presented in Chapter 1 of Jones, Farina, Hastorf, et al. (1984) are not entirely coincidental. There the emphasis was more on the interweaving of information about a stigmatizing condition into the processes of interaction and impression formation.

7. The best recent review of the literature on physical attractiveness and personal attraction is by Hatfield and Sprecher (1986). See also Huston and Levinger (1978); Berscheid (1985).

8. A provocative discussion by McArthur (1982) is a promising beginning. She discusses some of the major theoretical links between physical characteristics and stereotype formation by emphasizing the roles of categorization and salience — topics discussed in Chapter 4. She is more concerned with the possibilities of physical distinctiveness and similarities than with physical attractiveness as an appearance cue.

9. But my experience may not apply in the realm of heterosexual dating. Mathes (1975) found that attractiveness actually increased in importance on subsequent dates.

CHAPTER 2

1. An excellent summary of early research on the recognition of emotion and judgmental accuracy may be found in Tagiuri (1969).

2. Many of these experiments are discussed under the heading "The Directive-State Theory of Perception" in Allport (1955).

3. Indeed, Bruner induced two of his students (myself and Renato Tagiuri) to do their dissertations on different aspects of person perception. See Jones (1954); Tagiuri (1952).

4. Tagiuri and Petrullo (1958).

5. Darwin (1872).

6. Woodworth (1938) showed that emotions can be ordered along a discriminability dimension, and he constructed a crude six-point scale. Schlosberg (1952) showed that opposite emotions (e.g., contempt and mirth) are difficult to discriminate, thus

suggesting a circular scale. He ended (1954) with a representation in terms of three dimensions: pleasantness/unpleasantness, attention/rejection, and level of activation.

7. Schachter (1964) and Schachter and Singer (1962)

8. So called "facial feedback" theories (Izard, 1977; Tomkins, 1962) view expressions of the face as determinants and not just outcomes of emotional state. Recent work by Zajonc, Murphy, and Inglehart (1989) supports a "vascular theory of emotional efference" in which affective reactions are determined by changes in blood flow to the brain, in turn influenced by facial muscular movements.

9. A point made by Tomkins (1981).

10. Zuckerman, DePaulo, and Rosenthal (1981).

11. Summarized in DePaulo, Stone, and Lassiter (1985).

12. Cronbach and Gleser (1953); Cronbach (1955); Cronbach, (1958); Gage and Cronbach (1955).

13. Cronbach (1955).

14. A useful review of the implicit personality concept and measurement possibilities can be found in Schneider (1973). See also D'Andrade (1965); Passini and Norman (1966); Shweder (1977).

15. Chapman and Chapman (1969).

16. Andersen (1984).

17. Ibid., p. 304.

18. Asch (1946).

19. A good summary of these studies is in Anderson (1974).

20. Ostrom (1977) argues that Anderson's averaging model is so flexible that it can account for meaning shifts of individual traits as a function of context. Regardless of the model one prefers, there is no question in my mind that context effects are important in person perception.

21. Asch and Zukier (1984).

22. Ibid., p. 1238.

23. Heider (1944).

24. Michotte (1963).

25. Heider and Simmel (1944).

26. Many illustrations of this point can be found in Jervis (1976).

27. Thibaut and Riecken (1955) conducted an early experiment showing some important social consequences of phenomenal causality. This experiment, pointing up the autocratic leader's dilemma in assessing the spontaneity of subjects' compliance, had a strong influence on my thinking about the implications of the attributional approach.

28. Examples of this empirical work include Bruner and Goodman (1947); Bruner and Postman (1948); Bruner and Rodrigues (1953).

29. Jones and Thibaut (1958).

30. Jones and deCharms (1957).

31. A recent review by Showers and Cantor (1985) of "motivated strategies" provides a good summary of research concerned with the influence of interaction goals on social cognition.

32. Swann (1984).

Chapter 3

1. Heider (1944).

2. Heider (1958).

3. Many instances of bias or error will dot the pages to come. Perhaps the best and most provocative discussion of inferential failings in the social domain may be found in Nisbett and Ross (1980).

4. Jones and deCharms (1957).

5. This figure is an adaptation of the diagram in Heider (1958, p. 84).

6. In the early 1960s I was invited to write a chapter for a new series of volumes entitled *Advances in Experimental Social Psychology*. I decided I would try to expand on these ideas of choice to see if the result might be a more systematic and useful formulation of the person perception process. I invited Keith Davis, a brilliant former student, to collaborate with me in developing a

preliminary theoretical statement. The result: Jones and Davis (1965).

7. In their theory of *action identification*, Vallacher and Wegner (1987) make it abundantly clear, with convincing data from their own experiments, that a given act can be identified in many different ways: as a means, as an end, as a "low-level" muscle movement. The statement that we are only concerned with effects, therefore, must depend to some extent on the context.

8. The original theoretical statement referred to effects of the chosen action that were not also effects of the nonchosen action as "noncommon effects." Students (and colleagues) have found this phrasing awkward, so in this treatment I have chosen the term "distinctive effects" to convey the same meaning.

9. In particular, Jones and McGillis (1976) consider the implications of different definitions of correspondence.

10. This variable was referred to in the original presentation of correspondent inference theory (Jones and Davis, 1965) as the social desirability of the behavior observed. "Prior probability" includes the notion of social desirability but is preferred here because it includes other possible reasons why a response might be highly likely or expected.

11. Kelley (1967).

12. In the interests of a more straightforward presentation, this simplifies a complicated set of possibilities. A specialized literature has developed to consider the "anomalous" cases where consensus is high and distinctiveness low, or where consensus is low and distinctiveness high (in terms of the Kelley cube, the HLH and LHH cells). Most of the debate concerns the frequency of expected "person and situation" versus "no" attributions, or whether one can make dispositional attributions even when the causes of behavior are ambiguous. Cf. Jaspars, Hewstone, and Fincham (1983); Hilton and Slugoski (1986); Cheng and Novick (1990).

13. I tried to justify and develop this suggestion in a retrospective review of Heider's 1958 book: Jones (1987).

14. Some unfortunate consequences followed this early neglect of multiple observations. Many interpreters of correspondent inference theory, in numerous introductory texts, stated boldly that the more improbable (culturally undesirable) an observed

action, the more correspondent would be the inference about causal dispositions in the actor. This seems to follow from the prior probability principle, but it does not always make good intuitive sense. When we see someone behaving in an unexpected manner, probably the first thing we do is rule out some obvious alternative explanations before jumping to conclusions about unique personal dispositions. We try to assimilate the perceived actions to our expectations, and when this is not completely successful, we reexamine the situation and try to find constraints that could reasonably explain the behavioral anomaly. This would be particularly likely if the perceiver had strong expectancies about a particular actor based on a significant range of prior experiences with him or her. A number of studies have since shown that violation of expectancies based on prior knowledge of the specific actor are attributed to the situation if this is at all plausible, i.e., if the situational constraints are sufficiently ambiguous. It is interesting that one could interpret Kelley's model as anticipating this correction. A *distinctive* response to an entity is, in effect, an unexpected one — one that should, according to cultural desirability principles, lead to a correspondent inference. In Kelley's model, however, it is one clue toward entity (i.e., situational) attribution — an outcome more in accord with the empirical results thus far in the literature (Bell, Wicklund, Manko, et al., 1976; Kulik, 1983). When McGillis and I (Jones and McGillis, 1976) reexamined correspondent inference theory some ten years after its initial formulation, we tried to address the issue of expectancy disconfirmation by suggesting a "credibility correction." Our notion was that extreme expectancy violations would raise a number of questions and would not automatically lead to a correspondent inference based on this newly observed action. This was a little like vague hand waving, however, and the issue of expectancy violation remains one of the most important and central ones in the entire person perception arena.

15. Most fully explicated in Bem (1972) and discussed extensively below in Chapter 8.

16. Festinger (1954, 1957); Schachter (1964). Social comparison is clearly involved in a perceiver's use of the "consensus" variable. Cognitive dissonance and labeling theories, more fully discussed in Chapter 8, can each be reinterpreted as involving the misattribution to the self that which more correctly should be attributed to the situation.

17. Medcof (1990) has developed a probabilistic expectancy model

that attempts to integrate covariation and correspondent inference theories.

18. Kelley (1971, p. 8).

19. Thibaut and Riecken (1955).

20. Jones, Davis, and Gergen (1961).

21. Jones and Harris (1967).

22. Newtson (1974).

23. McArthur (1972).

24. Ruble and Feldman (1976); Cheng and Novick (1990).

25. Hilton and Slugoski (1986).

26. McGill (1989).

27. Gibson (1979).

28. McArthur and Baron (1983).

29. Ibid., p. 218

30. Ibid., p. 220

31. Ibid., p. 222

32. Ekman's work (e.g., Ekman, Friesen, and Ellsworth, 1972) provides the fullest account of the relations between facial configurations and emotions.

33. Johansson (1973).

34. Kozlowski and Cutting (1977).

35. Trope (1986).

36. McArthur and Baron (1983, p. 215).

37. Trope (1986, p. 242).

38. Snyder and Frankel (1976).

39. Weiner (1985).

40. Hastie (1984); Hamilton (1988).

CHAPTER 4

1. Jones and Davis (1965); Kelley (1967); Trope (1986).

2. Jones and McGillis (1976).

3. The following discussion presents a taxonomy that differs somewhat from the taxonomy presented in Jones and McGillis (1976). The differences are fairly trivial: McGillis and I divide category-based expectancies into "stereotype" and "normative," but the former is essentially equivalent to the current "dispositional" subcategory. Also, we add a third subcategory to target-based expectancies, "conceptual replications," to cover occasions where there is consistency across similar but not identical situations. Unlike "structural" target-based expectancies, conceptual replicative expectancies do not require a "structural" theory of personality or belief system.

4. Weisz and Jones (unpublished). This paper describes many studies in the literature that generally support the importance of the distinction between inconsistent behavior and behavior by idiosyncratic individuals.

5. Thibaut and Ross (1969).

6. Trope (1986).

7. Asch (1946).

8. These studies are reviewed in Jones and Goethals (1971).

9. Stewart (1965).

10. Tetlock (1983); Tetlock and Kim (1987).

11. Silka (1984).

12. Anderson's work (e.g., 1974) provides confirmation of such a tendency to ignore or discount recent information. Perhaps one way to handle new information that is not consistent with old information is simply to stop paying attention.

13. Fiske and Taylor (1984, pp. 139–154) provide a useful discussion of the social schema and related terms. This definition is essentially theirs.

14. Brewer (1988).

15. Quattrone (1986).

16. E.g., Hilton and Slugoski (1986); McGill (1989); Medcof (1990).

17. Kelley (1967).

18. Nisbett and Ross (1980).

19. Mischel and Gilligan (1964).

20. Useful discussions of the stereotype concept can be found in Allport (1954); Miller (1982); Brigham (1971); Brown (1986).

21. Quattrone, in an unpublished grant proposal, reports several correlational studies showing that the more a group of target persons are seen to look alike, the more they are assumed to share specific traits of character.

22. Fiske and Taylor (1984, p. 12) use this term to refer to a "capacity-limited thinker."

23. Dollard, Doob, Miller, et al. (1939). See also Miller (1941).

24. Miller (1944).

25. Adorno, Frenkel-Brunswik, Levinson, et al. (1950). Unfortunately, the force of this evidence was weakened by the recognition that at least some of this interconnectedness was an artifact of "response bias": Since items on the various scales were all worded so that agreement meant greater prejudice or more authoritarianism, those subjects who tended to agree regardless of content probably inflated the intercorrelations among the superficially different but theoretically related scales.

26. Hamilton (1979).

27. Hamilton and Gifford (1976).

28. Eagly and Steffen (1984).

29. Ross, Amabile, and Steinmetz (1977).

30. Taylor and Fiske (1975).

31. As discussed in Taylor and Fiske (1978). The authors concede that the evidence is largely "inferential" rather than direct, but more recent studies by Eisen and McArthur (1979), McArthur and Solomon (1978), and Taylor, Crocker, Fiske, et al. (1979) add to the empirical support of the hypothesis that salience leads to more extreme evaluations.

32. McArthur and Post (1977).

33. Taylor, Fiske, Etcoff, et al. (1978).

34. Quattrone and Jones (1980). Quattrone has written more recently (1986) and more generally on the topic.

35. Jones, Wood, and Quattrone (1981).

36. Park and Rothbart (1982).

37. Linville and Jones (1980).

38. Linville (1982); (1987).

39. Perdue (1983).

40. Locksley, Borgida, Brekke, et al. (1980); Locksley, Hepburn, and Ortiz (1982). See also the lucid discussion in Brown (1986).

41. Rasinski, Crocker, and Hastie (1985).

42. Darley and Gross (1983).

43. As noted earlier in this chapter (and in Note 4), Carolyn Weisz and I, in an unpublished paper, pursue the distinction between category-based and target-based expectations, emphasizing that the former are more likely to be probabilistic in predictive strength. We present results that are generally consistent with this distinction: A category-based expectancy has little influence, in our study, over the perception of an expectancy violator. Our results are similar to those of Locksley and her collaborators.

CHAPTER 5

1. Lewin (1951, pp. 239–240).

2. An influential example of this is the treatment by Dollard and Miller (1950). This was the forerunner of "social learning theory" (e.g., Rotter, 1954), an important alternative to the conventional psychodynamic position championed by Freud.

3. Heider (1958).

4. Skinner (1971, p. 14).

5. Bowers (1973, p. 319).

6. Cantor and Kihlstrom (1987, p. 84).

7. Ever since Thomas and Znaniecki (1918–1920) introduced the term "definition of the situation," arguing that "if men define situations as real, they are real in their consequences," there has been a persistent interest in defining situations within sociology. A useful review of this tradition of concern may be found in Stebbins (1986).

8. Nisbett and Ross (1980).

9. Nisbett and Wilson (1977).

10. Skinner (1971, p. 183).

11. Discussed more fully in the next chapter and also in Jones (1979).

12. These concepts come variously from liberalized S–R Theory (Miller, 1959), game theory (Luce and Raiffa, 1957), need-press theory (Murray, 1938), and field theory (Lewin, 1951).

13. This tendency has long been built into models of decision making. In fact, the preference for a sure thing over a 50–50 gamble for twice the amount of the sure thing can be traced at least as far back as Bernouilli (1738), who proposed an expected utility principle, suggesting that the psychological value of money does not increase as fast as its objective amount increases. Thus, an objective twice the amount of the sure thing is not twice the amount psychologically.

14. In Kahneman and Tversky's (1979) *Prospect Theory*, the preference for or against risk hinges on the reference point, whether the decision maker starts "in the hole" or "ahead of the game." This in turn may depend decisively on how the decision is framed.

15. Newtson's (1974) experimental evidence on this point was discussed in Chapter 3.

16. Jones and Gerard (1967).

17. Skinner (1938, 1953).

18. Thibaut and Kelley (1959).

19. Langer (1989) provides numerous anecdotal and experimental examples of mindless social interactions in which one person "controls" the behavior of another by using familiar cues. Thus, in one experiment a person about to use the Xerox machine was interrupted by a confederate who either said, "Excuse me, may I use the Xerox machine," "Excuse me, may I use the Xerox machine, because I want to make copies," or "Excuse me, may I use the Xerox machine because I'm in a rush." The second request produced just as much compliance as the third and more than the first, even though "because I want to make copies" hardly provides a reason why one person should relinquish the Xerox machine to another.

20. A familiar example to most psychologists are the classic Luchins (1942) experiments, in which subjects learn one way to solve a series of water jug problems and then proceed with this rather

laborious solution procedure when the problems change and an alternative procedure is simpler and more efficient.

21. See Figure 3-1 and Heider (1958).

22. Jones (1986).

23. Chapters in Magnusson (1981) — e.g., "Wanted: A Psychology of Situations" — suggest that help may be on the way, but it is not yet here. Also, Snyder and Ickes (1985) present a very useful summary of the issues that must be considered in developing an approach that relates conceptions of personalities to conceptions of situations.

24. Jones and Nisbett (1971–1972).

25. E.g., Bem (1981).

26. Ross, Greene, and House (1977).

27. Jones and Nisbett (1971–1972).

28. Ibid., p. 80.

29. Trope (1986).

30. Kulik (1983).

31. Weisz and Jones (unpublished).

32. Wachtel (1973). This critique of "situationism" is enthusiastically endorsed by Bowers (1973), who strongly advocates a view that emphasizes the interaction between predispositions and situational factors as behavior determinants. Wachtel's argument is also cited favorably in Monson and Snyder's (1977) critique of the actor–observer divergence proposition (Jones and Nisbett, 1971–1972).

33. Trope (1986).

34. Abelson (1981).

CHAPTER 6

1. Ross (1977); it is controversial because some contend that it is not necessarily an "error" and some argue that other attributional biases are more fundamental.

2. Ichheiser (1949).

3. Heider (1958, p. 54).

4. Jones and Nisbett (1971–1972).

5. Watson (1982).

6. Jones and Harris (1967).

7. Jones, Worchel, Goethals, et al. (1971); Snyder and Jones (1974); Miller (1976). General summary in Jones (1979).

8. Snyder and Jones (1974).

9. Ajzen et al. (1979).

10. Yandell and Insko (1977) present and attempt to defend this position.

11. Ross, Amabile, and Steinmetz (1977).

12. Snyder and Frankel (1976).

13. Miller, Jones, and Hinkle (1981).

14. Miller, Schmidt, Meyer, et al. (1984).

15. Miller, Jones, and Hinkle (1981).

16. Zuckerman, DePaulo, and Rosenthal (1981).

17. Jones (1979, p. 114).

18. Tversky and Kahneman (1974).

19. Quattrone (personal communication).

20. Quattrone and Sherman (personal communication).

21. Heider (1944).

22. Starting with Gilbert, Jones, and Pelham (1987).

23. Gilbert and Krull (1988).

24. Gilbert, Krull, and Pelham (1988).

25. Gilbert (personal communication).

26. Quattrone (1982).

27. Ross, Amabile, and Steinmetz (1977).

28. As described by Fiske and Taylor (1984, pp. 11–12).

29. This theme runs throughout Goffman's essays but is most sharply drawn in Goffman (1955).

30. Swann (1984).

31. Miller (1984).

32. This will be developed more fully when the phenomena associated with self-fulfilling prophecies are discussed in Chapter 9.

33. Described in greater detail in Gilbert and Jones (1986b).

34. Gilbert, Pelham, and Krull (1988).

35. Gilbert, Jones, and Pelham (1987).

36. My hunch is that these results suggesting that perceivers generally underestimate the effects of their own constraining influence are but the beginning of what will turn out to be a long and complicated story. Surely, given the well-known tendencies toward egocentric attributions and self-preoccupation, there must be occasions when we are inclined to exaggerate our own impact on others. Also, each of us probably has theories about how and when we are typically influential, and these theories should affect our use of the attributional discounting principle.

37. Ginzel, Jones, and Swann (1987).

CHAPTER 7

1. Jones and Thibaut (1958).

2. The first phase of this theorizing was presented in Jones (1964).

3. Baumeister (1982).

4. Thibaut and Kelley (1959).

5. See also the discussion of power with respect to interactions involving handicapped or otherwise stigmatized persons (Jones, Farina, Hastorf, et al., 1984).

6. Arkin (1981) in his discussion of self-presentation styles, draws an interesting distinction between "acquisitive" and "protective" self-presentations, the former concerned with gaining rewards (i.e., power), and the latter with the avoidance of losing power. This may turn out to be an important theoretical distinction, but for my purposes it suffices to lump them together as power maintenance and augmentation.

7. Stryker and Statham (1985, p. 314).

8. His major contribution was Mead (1934).

9. E.g., Swann (1987).

10. Jones and Pittman (1982 p. 233).

11. Hogan, Jones, and Check (1985) note that all behavior has "symbolic components,"

12. Ringer (1973).

13. Korda (1975).

14. Carnegie (1936).

15. Jones (1964, p. 11).

16. Godfrey, Jones, and Lord (1986).

17. Jones and Pittman (1982, p. 236).

18. Chesterfield (1901, p. 139).

19. Ibid., p. 28

20. Summarized in Jones and Wortman (1973).

21. This model, or formula, goes back at least as far as 1940, with the paper by Escalona introducing the resultant valence notion, of which variants have appeared in the writing of Rotter (1954), Tolman (1955), and Atkinson (1957). Schlenker (1980) presents a similar "expected value" model.

22. Jones (1965).

23. Ginzel (1989).

24. Cialdini and de Nicholas (1989).

25. Stires and Jones (1969).

26. Introduced and more fully discussed in Jones and Pittman (1982).

27. Jones, Gergen, and Davis (1962).

28. Godfrey, Jones, and Lord (1986); also mentioned earlier in the chapter when discussing the degree of consensus people share about useful ingratiation tactics.

29. Ginzel (1989).

30. First described by Jones and Pittman (1982).

31. Cf. Reeder and Brewer (1979).

32. Jones (1989).

33. Quattrone and Jones (1978).

34. The results of one experiment by Jones, Schwartz, and Gilbert (1983–1984) suggest that this intuition may need to be qualified. A target person who claimed to be invariably honest but who behaved deceptively was seen as lacking in insight but not as exploitative or duplicitous. Also, Gilbert and Jones (1986a) found that subjects draw a distinction between hypocrisy and self-deception, on the one hand, and exploitativeness, on the other. An exemplifier (one who presents himself as morally virtuous) who is seen to cheat is judged to be hypocritical but not as exploitative as a cheater who previously presented him- or herself as morally adaptable. There is evidence in this latter paper, however, that one who is victimized by a cheating exemplifier may feel that another who does not live up to the virtue he or she claims is indeed exploitative.

35. Goffman (1968) provides an acute analysis of the "voluntary exposure to fateful moments" that is consistent with this theme of effective exemplification in his essay, "Where the Action Is."

36. There seems to be a broad journalistic consensus that Reagan's popularity was somehow impervious to events in his presidency for which he was responsible. As an example, Steven Weisman in the *New York Times* wrote: "He has committed untold public bloopers and been caught in dozens of factual mistakes and misrepresentations. He has presided over the worst recession since the Great Depression. The abortive mission in Beirut cost 265 American lives, and there has been a sharp escalation of military involvement in Central America. An extraordinary number of Mr. Reagan's political appointees have come under fire, with many forced to resign, because of ethical or legal conflicts. Yet he is *The Man in the Teflon Suit*; nothing sticks to him" (Weisman, 1984). Ostrom and Simon (1989) present some data indicating that Reagan's approval ratings fluctuated with environmental events (such as the economy and the Irangate scandal) much more than with controllable "political drama" (TV speeches and presidential trips), and presumably in a fashion similar to that of previous presidents. However, they do not offer quantitative comparative data and do not explain why Reagan's popularity rebounded so quickly after negative environmental events.

CHAPTER 8

1. Cooley (1902).

2. Jones and Gerard (1967).

3. Ross, Greene, and House (1977). The implications of this work were also presented in Chapter 5 when discussing the consensual definition of "situational constraint."

4. The term "pluralistic ignorance" was coined by F. H. Allport (1924) to describe a situation in which members of a group privately reject group norms yet believe others accept them. Miller and McFarland (1987) have confirmed the contributing hypothesis that people believe they are more socially inhibited and more affected by embarrassment than others.

5. Kelley (1967).

6. Festinger (1957).

7. Bem (1965). Bem took it for granted that the perception of one's own behavior is a straightforward matter. Vallacher and Wegner (1987) point out that actions can be "identified" in many different ways, depending on numerous contextual factors. In addition, they argue that *how* an actor represents his or her own behavior can have an important effect on subsequent behavior —and certainly on the actor's self-perception.

8. Bem (1967).

9. Festinger (personal communication, 1968).

10. Bem (1972, p. 2), italics added.

11. Ibid., p. 44.

12. Schachter and Singer (1962); Schachter (1964).

13. E.g., Leventhal and Tomarken (1986) carefully consider the evidence supporting "cognition–arousal theory" and find it damaging to the theory in a number of respects, including the accumulation of subsequent evidence that there is much more autonomic specificity to different emotions than Schachter was willing to assume.

14. Though I say this without any inside information from Schachter or his colleagues.

15. Ross and Olson (1981).

16. Lepper and Greene (1978).

17. Zillmann, Katcher, and Milavsky (1972).

18. Cantor, Bryant, and Zillman (1974); Bryant and Zillmann (1979).

19. Bem (1972, p. 33).

20. Zanna and Cooper (1974).

21. Cooper, Zanna, and Taves (1978).

22. Fazio, Zanna, and Cooper (1977).

23. Sherif and Hovland (1961).

24. Aronson (1969).

25. Cooper and Fazio (1984).

26. This is experiment III reported in Jones, Rhodewalt, Berglas, et al. (1981).

27. Bem (1972).

28. Rhodewalt and Agustdottir (1986). A subsequent study by Schlenker and Trudeau (1990) raises some doubts about the applicability of the complete Fazio et al. perspective in a case where a specific trait attribution (rather than global self-esteem) is involved.

29. Beck, Ward, Mendelson, et al. (1961).

30. Jones and Gerard (1967, p. 716).

31. Tversky and Kahneman (1973, 1974, 1982). A useful discussion of heuristics can also be found in Nisbett and Ross (1980).

32. Greenwald (1980) identifies three cognitive biases: egocentricity (the self as focus of knowledge), beneffectance (attribution of personal responsibility for desired but not for undesired outcomes), and cognitive conservatism. The present discussion emphasizes the equivalents of the first two.

33. Heider (1958, pp. 119–120).

34. Jones and Davis (1965).

35. Cf. Russell (1950).

36. Jones and deCharms (1957).

37. The same may be said for a study by Chaikin and Cooper (1973)

showing that a person doing a good or bad (i.e., hedonically relevant) thing out of role is evaluated more extremely than one doing the same thing in role: Thus, a northern professor who joins the Ku Klux Klan is less admired and respected than a southern millworker who joins the Klan. This is a twist on predictions of hedonic relevance made by correspondent inference theory. Instead of hedonic relevance leading to greater correspondence, in this case correspondence (out-of-role behavior) leads to an extreme evaluation.

38. Enzle, Harvey, and Wright (1980).

39. Kelley (1967).

40. Ross and Sicoly (1979).

41. Snyder and Fromkin (1980).

42. Snyder and Wicklund (1981).

43. See the summary in Ross and Fletcher (1985, p. 104).

44. Miller and Ross (1975)

45. Tetlock and Manstead (1985)

46. Ross and Fletcher (1985, p. 105).

47. Jones and Gerard (1967, pp. 227–229).

48. Snyder, Higgins, and Stucky (1983).

49. Scott and Lyman (1968).

50. Jones and Berglas (1978).

51. Seligman (1975); Huesmann (1978).

52. Taylor and Brown (1988).

53. Showers (1986).

54. Reviewed in Swann (1987).

55. Swann and Pelham (under review).

56. Swann (1987, p. 1040).

57. Jones (1973).

58. Tesser (1986).

59. Steele (1988).

60. Swann (in press).

61. Swann, Pelham, and Krull (1989).

62. Which reminds us of the third cognitive bias mentioned by Greenwald (1980): resistance to change in the cognitive self structure.

63. Jones (1990).

64. Hochschild (1983).

65. Athough the more adaptable survivors report success in emotional control, such efforts can miscarry, and many attendants complained in their interviews of self-alienation and self-estrangement.

Chapter 9

1. Merton (1948, p. 195).

2. And also including the confirmation of prejudice-based racial stereotypes, as Merton noted and Allport (1954) implied with his discussion of "traits of victimization."

3. Jervis (1976) presents other specific examples like this in discussing "the spiral model" of deterrence (pp. 62–113).

4. Rosenthal and Jacobson (1968).

5. Rosenthal and Rubin (1978).

6. Snyder, Tanke, and Berscheid (1977).

7. To pick just one general source, Fiske and Taylor (1984).

8. Snyder and Swann (1978a).

9. Trope and Bassok (1982).

10. Swann and Guiliano (1987).

11. Snyder and Swann (1987b).

12. Davis (1962). This pathbreaking study has, alas, never been prepared for publication.

13. Skrypnek and Snyder (1982).

14. Baumeister, Hutton, and Tice (1989).

15. Reeder and Brewer (1979).

16. Darley, Fleming, Hilton, et al. (1988).

17. Swann and Read (1981).

18. Ginzel (1989).

19. Schoenberger (1988).

20. Hilton and Darley (1985).

21. Jones (1986, p. 45).

22. Darley, Fleming, Hilton, et al. (1988).

23. Cooper and Fazio (1984).

24. Bem (1972).

25. Tice (1987).

26. Kulik, Sledge, and Mahler (1986). These investigators documented the reasonable expectation that subjects who are induced to act in a characteristic way will attribute their actions to a correspondent disposition, whereas those whose actions are uncharacteristic (in the same setting) will attribute them to the situation.

27. After waiting in the hall and being "debriefed" about the confederate, subjects were asked to help in coding the videotaped responses of some previous subjects. In this way the similarity manipulation was introduced. All subjects had participated earlier in the semester in a testing session involving many self-rating instruments. Thus, it was plausible to tell them that, on the basis of the test results, a personality profile was constructed. Subjects were then led to believe that two of the tapes they were watching were of subjects highly similar to themselves, whereas the other two were definitely dissimilar. During the process of observing and trying to code the three-minute "interactions" between the confederate and the prior subjects, each naive subject could readily discern whether any of the four videotaped predecessors had carried on a conversation.

28. Fazio, Effrein, and Falender (1981).

References

Abelson, R. P. (1981). Psychological status of the script concept. *American Psychologist, 36,* 715–729.

Adorno, T. W., Frenkel-Brunswik, E., Levinson, D. J., and Sanford, R. N. (1950). *The authoritarian personality.* New York: Harper & Row.

Ajzen, I., Dalto, C. A., and Blyth, D. P. (1979). Consistency and bias in the attribution of attitudes. *Journal of Personality and Social Psychology 37,* 1871–1876.

Allport, F. H. (1924). *Social psychology,* Boston: Houghton Mifflin.

Allport, F. H. (1955). *Theories of perception and the concept of structure.* New York: Wiley.

Allport, G. W. (1954). *The nature of prejudice.* Cambridge, Mass. Addison-Wesley.

Andersen, S. M. (1984). Self-knowledge and social inference: II. The diagnosticity of cognitive/affective and behavioral data. *Journal of Personality and Social Psychology, 46,* 294–307.

Anderson, N. H. (1974). Cognitive algebra: Integration theory applied to social attribution. In L. Berkowitz (Ed.), *Advances in experimental social psychology* (Vol. 7, pp. 1–101). New York: Academic Press.

Arkin, R. M. (1981). Self-presentation styles. In J. T. Tedeschi, (Ed.), *Impression management theory and social psychological research* (pp. 311–333). New York: Academic Press.

Aronson, E. (1969). The theory of cognitive dissonance: A current perspective. In L. Berkowitz (Ed.), *Advances in experimental social psychology* (Vol. 4, pp. 2–35). New York: Academic Press.

Asch, S. E. (1946). Forming impressions of personality. *Journal of Abnormal and Social Psychology, 41,* 258–290.

Asch, S. E., and Zukier, H. (1984). Thinking about persons. *Journal of Personality and Social Psychology, 46,* 1230–1240.

Atkinson, J. W. (1957). Motivational determinants of risk-taking behavior. *Psychological Review, 64,* 359–373.

Baumeister, R. F. (1982). A self-presentational view of social phenomena. *Psychological Bulletin, 91,* 3–26.

Baumeister, R. F., Hutton, D. G., and Tice, D. M. (1989). Cognitive processes during deliberate self-presentation: How self-presenters alter and misinterpret the behavior of their interaction partners. *Journal of Experimental Social Psychology, 25,* 59–78.

Beck, A. T., Ward, C. H., Mendelson, M., Mock, J., and Erbaugh, J. (1961). An inventory for measuring depression. *Archives of General Psychiatry, 4,* 561–571.

Bell, L. G., Wicklund, R. A., Manko, G., and Larkin, C. (1976). When unexpected behavior is attributed to the environment. *Journal of Research in Personality, 10,* 316–327.

Bem, D. J. (1965). An experimental analysis of self-persuasion. *Journal of Experimental Social Psychology, 1,* 199–218.

Bem, D. J. (1967). Self-perception: An alternative interpretation of cognitive dissonance phenomena. *Psychological Review, 74,* 183–200.

Bem, D. J. (1972). Self-perception theory. In L. Berkowitz (Ed.),

Advances in experimental social psychology (Vol. 6, pp. 1–62). New York: Academic Press.

Bem, D. J. (1981). Assessing situations by assessing persons. In D. Magnusson (Ed.), *Toward a psychology of situations: An interactional perspective* (pp. 245–257). Hillsdale, N.J.: Erlbaum.

Bernouilli, D. (1738). Specimen theoriae novae de mensura sortis. St Petersburg. Translated in *Econometrica*, 1954, 22, 23–36.

Berscheid, E. (1985). Interpersonal attraction. In G. Lindzey & E. Aronson (Eds.), *The handbook of social psychology* (3rd ed., Vol. 2, 413–484). New York: Random House.

Bowers, K. S. (1973). Situations in psychology: An analysis and critique. *Psychological Review, 80*, 307–336.

Brewer, M. (1988). A dual process model of impression formation. In T. K. Srull and R. S. Wyer (Eds.), *Advances in social cognition* (Vol. 1, pp. 1–36). Hillsdale, N.J.: Erlbaum.

Brigham, J. C. (1971). Ethnic stereotypes. *Psychological Bulletin, 76*, 15–38.

Brown, R. (1986). *Social psychology the second edition.* New York: Free Press.

Bruner, J. S., and Goodman, C. C. (1947). Value and need as organizing factors in perception. *Journal of Abnormal Social Psychology, 42*, 33–44.

Bruner, J. S., and Postman, L. (1948). Symbolic value as an organizing factor in perception. *Journal of Social Psychology, 27*, 203–208.

Bruner, J. S., and Rodrigues, J. S. (1953). Some determinants of apparent size. *Journal of Abnormal and Social Psychology, 48*, 17–24.

Bryant, J., and Zillmann, D. (1979). Effect of intensification of annoyance through unrelated residual excitation of subsequently delayed hostile behavior. *Journal of Experimental Social Psychology, 15*, 470–480.

Cantor, J. R., Bryant, J., and Zillmann, D. (1974). Enhancement of human appreciation by transferred excitation. *Journal of Personality and Social Psychology, 30*, 812–821.

Cantor, N., and Kihlstrom, J. F. (1987). *Personality and social intelligence.* Englewood Cliffs, N.J.: Prentice-Hall.

Carnegie, D. (1936). *How to win friends and influence people.* New York: Simon & Schuster.

Chaikin, A., and Cooper, J. (1973). Evaluation as a function of correspondence and hedonic relevance. *Journal of Experimental and Social Psychology, 9,* 257–264.

Chapman, L. J., and Chapman, J. P. (1969). Illusory correlation as an obstacle to the use of valid psychodiagnostic signs. *Journal of Abnormal Psychology, 74,* 271–280.

Cheng, P. W., and Novick, L. R. (1990). A probabilistic contrast model of causal induction. *Journal of Personality and Social Psychology, 58,* 545–567.

Chesterfield, Earl of (Philip Darner Stanhope) (1901). Letters to his son. Walker M. Dunne (Ed.). New York: Wiley. (Originally published, 1774.)

Cialdini, R., and de Nicholas, M. E. (1989). Self-presentation by association. *Journal of Personality and Social Psychology, 57,* 626–631.

Cooley, C. H. (1902). *Human nature and the social order.* New York: Scribner's.

Cooper, J., and Fazio, R. H. (1984). A new look at dissonance theory. In L. Berkowitz (Ed.), *Advances in experimental social psychology* (Vol. 17, pp. 229–267). New York: Academic Press.

Cooper, J., Zanna, M. P., and Taves, P. A. (1978). Arousal as a necessary condition for attitude change following induced compliance. *Journal of Personality and Social Psychology, 36,* 1101–1106.

Cronbach, L. J. (1955). Processes affecting scores on "understanding of others" and "assumed similarity." *Psychological Bulletin, 52,* 177–193.

Cronbach, L. J. (1958). Proposals leading to analytic treatment of social perception scores. In R. Tagiuri and L. Petrullo (Eds.), *Person perception and interpersonal behavior.* Stanford: Stanford University Press.

Cronbach, L. J., and Gleser, G. C. (1953). Assessing similarity between profiles. *Psychological Bulletin, 50,* 456–474.

D'Andrade, R. G. (1965). Trait psychology and componential analysis. *American Anthropologist, 67,* 215–228.

Darley, J. M., and Fazio, R. H. (1980). Expectancy confirmation processes arising in the social interaction sequence. *American Psychologist, 35,* 867–881.

Darley, J. M., Fleming, J. H., Hilton, J. L., and Swann, W. B., Jr. (1988). Dispelling negative expectancies: The impact of interaction goals and target characteristics on the expectancy confirmation process. *Journal of Experimental Social Psychology, 24,* 19–36.

Darley, J. M., and Gross, P. H. (1983). A hypothesis-confirming bias in labeling effects. *Journal of Personality and Social Psychology, 44,* 20–33.

Darwin, C. (1872). *The expression of emotions in man and animals.* London: Murray.

Davis, K. E. (1962). *Impressions of others and interaction context as determinants of social interaction and perception in two-person discussion groups.* Unpublished doctoral dissertation, Duke University.

DePaulo, B. M., Stone, J. I., and Lassiter, G. D. (1985). Deceiving and detecting deceit. In B. R. Schlenker (Ed.), *The self and social life* (pp. 323–370). New York: McGraw-Hill.

Dollard, J., Doob, L. W., Miller, N. E., Mowrer, O. H., and Sears, R. R. (1939). *Frustration and aggression.* New Haven Conn.: Yale University Press.

Dollard, J., and Miller, N. E. (1950). *Personality and psychotherapy.* New York: McGraw-Hill.

Eagly, A. H., and Steffen, V. J. (1984). Gender stereotypes stem from the disruption of men and women into social roles. *Journal of Personality and Social Psychology, 46,* 735–754.

Eisen, S. V., and McArthur, L. Z. (1979). Evaluating and sentencing a defendant as a function of his salience and the observer's set. *Personality and Social Psychology Bulletin, 5,* 48–52.

Ekman, P., Friesen, W. V., and Ellsworth, P. (1972). *Emotion in the human face.* New York: Pergamon Press.

Enzle, M. E., Harvey, M. D., and Wright, E. F. (1980). Personalism and distinctiveness. *Journal of Personality and Social Psychology, 39,* 542–552.

Escalona, S. K. (1940). The effect of success and failure upon the level of aspiration and behavior in manic-depressive psychoses. *University of Iowa Studies in Child Welfare, 16,* #3, 199–302.

Fazio, R. H., Effrein, E. A., and Falender, V. J. (1981). Self-perceptions following social interaction. *Journal of Personality and Social Psychology, 41*, 232–242.

Fazio, R. H., Zanna, M. P., and Cooper, J. (1977). Dissonance and self-perception: An integrative view of each theory's proper domain of application. *Journal of Experimental Social Psychology, 13*, 464–479.

Festinger, L. (1954). A theory of social comparison processes. *Human Relations, 7*, 117–140.

Festinger, L. (1957). *A theory of cognitive dissonance*. Evanston, Ill.: Row-Peterson.

Fiske, S. T., and Taylor, S. E. (1984). *Social cognition*. Reading, Mass.: Addison Wesley.

Gage, N. L., and Cronbach, L. J. (1955). Conceptual and methodological problems in interpersonal perception. *Psychological Review, 62*, 411–423.

Gibson, J. J. (1979). *The ecological approach to visual perception*. Boston: Houghton Mifflin.

Gilbert, D. T. (1989). Thinking lightly about others: Automatic components of the social inference process. In J. S. Uleman and J. A. Bargh (Eds.), *Unintended thought: Causes and consequences for judgment, emotion, and behavior* (pp. 189–211). New York: Guilford.

Gilbert, D. T., and Jones, E. E. (1986a). Exemplification: The self-presentation of moral character. *Journal of Personality, 54*, 593–615.

Gilbert, D. T., and Jones, E. E. (1986b). Perceiver-induced constraint: Interpretations of self-generated reality. *Journal of Personality and Social Psychology, 50*, 269–280.

Gilbert, D. T., Jones, E. E., and Pelham, B. W. (1987). What the active perceiver overlooks. *Journal of Personality and Social Psychology, 52*, 861–870.

Gilbert, D. T., and Krull, D. S. (1988). Seeing less and knowing more: The benefits of perceptual ignorance. *Journal of Personality and Social Psychology, 54*, 193–202.

Gilbert, D. T., Krull, D. S., & Pelham, B. W. (1988). Of thoughts unspoken: Social inference and the self-regulation of behavior. *Journal of Personality and Social Psychology, 55*, 685–694.

Gilbert, D. T., Pelham, B. W., and Krull, D. S. (1988). On cognitive busyness: When person perceivers meet persons perceived. *Journal of Personality and Social Psychology, 54*, 733–740.

Ginzel, L. E. (1989). *The effect of perceiver-induced constraint on performance judgments: The role of the target person.* Unpublished doctoral dissertation, Princeton University.

Ginzel, L., Jones, E. E., & Swann, W. B., Jr. (1987). How "naive" is the naive attributor?: Discounting and augmentation in attitude attribution. *Social Cognition, 5*, 108–130.

Godfrey, D., Jones, E. E., and Lord, C. (1986). Self-promotion is not ingratiating. *Journal of Personality and Social Psychology, 50*, 106–115.

Goffman, E. (1955). On face work: An analysis of ritual elements in social interaction. *Psychiatry, 18*, 213–231.

Goffman, E. (1959). *The presentation of self in everyday life.* Garden City, N.Y.: Doubleday Anchor Books.

Goffman, E. (1968). *Interaction ritual: Essays on face-to-face behavior.* Chicago: Aldine.

Greenwald, A. G. (1980). The totalitarian ego: Fabrication and revision of personal history. *American Psychologist, 35*, 603–618.

Hamilton, D. L. (1979). A cognitive attributional analysis of stereotyping. In L. Berkowitz (Ed.), *Advances in experimental social psychology* (Vol. 12, pp. 53–84). New York: Academic Press.

Hamilton, D. L. (1988). Causal attribution viewed from an information processing perspective in D. Bar-Tal and A. W. Kruglanski (Eds.), *The social psychology of knowledge* (pp. 359–385). New York: Cambridge University Press.

Hamilton, D. L., and Gifford, R. K. (1976). Illusory correlation in interpersonal perception: A cognitive basis of stereotypic judgments. *Journal of Experimental Social Psychology, 12*, 392–407.

Hastie, R. (1984). Causes and effects of causal attribution. *Journal of Personality and Social Psychology, 46*, 44–56.

Hatfield, E., and Sprecher, S. (1986). *Mirror, mirror: The importance of looks in everyday life.* Albany: State University of New York Press.

Heider, F. (1944). Social perception and phenomenal causality. *Psychological Review, 51*, 258–374.

Heider, F. (1958). *The psychology of interpersonal relations*. New York: Wiley.

Heider, F., and Simmel, M. (1944). An experimental study of apparent behavior. *American Journal of Psychology, 57*, 243–259.

Hilton, D. J., and Slugoski, B. R. (1986). Knowledge-based causal attribution: The abnormal conditions focus model. *Psychological Review, 93*, 75–88.

Hilton, J. L., and Darley, J. M. (1985). Constructing other persons: A limit on the effect. *Journal of Experimental Social Psychology, 21*, 1–18.

Hochschild, A. R. (1983). *The managed heart: The commercialization of human feeling*. Berkeley, Calif. University of California Press.

Hogan, R., Jones, W., and Check, J. (1985). Socioanalytic theory: An alternative to armadillo psychology. In B. R. Schlenker (Ed.), *The self and social life* (pp. 175–198). New York: McGraw-Hill.

Huesmann, L. R. (Ed.) (1978). Learned helplessness as a model of depression. *Journal of Abnormal Psychology, 87*, 1–98.

Huston, T. L., and Levinger, G. (1978). Interpersonal attraction and relationships. *Annual Review of Psychology, 29*, 115–156.

Ichheiser, G. (1949). Misunderstandings in human relations. *American Journal of Sociology, 55*, #2, Part 2.

Izard, C. E. (1977). *Human emotions*. New York: Plenum Press.

Jaspars, J., Hewstone, M., and Fincham, F. D. (1983). Attribution theory and research: The state of the art. In J. Jaspars, F. D. Fincham, and M. Hewstone (Eds.), *Attribution theory and research: Conceptual development and social dimensions* (pp. 3–36). London: Academic Press.

Jennings, D., Amabile, T. M., and Ross, L. (1980). Informal covariation assessment: Data-based vs. theory-based judgments. In D. Kahneman, A. Tversky, and P. Slovic (Eds.), *Judgment under uncertainty: Heuristics and biases* (pp. 211–230). New York: Cambridge University Press.

Jervis, R. (1976). *Perception and misperception in international politics*. Princeton, N.J.: Princeton University Press.

Johansson, G. (1973). Visual perception of biological motion and a model for its analysis. *Perception and Psychophysics, 14*, 201–211.

Jones, E. E. (1954). Authoritarianism as a determinant of first impression formation. *Journal of Personality, 23*, 107–127.

Jones, E. E. (1964). *Ingratiation*. New York: Appleton-Century-Crofts.

Jones, E. E. (1965). Conformity as a tactic of ingratiation. *Science, 149*, 144–150.

Jones, E. E. (1979). The rocky road from acts to dispositions. *American Psychologist, 34*, 107–117.

Jones, E. E. (1986). Interpreting interpersonal behavior: The effects of expectancies. *Science, 234*, 41–46.

Jones, E. E. (1987). Retrospective review: The seer who found attributional wisdom in naivety. *Contemporary Psychology, 32*, 213–216.

Jones, E. E. (1989). The framing of competence. *Personality and Social Psychology Bulletin, 15*, 477–492.

Jones, E. E. (1990). Constrained behavior and self-concept change. In J. Olson and M. P. Zanna (Eds.), *Self-inference processes. The Ontario Symposium* (Vol. 6). Hillsdale, N.J.: Erlbaum.

Jones, E. E., and Berglas, S. (1978). Control of attributions about the self through self-handicapping strategies: The role of alcohol and underachievement. *Personality and Social Psychology Bulletin, 4*, 200–206.

Jones, E. E., and Davis, K. E. (1965). From acts to dispositions: The attribution process in person perception. In L. Berkowitz (Ed.), *Advances in experimental social psychology* (Vol. 2, pp. 219–266). New York: Academic Press.

Jones, E. E., Davis, K. E., and Gergen, K. J. (1961). Role playing variations and their informational value for person perception. *Journal of Abnormal and Social Psychology, 63*, 302–310.

Jones, E. E., and deCharms, R. (1957). Changes in social perception as a function of the personal relevance of behavior. *Sociometry, 20*, 75–85.

Jones, E. E., Farina, A., Hastorf, A. H., Markus, H., Miller, D. T., and Scott, R. (1984). *Social stigma: The psychology of marked relationships*. New York: W. H. Freeman.

Jones, E. E., Gergen, K. J., and Davis, K. E. (1962). Some determinants of reactions to being approved or disapproved as a person. *Psychological Monographs, 76,* whole #521.

Jones, E. E., and Gerard, H. B. (1967). *Foundations of social psychology.* New York: Wiley.

Jones, E. E., and Goethals, G. R. (1971). Order effects in impression formation: Attribution context and the nature of the entity. In E. E. Jones, D. E. Kanouse, H. H. Kelley, et al., *Attribution: Perceiving the causes of behavior* (pp. 27–46). New York: General Learning Press.

Jones, E. E., and Harris, V. A. (1967). The attribution of attitudes. *Journal of Experimental Social Psychology, 3,* 1–24.

Jones, E. E., Kanouse, D., Kelley, H. H., Nisbett, R., Valins, S., and Weiner, D. (1971–1972). *Attribution: Perceiving the causes of behavior.* Morristown, N.J.: General Learning Press.

Jones, E. E., and McGillis, D. (1976). Correspondent inferences and the attribution cube: A comparative reappraisal. In J. H. Harvey, W. J. Ickes, and R. F. Kidd (Eds.), *New direction in attribution research* (Vol. 1, pp. 389–420). Hillsdale, N.J.: Erlbaum.

Jones, E. E., and Nisbett, R. E. (1971–1972). The actor and the observer: Divergent perceptions of the causes of behavior. In E. E. Jones, D. Kanouse, H. H. Kelley, et al., *Attribution: Perceiving the causes of behavior* (pp. 79–94). Morristown, N.J.: General Learning Press.

Jones, E. E., and Pittman, T. S. (1982). Toward a general theory of strategic self presentation. In J. Suls (Ed.), *Psychological perspectives on the self* (Vol. 1, pp. 231–262). Hillsdale, N.J.: Erlbaum.

Jones, E. E., Rhodewalt, F., Berglas, S. E., and Skelton, J. A. (1981). Effects of strategic self-presentation on subsequent self-esteem. *Journal of Personality and Social Psychology, 41,* 407–421.

Jones, E. E., Schwartz, J., and Gilbert, D. T. (1983–1984). Perceptions of moral-expectancy violation: The role of expectancy source. *Social Cognition, 2,* 273–293.

Jones, E. E., and Thibaut, J. W. (1958). Interaction goals as bases of inference in interpersonal perception. In R. Tagiuri & L. Petrullo (Eds.), *Person perception and interpersonal behavior* (pp. 151–178). Stanford: Stanford University Press.

Jones, E. E., Wood, G. C., and Quattrone, G. A. (1981b). Perceived variability of personal characteristics in in-groups and out-groups:

The role of knowledge and evaluation. *Personality and Social Psychology Bulletin, 7,* 523–528.

Jones, E. E., Worchel, S., Goethals, G. R., and Grumet, J. F. (1971). Prior expectancy and behavioral extremity as determinants of attitude attribution. *Journal of Experimental Social Psychology, 7,* 59–80.

Jones, E. E., and Wortman, C. (1973). *Ingratiation: An attributional approach.* Morristown, N.J.: General Learning Press.

Jones, R. A. (1977). *Self-fulfilling prophecies: Social psychological, and physiological effects of expectancies.* Hillsdale, N.J.: Erlbaum.

Jones, S. C. (1973). Self and interpersonal evaluations: Esteem theory versus consistency theories. *Psychological Bulletin, 79,* 185–199.

Kahneman, D., and Tversky, A. (1979). Prospect theory: An analysis of decision under risk. *Econometrica, 47,* 263–291.

Kelley, H. H. (1967). Attribution theory in social psychology. *Nebraska symposium on motivation, 14,* 192–241.

Kelley, H. H. (1971). Attribution in social interaction. In E. E. Jones, D. Kanouse, H. H. Kelley, et al., *Attribution: Perceiving the causes of behavior* (pp. 1–26). Morristown, N.J.: General Learning Press.

Korda, M. (1975). *Power: How to get it, how to use it.* New York: Random House.

Kozlowski, L. T., and Cutting, J. E. (1977). Recognizing the sex of a walker from a dynamic point-light display. *Perception and Psychophysics, 21,* 575–580.

Kulik, J. A. (1983). Confirmatory attribution and the perpetuation of social beliefs. *Journal of Personality and Social Psychology, 44,* 1171–1181.

Kulik, J. A., Sledge, P., and Mahler, H. J. M. (1986). Self-confirmatory attribution, egocentricism, and the perpetuation of self-beliefs. *Journal of Personality and Social psychology, 50,* 587–594.

Langer, E. (1989). *Mindfulness.* Cambridge, Mass.: Addison Wesley.

Lepper, M. R., and Greene, D. (1978). *The hidden costs of reward: New perspectives on the psychology of human motivation.* Hillsdale, N.J.: Erlbaum.

Leventhal, H., and Tomarken, A. J. (1986). Emotion: Today's problems. *Annual Review of Psychology, 37,* 565–610.

Lewin, K. (1951). In D. Cartwright, (Ed.), *Field theory in social science*. New York: Harper & Bros.

Linville, P. (1982). The complexity-extremity effect and age-based stereotyping. *Journal of Personality and Social Psychology, 42,* 193–211.

Linville, P. (1987). Self-complexity as a cognitive buffer against stress-related illness and depression. *Journal of Personality and Social Psychology, 52,* 663–676.

Linville, P., and Jones, E. E. (1980). Polarized appraisals of outgroup members. *Journal of Personality and Social Psychology, 38,* 689–703.

Lippmann, W. (1922). *Public opinion*. New York: Harcourt, Brace.

Locksley, A., Borgida, E., Brekke, N., and Hepburn, C. (1980). Sex stereotypes and social judgment. *Journal of Personality and Social Psychology, 39,* 821–831.

Locksley, A., Hepburn, C., and Ortiz, V. (1982). Social stereotypes and judgments of individuals: An instance of the base-rate fallacy. *Journal of Experimental and Social Psychology, 18,* 23–42.

Luce, R. D., and Raiffa, H. (1957). *Games and decisions*. New York: Wiley.

Luchins, A. S. (1942). Mechanization in problem solving. *Psychological Monographs, 54,* whole #248.

Magnusson, D. (Ed.) (1981). *Toward a psychology of situations: An interactional perspective*. Hillsdale, N.J.: Erlbaum.

Mathes, E. (1975). The effects of physical attractiveness and anxiety on heterosexual attraction over a series of five encounters. *Journal of Marriage and the Family, 37,* 769–774.

McArthur, L. Z. (1972). The how and what of why: Some determinants and consequences of causal attribution. *Journal of Personality and Social Psychology, 22,* 171–193.

McArthur, L. Z. (1982). Judging a book by its cover: A cognitive analysis of the relationship between physical appearance and stereotyping. In A. H. Hastorf and A. M. Isen (Eds.), *Cognitive social psychology* (pp. 149–212). New York: Elsevier North Holland.

McArthur, L. Z., and Baron, R. M. (1983). Toward an ecological theory of social perception. *Psychological Review, 90,* 215–238.

McArthur, L. Z., and Post, D. L. (1977). Figural emphasis and person perception. *Journal of Experimental and Social Psychology*, *13*, 520–535.

McArthur, L. Z., and Solomon, L. K. (1978). Perceptions of an aggressive encounter as a function of the victim's salience and the perceiver's arousal. *Journal of Personality and Social Psychology*, *36*, 1278–1290.

McGill, A. L. (1989). Context effects in judgments of causation. *Journal of Personality and Social Psychology*, *57*, 189–200.

Mead, G. H. (1934). *Mind, self, and society*. Chicago: University of Chicago Press.

Medcof, J. W. (1990). PEAT: An integrative model of attribution processes. In M. Zanna (Ed.), *Advances in experimental social psychology* (Vol. 23, pp. 111–210). New York: Academic Press.

Merton, R. K. (1948). The self-fulfilling prophecy. *Antioch Review*, *8*, 193–210.

Michotte, A. (1963). *The perception of causality*. New York: Basic Books. (Originally published as *La perception de la causalité* by Publications Universitaires de Louvain, 1946.)

Miller, A. G. (1976). Constraint and target effects in the attribution of attitudes. *Journal of Experimental Social Psychology*, *12*, 325–339.

Miller, A. G. (Ed.). (1982). *In the eye of the beholder: Contemporary issues in stereotyping*. New York: Praeger.

Miller, A. G., Jones, E. E., and Hinkle, S. (1981). A robust attribution error in the personality domain. *Journal of Experimental Social Psychology*, *17*, 587–600.

Miller, A. G., Schmidt, D., Meyer, C., and Colella, A. (1984). The perceived value of constrained behavior: Pressures toward biased inference in the attitude attribution paradigm. *Social Psychology Quarterly*, *47*, 160–171.

Miller, D. T., and McFarland, C. (1987). Pluralistic ignorance: When similarity is interpreted as dissimilarity. *Journal of Personality and Social Psychology*, *53*, 298–305.

Miller, D. T., and Ross, M. (1975). Self-serving biases in the attribution of causality: Fact or fiction? *Psychological Bulletin*, *82*, 213–225.

Miller, J. (1984). Culture and the development of everyday social explanation. *Journal of Personality and Social Psychology*, *46*, 961–978.

Miller, N. E. (1941). Frustration – aggression hypothesis. *Psychological Review, 48,* 337 – 342.

Miller, N. E. (1944). Experimental studies in conflict. In J. McV. Hunt (Ed.), *Personality and the behavior disorders* (pp. 431 – 465). New York: Ronald.

Miller, N. E. (1959). Liberalization of basic S – R concepts: Extension to conflict behavior, motivation, and social learning. In S. Koch (Ed.), *Psychology: A study of a science* (Vol. 2, pp. 196 – 292). New York: McGraw-Hill.

Mischel, W., and Gilligan, C. (1964). Delay of gratification, motivation for the prohibited gratification, and responses to temptation. *Journal of Abnormal and Social Psychology, 64,* 411 – 417.

Monson, T. C., and Snyder, M. (1977). Actors, observers, and the attribution process: Toward a reconceptualization. *Journal of Experimental Social Psychology, 13,* 89 – 111.

Murray, H. A. (1938). *Explorations in personality.* New York: Oxford University Press.

Newtson, D. (1974). Dispositional inference from effects of actions: Effects chosen and effects foregone. *Journal of Experimental Social Psychology, 10,* 489 – 496.

Nisbett, R. E., and Ross, L. (1980). *Human inference strategies and shortcomings of social judgment.* Englewood Cliffs, N.J.: Prentice-Hall.

Nisbett, R. E., and Wilson, T. D. (1977). Telling more than we can know: Verbal reports on mental processes. *Psychological Review, 84,* 231 – 259.

Ostrom, C. W., Jr., and Simon, D. M. (1989). The man in the Teflon suit: The environmental connection, political drama, and popular support in the Reagan presidency. *Public Opinion Quarterly, 53,* 353 – 387.

Ostrom, T. M. (1977). Between-theory and within-theory conflict in explaining context effects in impression formation. *Journal of Experimental Social Psychology, 13,* 492 – 503.

Park, B., and Rothbart, M. (1982). Perception of out-group homogeneity and levels of social categorization: Memory for the subordinate attributes of in-group and out-group members. *Journal of Personality and Social Psychology, 42,* 1051 – 1068.

Passini, F. T., and Norman, W. T. (1966). A universal conception of personality structure? *Journal of Personality and Social Psychology,* 4, 44–49.

Perdue, C. (1983). *Perceived ingroup heterogeneity and evaluative complexity: Evidence for a bias in information acquisition.* Unpublished doctoral dissertation, Princeton University.

Quattrone, G. A. (1982). Behavioral consequences of attributional bias. *Social Cognition, 1,* 358–378.

Quattrone, G. A. (1986). On the perception of a group's variability. In S. Worchel and W. G. Austin (Eds.), *Cognitive social psychology* (pp. 149–211). New York: Elsevier.

Quattrone, G. A., and Jones, E. E. (1978). Selective self-disclosure with and without correspondent performance. *Journal of Experimental Social Psychology, 14,* 511–526.

Quattrone, G. A., and Jones, E. E. (1980). The perception of variability within in-groups and out-groups: Implication for the law of small numbers. *Journal of Personality and Social Psychology, 38,* 141–152.

Rasinski, K. A., Crocker, J., and Hastie, R. (1985). Another look at sex stereotypes and social judgments: An analysis of the social perceiver's use of subjective probabilities. *Journal of Personality and Social Psychology, 49,* 317–326.

Reeder, G. D., and Brewer, M. B. (1979). A schematic model of dispositional attribution in interpersonal perception. *Psychological Review, 86,* 61–79.

Rhodewalt, F., and Agustdottir, S. (1986). Effects of self-presentation on the phenomenal self. *Journal of Personality and Social Psychology, 50,* 47–55.

Ringer, R. J. (1973). *Winning through intimidation.* Los Angeles: Los Angeles Publishing.

Rosenthal R., and Jacobson, L. (1968). *Pygmalion in the classroom.* New York: Holt, Rinehart & Winston.

Rosenthal, R., and Rubin, D. B. (1978). Interpersonal expectancy effects: The first 345 studies. *Behavioral and Brain Sciences, 3,* 377–415.

Ross, L. (1977). The intuitive psychologist and his shortcomings: Distortions in the attribution process. In L. Berkowitz (Ed.), *Advances in experimental social psychology* (Vol. 10, pp. 174–221). New York: Academic Press.

Ross, L., Amabile, T., and Steinmetz, J. L. (1977). Social roles, social control, and biases in social-perception processes. *Journal of Personality and Social Psychology, 35,* 484–494.

Ross, L., Greene, D., and House, P. (1977). The "false consensus effect": An egocentric bias in social perception and attribution processes. *Journal of Experimental Social Psychology, 13,* 279–301.

Ross, M., and Fletcher, G. J. O. (1985). Attribution and social perception. In G. Lindzey and E. Aronson (Eds.), *The handbook of social psychology* (3rd ed., pp. 73–122). New York: Random House.

Ross, M., and Olson, J. M. (1981). An expectancy-attribution model of the effects of placebos. *Psychological Review, 88,* 408–437.

Ross, M., and Sicoly, F. (1979). Egocentric biases in availability and attribution. *Journal of Personality and Social Psychology, 37,* 322–336.

Rotter, J. B. (1954). *Social learning and clinical psychology.* Englewood Cliffs, N.J.: Prentice-Hall.

Ruble, D. N., and Feldman, N. S. (1976). Order of consensus, distinctiveness, and consistency information and causal attribution. *Journal of Personality and Social Psychology, 34,* 930–937.

Russell, B. (1950). *Unpopular essays.* New York: Simon & Schuster, Readers' Editions.

Schachter, S. (1964). The interaction of cognitive and physiological determinants of emotional state. In L. Berkowitz (Ed.), *Advances in experimental social psychology* (Vol. 1, pp. 49–80). New York: Academic Press.

Schachter, S., and Singer, J. E. (1962). Cognitive, social, and physiological determinants of emotional state. *Psychological Review, 69,* 379–399.

Schlenker, B. R. (1980). *Impression management.* Monterey, Calif.: Brooks/Cole.

Schlenker, B. R. and Trudeau, J. V. (1990). Impact of self-presentations on private self-beliefs: Effects of prior self-beliefs and misattribution. *Journal of Personality and Social Psychology, 58,* 22–32.

Schlosberg, H. (1952). The description of facial expressions in terms of two dimensions. *Journal of Experimental Psychology, 44,* 229–237.

Schlosberg, H. (1954). Three dimensions of emotion. *Psychological Review, 61*, 81–88.

Schneider, D. J. (1973). Implicit personality theory: A review *Psychological Bulletin, 79*, 294–309.

Schoenberger, N. E. (1988). *Maintaining self-esteem in the face of behavioral pressures for change: Support for the theory of self-verification.* Unpublished senior thesis, Princeton University.

Shweder, R. A. (1977). Likeness and likelihood in everyday thought: Magical thinking in judgments about personality. *Current Anthropology, 18*, 637–648.

Scott, M. B., and Lyman, S. M. (1968). Accounts. *American Sociological Review, 33*, 46–62.

Seligman, M. G. P. (1975). *Helplessness: On depression, development, and death.* San Francisco: W. H. Freeman.

Sherif, M., and Hovland, C. T. (1961). *Social judgment: Assimilation and contrast effects in communication and attitude change.* New Haven: Yale University Press.

Showers, C. J. (1986). *Anticipatory cognitive strategies: The positive side of negative thinking.* Unpublished doctoral dissertation, University of Michigan.

Showers, C. J., and Cantor, N. (1985). Social cognition: A look at motivated strategies. *Annual Review of Psychology, 36*, 275–305.

Silka, L. (1984). Intuitive perceptions of change: An overlooked phenomenon in person perception? *Personality and Social Psychology Bulletin, 10*, 180–190.

Skinner, B. F. (1983). *The behavior of organisms.* New York: Appleton-Century.

Skinner, B. F. (1953). *Science and human behavior.* New York: Macmillan.

Skinner, B. F. (1971). *Beyond freedom and dignity.* New York: Knopf.

Skrypnek, B. J., and Snyder, M. (1982). On the self-perpetuating nature of stereotypes about women and men. *Journal of Experimental Social Psychology, 18*, 277–291.

Snyder, C. R., and Fromkin, H. L. (1980). *Uniqueness: The human pursuit of difference.* New York: Plenum Press.

Snyder, C. R., Higgins, R. L., and Stuckey R. J. (1983). *Excuses: Masquerades in search of grace.* New York: Wiley.

Snyder, M., and Ickes, W. (1985). Personality and social behavior. In G. Lindzey and E. Aronson (Eds.), *The handbook of social psychology* (3rd ed., Vol. 2, pp. 883–948). New York: Random House.

Snyder, M. and Swann, W. B., Jr. (1978a) Hypothesis testing processes in social interaction. *Journal of Personality and Social Psychology, 36,* 1202–1212.

Snyder, M., and Swann, W. B., Jr. (1978b). Behavioral confirmation in social interaction: From social perception to social reality. *Journal of Experimental Social Psychology, 14,* 148–162.

Snyder, M., Tanke, E. D., and Berscheid, E. (1977). Social perception and interpersonal behavior: On the self-fulfilling nature of stereotypes. *Journal of Personality and Social Psychology, 35,* 656–666.

Snyder, M. L., and Frankel, A. (1976). Observer bias: A stringent test of behavior engulfing the field. *Journal of Personality and Social Psychology, 34,* 857–864.

Snyder, M. L., and Jones, E. E. (1974). Attitude attribution when behavior is constrained. *Journal of Experimental Social Psychology, 10,* 585–600.

Snyder, M. L., and Wicklund, R. A. (1981). Attribute ambiguity. In J. H. Harvey, W. Ickes, and R. F. Kidd (Eds.), *New directions in attribution research* (Vol. 3, pp. 197–221). Hillsdale, N.J.: Earlbaum.

Stebbins, R. A. (1986). The definition of the situation: A review. In A. Furnham (Ed.), *Social behavior in context* (pp. 134–154). Boston: Allyn & Bacon.

Steele, C. M. (1988). The psychology of self-affirmation: Sustaining the integrity of the self. In L. Berkowitz (Ed.), *Advances in experimental social psychology* (Vol. 21, pp. 261–302). New York: Academic Press.

Stewart, R. H. (1965). Effect of continuous responding on the order effect in personality impression formation. *Journal of Personality and Social Psychology, 1,* 161–165.

Stires, L. K., and Jones, E. E. (1969). Modesty versus self-enhancement as alternative forms of ingratiation. *Journal of Experimental Social Psychology, 5,* 172–188.

Stryker, S., and Statham, A. (1985). Symbolic interaction and role theory. In G. Lindzey and E. Aronson (Eds.), *The handbook of social psychology* (3rd ed., Vol. 1, pp. 311–378). New York: Random House.

Swann, W. B., Jr. (1984). Quest for accuracy in person perception: A matter of pragmatics. *Psychological Review, 91,* 457–477.

Swann, W. B., Jr. (1987). Identity negotiation: Where two roads meet. *Journal of Personality and Social Psychlogy, 53,* 1038–1051.

Swann, W. B., Jr. (in press). To be adored or to be known? The interplay of self-enhancement and self-verification. In R. M. Sorrentino and E. T. Higgins (Eds.), *Motivation and cognition* (Vol. 2). New York: Guilford Press.

Swann, W. B., Jr., and Guiliano, T. (1987). Confirmatory search strategies in social interaction: When, how, why, and with what consequences. *Journal of Clinical and Social Psychology, 5,* 511–524.

Swann, W. B., Jr., and Pelham, B. W. (under review). Getting out when the going gets good: Choice of relations by partners and the self.

Swann, W. B., Jr., Pelham, B. W., and Krull, D. S. (1989). Agreeable fancy or disagreeable truth? Reconciling self-enhancement and self-verification. *Journal of Personality and Social Psychology, 57,* 782–791.

Swann, W. B., Jr., and Read, S. J. (1981) Self-verification processes: How we sustain our self-conceptions. *Journal of Experimental Social Psychology, 17,* 351–372.

Tagiuri, R. (1952). Relational analysis: An extension of sociometric method with emphasis on social perception. *Sociometry, 15,* 91–104.

Tagiuri, R. (1969). Person perception. In G. Lindzey and E. Aronson (Eds.), *The handbook of social psychology* (Vol. 3, pp. 395–449).

Tagiuri, R., and Petrullo, L. (1958). *Person perception and interpersonal behavior.* Stanford: Stanford University Press.

Taylor, S. E., and Brown, J. D. (1988). Illusion and well-being: A social psychological perspective on mental health. *Psychological Bulletin, 103,* 193–210.

Taylor, S. E., Crocker, J., Fiske, S. T., Springer, M., and Winkler, J. D. (1979). The generalizability of salience effects. *Journal of Personality and Social Psychology, 37,* 357–368.

Taylor, S. E., and Fiske, S. T. (1975). Point of view and perceptions of causality. *Journal of Personality and Social Psychology, 32*, 439–445.

Taylor, S. E., and Fiske, S. T. (1978). Salience, attention, and attribution: Top of the head phenomena. In L. Berkowitz (Ed.), *Advances in experimental social psychology* (Vol. 11, pp. 249–288). New York: Academic Press.

Taylor, S. E., Fiske, S. T., Etcoff, N. L., and Ruderman, A. J. (1978). Categorical bases of person memory and stereotyping. *Journal of Personality and Social Psychology, 36*, 778–793.

Tesser, A. (1986). Some effects of self-evaluation maintenance on cognition and action. In R. M. Sorrentino and E. T. Higgins (Eds.), *Handbook of motivation and cognition* (pp. 435–464). New York: Guilford Press.

Tetlock, P. E. (1983). Accountability and the perseverance of first impressions. *Social Psychology Quarterly, 46*, 285–292.

Tetlock, P. E., and Kim, J. I. (1987). Accountability and judgment processes in a personality prediction task. *Journal of Personality and Social Psychology, 52*, 700–709.

Tetlock, P. E., and Manstead, A. S. R. (1985). Impression management versus intrapsychic explanations in social psychology: A useful dichotomy? *Psychological Review, 92*, 59–77.

Thibaut, J. W., and Kelley, H. H. (1959). *The social psychology of groups*. New York Wiley.

Thibaut, J. W., and Riecken, H. W. (1955). Some determinants and consequences of the perception of social causality. *Journal of Personality, 1955, 24*, 113–133.

Thibaut, J. W., and Ross, M. (1969). Commitment and experience as determinants of assimilation and contrast. *Journal of Personality and Social Psychology, 13*, 322–330.

Thomas, W. I., and Znaniecki, F. (1918–1920). *The Polish peasant in Europe and America*. (5 vols.) Boston: Richard G. Badger.

Tice, D. M. (1987). *Similarity of others and dispositional versus situational attributions*. Unpublished doctoral dissertation, Princeton University.

Tolman, E. C. (1955). Principles of performance. *Psychological Review, 62*, 315–326.

Tomkins, S. S. (1962). *Affect, imagery, consciousness: I. The positive affects*. New York: Springer Verlag.

Tomkins, S. S. (1981). The quest for primary motives: Biography and autobiography of an idea. *Journal of Personality and Social Psychology, 41*, 306–329.

Trope, Y. (1986). Identification and inference processes in dispositional attribution. *Psychological Review, 93*, 239–257.

Trope, Y., and Bassok, M. (1982). Confirmatory and diagnosing strategies in social information gathering. *Journal of Personality and Social Psychology, 43*, 22–34.

Tversky, A., and Kahneman, D. (1973). Availability: A heuristic for judging frequency and probability. *Cognitive Psychology, 5*, 207–232.

Tversky A., and Kahneman, D. (1974). Judgment under uncertainty: Heuristics and biases. *Science, 185*, 1124–1131.

Tversky, A., and Kahneman, D. (1982). Judgements of and by representativeness. In D. Kahneman, P. Slovic, and A. Tversky (Eds.), *judgement under uncertainty: Heuristics and biases* (pp. 84–98). New York: Cambridge University Press.

Vallacher, R. R., and Wegner, D. M. (1987). What do people think they're doing? Action identification and human behavior. *Psychological Review, 94*, 3–15.

Wachtel, P. (1973). Psychodynamics, behavior therapy, and the implacable experimenter: An inquiry into the consistency of personality. *Journal of Abnormal Psychology, 82*, 324–334.

Watson, D. (1982). The actor and the observer: How are their perceptions of causality divergent? *Psychological Bulletin, 92*, 682–700.

Weiner, B. (1985). Spontaneous causal search. *Psychological Bulletin, 97*, 74–84.

Weisman, S. R. (1984). Can the magic prevail? *New York Times Magazine, 29* (April), 38–56.

Weisz, C., and Jones, E. E. (unpublished). Some consequences of expectancies for person perception: Target-based versus category-based expectancies.

Woodworth, R. S. (1938). *Experimental psychology*. New York: Holt.

Wright, J. C., and Dawson, V. L. (1988). Person perception and the bounded rationality of social judgment. *Journal of Personality and Social Psychology, 55,* 780–794.

Yandell, B., and Insko, C. A. (1977). Attribution of attitudes to speakers and listeners under assigned behavior conditions: Does behavior engulf the field? *Journal of Experimental Social Psychology, 13,* 269–278.

Zajonc, R., Murphy, S. T., and Inglehart, M. (1989). Feeling and facial efference: Implications of the vascular theory of emotion. *Psychological Review, 96,* 395–416.

Zanna, M. P., and Cooper, J. (1974). Dissonance and the pill: An attribution approach to studying the arousal properties of dissonance. *Journal of Personality and Social Psychology, 29,* 703–709.

Zillmann, D., Katcher, A. H., and Milavsky, B. (1972). Excitation transfer from physical exercise to subsequent aggressive behavior. *Journal of Experimental Social Psychology, 8,* 247–259.

Zuckerman, M., DePaulo, B. M., and Rosenthal, R. (1981). Verbal and nonverbal communication of deception. In L. Berkowitz (Ed.), *Advances in experimental social psychology* (Vol. 14, pp. 2–60). New York: Academic Press.

Author Index

Subject Index